Mean Streets and Raging Bulls

The Legacy of Film Noir in Contemporary American Cinema

Richard Martin

The Scarecrow Press, Inc.
Lanham, Maryland, and London
1999

SCARECROW PRESS, INC.

Published in the United States of America
by Scarecrow Press, Inc.
4720 Boston Way
Lanham, Maryland 20706

4 Pleydell Gardens, Folkestone
Kent CT20 2DN, England

This book is adapted from a doctoral dissertation submitted to the University of Newcastle upon Tyne, England, in November 1995.

British Library Cataloguing in Publication Information Available

Library of Congress Cataloging-in-Publication Data

Martin, Richard, 1969-
    Mean streets and raging bulls : the legacy of film noir in contemporary American cinema / Richard Martin. -- 1st pbk. ed.
        p.   cm.
    Filmography : p.
    Includes bibliographical references and index.
    ISBN 0-8108-3642-4 (pbk.)
    1. Film noir--United States--History and criticism.   I. Title.
PN1995.9.F54M37
791.43'655--dc21   99-17309
                                                              CIP

⊖™ The paper used in this publication meets the minimum requirements of American National Standard for Information Sciences—Permanence of Paper for Printed Library Materials, ANSI/NISO Z39.48–1992.
Manufactured in the United States of America.

For Abi

Contents

Acknowledgments

Many people have provided advice, encouragement, and resources during the inception and ultimate realization of *Mean Streets and Raging Bulls*. To this end I would like to thank Bruce Babington, Peter Evans, Celestino Deleyto, Paco Collado, Phil Powrie, Deborah Thomas, John Saunders, Agustín Sánchez Vidal, Isabel Santaolalla, Ginette Vincendeau, Briony Hanson, David Thompson, Les Keyser, Ian Bahrami, Tony and Traude Murray, Gavin McAulay, Simon Duncombe, Mike Scoging, and the staffs of the British Film Institute library and the British Academy. Finally, I would like to express my gratitude for the unstinting generosity and encouragement of my parents, Jean and Andrew Martin, and my wife, Abigail Murray, all of whom have done so much to help this project come to fruition. Abi, in particular, has been a constant source of motivation and inspiration, and it is to her that this book is dedicated.

Preface

Classic film noir was Hollywood's "dark cinema" of crime and corruption, a genre underpinned by a tone of existential cynicism, which stripped bare the myth of the American Dream and offered a bleak nightmare vision of a fragmented society that rhymed with many of the social realities of post-war America. *Mean Streets and Raging Bulls* explores how, since its apparent demise in the late fifties, the noir genre has been revitalized in the post-studio era, post-Vietnam context of recent American cinema. The book is divided into two sections. In the first, the evolution of film noir, indeed its metamorphosis into post-sixties neo-noir, is contextualized in relation to both industrial transformation (that is, studio policy, technological innovation, and the influx of new personnel) and the post-Depression political history of the United States from the Second World War to the present. In the second, the evolution of neo-noir and its relation to classic film noir is illustrated by detailed reference to temporally specific texts: *Chinatown, Night Moves,* and *Taxi Driver* in the seventies; *After Hours, Blood Simple,* and *Sea of Love* in the eighties; and *Reservoir Dogs, Romeo is Bleeding,* and *One False Move* in the nineties. Not only do these films suggest noir's continuing exploration of the collective anxieties of American society, but they also reflect a sustained tradition of artistic creativity and technical virtuosity nurtured within the confines of American genre cinema. Such a tradition is epitomized by the work of neo-noir auteur Martin Scorsese, whose influence on the recent evolution of the genre is considered in some detail.

Introduction

Film noir is a descriptive term for the American crime film as it flourished, roughly, from the early forties to the late fifties. It embraces a variety of crime dramas ranging from the claustrophobic studies of murder and psychological entrapment to more general treatments of criminal organizations. From stylized versions of the city at night to documentary-like reports of the city at midday, from the investigations of the wry, cynical sleuth to the "innocent" man momentarily and fatally tempted by luxury, to the desperate failings of the confirmed and inveterate criminal, the genre covers a heterogeneous terrain. In range of theme and visual style, it is both varied and complex, and in level of achievement it is consistently high.

Foster Hirsch, *The Dark Side of the Screen*

What are we doing when, to practice a "genre," we quote a genre, represent it, stage it, expose its *generic law,* analyze it practically? Are we still practicing the genre?

Jacques Derrida, "Living On: Borderlines"

A feature of American film production throughout the forties and much of the fifties, film noir was not at first recognized as distinct from other Hollywood genres in the nation of its origin. In fact, it was in post-war France, where American forties productions unavailable during the Nazi occupation were finally being screened, that films like *The Maltese Falcon* (John Huston, 1941), *Double Indemnity* (Billy Wilder, 1944), *Laura* (Otto Preminger, 1944), and *Murder, My Sweet* (Edward Dmytryk, 1944) were initially celebrated for their thematic and stylistic departure from the conventions of traditional Hollywood studio filmmaking. Given the darkness of their tone and mood such films were collectively dubbed *film noir,* or "dark cinema," by the French, and were considered a cinematic correlative to the American hard-boiled fiction of

1

Dashiell Hammett, Horace McCoy, Raymond Chandler, James M. Cain, and Cornell Woolrich, a type of crime fiction popularized in France by collections such as Marcel Duhamel's "Série Noire," which similarly debunked notions of the American Dream and offered a nightmare vision of contemporary urban society in the United States. Indeed, a recent definition of hard-boiled fiction applies in equal measure to film noir, which, as the authors themselves acknowledge, has always "proved fertile ground for the hard-boiled movement":

> The hard-boiled crime story deals with disorder, disaffection, and dissatisfaction. Throughout the genre's seventy-year history, this has remained a constant and central tenet. The typical hard-boiled character (if not the typical hard-boiled writer) has a jaundiced view of government, power, and the law. He (or, sometimes she) is often a loner, a social misfit. If he is on the side of angels, he is likely to be a cynical idealist: he believes that society is corrupt, but he also believes in justice and will make it his business to do whatever is necessary to see that justice is done. If he walks the other side of the mean streets, he walks them at night; he is likely a predator, and as morally bankrupt as any human being can be. In the noir world, extremes are the norm; clashes between good and evil are never petty, and good does not always triumph, nor is justice always done.[1]

Film noir, then, and by extension the hard-boiled movement in general, represented for those early European commentators like Nino Frank, Raymond Borde, and Étienne Chaumeton[2] a body of work which offered a bleak and, to a certain degree, subversive worldview that contrasted starkly with the self-promoting American myths that had characterized many of the Depression-era Hollywood films.

As a descriptive term *film noir* first appeared in print in 1946 in Nino Frank's *L'Ecran Français* article "Un nouveau genre 'policier': l'aventure criminelle."[3] It was not until the late sixties and seventies, though, that it gained widespread currency in anglophone film culture, adopted by writers such as Raymond Durgnat, Paul Schrader, Janey Place and Lowell Peterson, Robert Porfirio, James Damico, and Alain Silver and Elizabeth Ward.[4] During this period, despite the early parallels drawn by the French between film noir and the literary hard-boiled genre, noir was subjected to such rigorous academic and critical investigation that the concept of what exactly constituted film noir became diffuse and fragmented. Noir was co-opted by different academic and theoretical factions, becoming many things for many people: it was a style, a tone, a mood, an existential worldview, and only occasionally a genre; it represented an American commodification and hybridization of German Expressionism, French Poetic Realism, and Italian Neo-Realism. It bore testament to

> the influx of German *emigrés* and the influence of expressionism; the influx of French *emigrés* and the influence of existentialism; Ernest Hemingway and the "hard boiled" school of writing; Edward Hopper and the "ash can" school of painting; pre-war photo-journalism, wartime news-reels and post-war neo-realism; the creators of *Kane*—Citizens Mankiewicz, Toland and Welles; the Wall Street crash and the rise of populism; the second world war and the rise of fascism; the cold war and the rise of McCarthyism . . . general American fears about bureaucracy, the bomb and the big city . . . the industrialisation of the female work-force during the war and the escalating corporatism of American capital throughout the Forties.[5]

In fact, film noir was all these things, its very attraction to film commentators grounded in the fact that it offered itself to interpretation in terms of numerous (occasionally conflicting) theoretical disciplines (sociopolitical contextualization, genre criticism, psychoanalysis, feminism, structuralism, even auteurism).

Academic and critical investigation has continued throughout the eighties and the nineties and has culminated in a flurry of recent book-length publications on the subject, including J. P. Telotte's *Voices in the Dark: The Narrative Patterns of Film Noir* (1989), Frank Krutnik's *In a Lonely Street: Film Noir, Genre, Masculinity* (1991), the third edition of Silver and Ward's encyclopedic reference guide *Film Noir* (1992), Carl Richardson's *Autopsy: An Element of Realism in American Film Noir* (1992), *The Movie Book of Film Noir* (1992) edited by Ian Cameron, *Shades of Noir* (1993) edited by Joan Copjec, R. Barton Palmer's *Hollywood's Dark Cinema: The American Film Noir* (1994), Michael Stephens's *Film Noir: A Comprehensive Illustrated Reference to Movies, Terms and Persons* (1995), James F. Maxfield's *The Fatal Woman: Sources of Male Anxiety in American Film Noir, 1941–1991* (1996), R. Barton Palmer's *Perspectives on Film Noir* (1996), and Alain Silver and James Ursini's *A Film Noir Reader* (1996). But it has been the parallel cinematic investigation and revival of film noir in the Hollywood cinema of the late sixties and its subsequent transformation through the cinema of the seventies, eighties, and nineties that has most significantly contributed to an evolving concept of what film noir actually is. The industrial assimilation of the term film noir, moreover, has contributed to its establishment as a contemporary Hollywood genre irrespective of how one is inclined to define the generic status of the classic films of the forties and fifties.

Although never employed in the United States either critically or industrially during the forties and fifties, today the term *noir,* having gained currency outside the domains of film criticism and academia, holds some significance for twentieth-century popular culture in general. It is applicable not only to the cinema but to all the arts. The noir sensibility manifests itself in fiction, exerting its influence beyond the pages of the crime novel and the short story, as witness David Thomson's *Suspects,*[6] Paul Auster's *The New York Trilogy,* Thomas Pynchon's *Vineland,* Theodore Roszak's *Flicker,* and Geoff Dyer's *The Search.* In painting, this sensibility is sustained by an enduring fascination among painters, filmmakers, and novelists with the frequently noirish work of Edward Hopper. It also can be perceived in photography, radio, theater (including musical productions like *City of Angels* and *Sunset Boulevard*), animation, and even comic strips such as Martin Rowson's Chandlerian *The Waste Land,* a postmodern reworking of T. S. Eliot's narrative poem of the same name. It is also, of course, a prevalent feature of network and cable television programming from the highly stylized eighties police procedural series *Miami Vice* to the nostalgic Showcase cable television series *Fallen Angels.*

In the United States of the nineties, film noir and its present-day counterpart, neo-noir, are terms now freely employed within the American film industry by both filmmakers and film reviewers to define the style, tone, and content of contemporary films (not to mention books, plays, television shows, and so forth). In fact, while classic film noir is the subject of countless publications and frequent retrospective seasons at film festivals and on television, in the mid-nineties the genre is enjoying one of the most prolific periods of production since the heyday of classic film noir in the mid-to-late forties. In 1995, for example, the fall season of U.S. cinema releases alone offered such neo-noirs or noir hybrids as *The Usual Suspects* (Bryan Singer, 1995), *Seven* (David Fincher, 1995), *Clockers* (Spike Lee, 1995), *Devil in a Blue Dress* (Carl Franklin, 1995), *Nick of Time* (John Badham, 1995), *Jade* (William Friedkin, 1995), *Strange Days* (Kathryn Bigelow, 1995), *Things To Do In Denver When You're Dead* (Gary Fleder, 1995), *Casino* (Martin Scorsese, 1995), and *Heat* (Michael Mann, 1995), and this in a year that had already witnessed the runaway commercial and critical success of Quentin Tarantino's neo-noir *Pulp Fiction* (1994). Similarly, the universal appeal of the genre was reflected during the same period in the United Kingdom, where two film noir seasons were programmed by the crime fiction writer James Ellroy at the National Film Theatre in London and at the "Shots in the Dark" film festival in Nottingham, and a number of classic films noirs including *Scarlet Street* (Fritz Lang, 1945), *The Strange Love of Martha Ivers* (Lewis Milestone, 1946), and *D.O.A.* (Rudolph Maté, 1950) were released on the new VHS label Second Sight Film Noir. There were also television broadcasts of the period noir series *Fallen Angels* and the documentaries *The Film Noir Story* (BBC2) and *Dark and Deadly* (Channel 4), both of which served as introductions to extended noir seasons on British television.[7]

As the term *film noir* has gradually permeated our culture, the evolution of the genre itself during the last fifty years has been informed both by the complex history of the American film industry and by the social and political change that has shaped the recent history of the United States. In part I of our exploration of film noir's metamorphosis into the neo-noir of contemporary American cinema, "From Film Noir to Neonoir," we shall consider how both these factors have affected the history of the genre. In chapter 1, "Industrial Evolution," we will explore how the genesis of film noir in the forties and its revival in the late sixties coincide with two periods marked by both tumultuous change within the infrastructure of the industry itself and an intense creative energy fueled by the emergence of new talent and technology. We also will analyze how the continuing evolution of the genre embraces changes in methods of production and marketing, technological innovation, and shifts in the popular taste of the filmgoing public. By so doing we will observe how film noir has evidenced those qualities associated by the film historians Robert Allen and Douglas Gomery with the longevity of Hollywood filmmaking itself, noting how "it has accommodated itself to economic changes, technological revolutions, influences from other stylistic systems, and the individual and aesthetic demands of thousands of filmmakers over half a century."[8] We will see, moreover, how the trajectory of film noir's evolution has seen it develop from a radical, slightly subversive alternative to mainstream Hollywood conservatism to its current status as one of the mainstays of contemporary genre film production. In chapter 2, "America Noir," we will contextualize recurrent noir motifs in relation to the post-Depression history of the United States, exploring how specific cultural movements and sociopolitical events have shaped our understanding of the evolution of the genre and examining how the recent history of the United States, with its wars, political scandals, and social injustices, itself reads as a noir narrative founded as it is on the traditional noir motifs of violence, corruption, greed, misogyny, and discrimination (sexual, racial, and class). Throughout we will attempt to illustrate how film noir has continued to serve as a public conscience, documenting the darker moments in the history of American politics and society in the latter half of the twentieth century.

The sociopolitical contextualization of film production remains a topic of considerable significance in part II of this study, "The Legacy of Film Noir," in which the revival of the genre and its transformation throughout the seventies, eighties, and nineties are explored in more depth. Indeed, beyond the exploration of dominant cultural tendencies suggested by the respective chapter titles, "Seventies Revisionism," "Eighties Pastiche," and "Nineties Irony," in this section we will consider how representative neo-noir films like *Chinatown* (Roman Polanski, 1974), *Night Moves* (Arthur Penn, 1975), *Taxi Driver* (Martin Scorsese, 1976), *Blood Simple* (Joel and Ethan Coen, 1984), *After Hours* (Martin Scorsese, 1985), *Sea of Love* (Harold Becker, 1989), *Reservoir Dogs* (Quentin Tarantino, 1992), *One False Move* (Carl Franklin, 1992), and *Romeo is Bleeding* (Peter Medak, 1994), intersect with the recent sociopolitical history of the United States and exploit the collective anxieties of contemporary American society. Additionally we will examine how these films draw from and develop traditions, both thematic and stylistic, inherited or borrowed from classic noir texts. We will also consider how, like many of the classic film noir and hard-boiled narratives, the post-sixties neo-noir constitutes a contemporary, nightmare-like correlative to classical mythology.

Like the archetypal hero adventure, in fact, these films are modeled on the paradigmatic identity quest, featuring dangerous journeys into the underworld of both the protagonists' habitats and their own fragmented psyches. Cynical and pessimistic in tone, these are essentially timeless narratives about the darker side of the human condition, modern fables that highlight the dangers of alienation, the fragmentation of society, the breakdown of human interaction, the debasement of love, the beguiling power of wealth, the corruption of government, and mankind's inherent propensity for inertia and impotence.

Finally, a note on the title of this study, which alludes to the work of Martin Scorsese, one of the first of the "Hollywood Renaissance" directors to return with some regularity to the noir genre, frequently taking the concept of film noir as a point of departure in personal narratives like

Mean Streets (1973), *Taxi Driver* (1976), *New York, New York* (1977), *Raging Bull* (1980), and *After Hours* (1985). In fact, Scorsese's neo-noir oeuvre stands as a testament to the enduring, if somewhat marginalized, principals of artistic creativity and technical virtuosity harnessed together in service of a personal cinematic vision, qualities that characterized the work of classic film noir auteurs like Joseph H. Lewis, Edgar G. Ulmer, Jacques Tourneur, André de Toth, Nicholas Ray, and Samuel Fuller. In part II of this study, Scorsese's *Taxi Driver* and *After Hours,* two seminal texts in the continuing evolution of the noir genre, will be analyzed in some detail, and further consideration will be given to the influence of Scorsese's work as both filmmaker and film historian on subsequent neo-noir filmmakers.

The allusive resonances of the title *Mean Streets and Raging Bulls,* it should be noted, are intended to embrace much more than the role Martin Scorsese has played in the evolution of contemporary film noir, however influential that may ultimately prove to be. After all, the film *Mean Streets* was named for a celebrated passage from Raymond Chandler's essay "The Simple Art of Murder," in which he endeavored to define the role of the hard-boiled detective.[9] That Scorsese's film is concerned with small-time hoodlums in New York's Little Italy is illustrative of how Chandler's passage (in the same way that the meaning of the term *film noir* has gradually evolved) has helped define a tradition that extends far beyond the author's own romanticized vision of the private investigator. In fact, as the proliferation of neo-noir road movies would suggest, today's "mean streets" are no longer confined to the urban sprawl of America's major cities but crisscross the nation, implicating the whole of the United States in the dark picture painted by the contemporary film noir.

Originally, in the crime fiction of the twenties and thirties and the films of the early forties, noir's "mean streets" were the province of the private eye. As hard-boiled fiction and film noir evolved, however, the detective was joined by the femme fatale, the naïve middle-class victim, the gangster, the corrupt patriarch, the homme fatal, and the psychopath. It is the latter "raging bull" figure that seems most representative of the modern era. Indeed, in one of the most influential anglophone studies of the noir phenomenon, "Notes on *Film Noir,*" Paul Schrader has observed that the fifties film noir was characterized by a mood of "psychotic action and suicidal impulse."[10] For me this remains a defining feature of the post-sixties' neo-noir, the protagonist's violence, paranoia, and fragmented psyche a response to the social realities of the modern experience. The power of many contemporary films noirs is that rather than allowing for an uplifting conclusion to the mythic/psychic hero adventure, as was the case in a number of the A-feature, studio-compromised films noirs of the classical Hollywood era, the crisis of identity that is at the core of the modern "raging bull" films has no potential for resolution. We simply watch the antisocial behavior of a psychotic figure result in his or her own self-destruction within an inhospitable and uncaring environment. The tragedy of it all (as witness, for example, John Hinckley's 1981 assassination attempt on President Ronald Reagan) is that in the post-assassination, post-Vietnam, post-Watergate context of contemporary American society such narratives frequently have a greater foundation in reality than in fiction.[11]

I

From Film Noir to Neo-noir

Industrial Evolution

1 conservative policies,
low-budget innovation

The history and evolution of film noir is inextricably tied to that of the American film industry of the post-Depression era. Noir, in its manifestation as both classic film noir of the forties and fifties and neo-noir of the seventies, eighties, and nineties, is symptomatic of the time and place in which it was produced, a reflection of the production policies, artistic tendencies, and technological developments prevalent within the film industry at any given moment in its history. The evolution of film noir, moreover, as we shall explore it in the following pages, is closely connected with three of the most intriguing developments in the American film culture of the sound era: the emergence of the B-film as an arena of low-budget innovation and experimentation, the fusion of mainstream and art cinema filmmaking techniques in the *nouvelle vague*–influenced Hollywood renaissance cinema of the late sixties and early seventies, and the revitalization of the independent sector in the late eighties and nineties. By necessity, given their impact on the subsequent three decades of filmmaking, our history of the genre starts some years prior to the release of the first American film noir with the film industry's conversion to sound and the development of the studio system of production.

CLASSICAL HOLLYWOOD

By the mid-twenties the Hollywood studios had adopted a system of production modeled on other American industries by which departmentalized contract personnel, including producers, screenwriters, art directors, cinematographers, directors, actors, and music directors, were involved in the mass production of feature films. However, although all Hollywood films were governed by standardized formal and thematic paradigms and regulated by the stringent requirements of the Motion

11

Picture Production Code, unlike other industries, the studios did not strive for absolute uniformity of product. Instead they sought by means of generic differentiation, exploitation of star popularity, and technological innovation to achieve a balance between the "qualities of difference and sameness upon which the continuing appeal of Hollywood entertainment depended."[1] The studios, that is, catered to the consumer desires of the cinema-going public which, paradoxically, were artificially created and manipulated by the studios' own production policies and marketing strategies, and by so doing garnered huge financial returns through box-office receipts.

From approximately 1930, when the conversion to sound was virtually complete and the Wall Street involvement in Hollywood had been consolidated, the American film industry was dominated by the five vertically integrated "major" corporations—Metro-Goldwyn-Mayer (MGM), Paramount Pictures, Radio-Keith-Orpheum (RKO), Twentieth Century-Fox, and Warner Brothers. In collusion with the three "minor" studios, Columbia Pictures, United Artists, and Universal Pictures, these companies exercised a monopoly on production, distribution, and exhibition. In 1938, however, the Justice Department filed an antitrust suit, *The United States v. Paramount Pictures et al.,* against this oligopoly. The suit was part of the Roosevelt administration's policy of reviving the economy and instigating codes of fair competition in the midst of the Depression, and it was prompted in part by the failure of the National Industrial Recovery Act (1933) which, considered by many to be instrumental in perpetuating industrial oligopoly rather than encouraging fair competition as intended, had been ruled unconstitutional by the Supreme Court in 1935.

In 1940, as a temporary measure of appeasement, the majors agreed to sign a Consent Decree that entitled them to maintain their exhibition outlets but necessitated the abandonment of their policy of block booking and blind selling to exhibitors, introducing legislation that required that *all* films, including B pictures, be sold to exhibitors on an individual basis. Nevertheless, as John Izod notes in *Hollywood and the Box Office,* owing to the refusal of the minor studios to comply with the changes in business practice demanded by the Consent Decree, by mid-1942 pre-decree patterns of business had been resumed by the eight big studios.[2] Ineffective as it may have been in regulating the business policies of the oligopoly, however, the Consent Decree was instrumental in creating a competitive environment for the B-film in the early forties and thus represents something of a landmark in the genesis of film noir.

B-film production was a consequence of the double feature exhibition policy introduced in the early thirties as a calculated measure designed to tempt back the cinema-going public during the Depression. This policy was based on the packaging of a relatively high-budget A-feature (rented out for a percentage of box-office receipts), newsreel, and cartoon with a low-budget B-feature (rented for a flat rate), thus providing the customer with some three hours of entertainment for the price of a single entry. Initially at least the bottom half of the bill was filled from a backlog of previously unreleased films, A-features that had been unsuccessful during their first run, or pictures produced by low-budget B-units at the eight big studios, with only a relatively small number provided by the so-called "Poverty Row" studios like Monogram Pictures, Producers Releasing Corporation (PRC), and Republic Pictures. The market share of independent producers changed significantly, however, after 1940.

Between the end of the thirties and 1946 the number of independent production companies in operation had risen to in excess of forty, a number that was to escalate rapidly during the following decade. This was due in part, at least in the early forties, to the free market provisions of the Consent Decree whereby each film, irrespective of budget, was now competing on an individual basis. There was a need in the lower-budget end of the market "to carve out identifiable and distinctive styles" in order to differentiate the product from that of the established A-feature production units at the eight big studios.[3] As the decade progressed, other factors came into play. First, the majors began to reduce their production output precisely at the moment when there was an exhibition boom during the war years, creating a gap in the market that the independents filled. This signaled the beginnings of a new manufacturing policy that would become increasingly widespread during the forties and into the fifties, whereby the majors assumed the role of financiers and distributors for independent production companies, often renting out both equipment and studio facilities. The pre-war policy of contracting artistic and technical personnel was abandoned in favor of producers contracting labor on a film-by-film basis.[4] Second, independent film production offered the possibility of creative freedom and substantial tax advantages, and therefore prompted several leading talents formerly under contract to the eight big studios to create their own companies. Ultimately, however, true creative freedom proved to be short-lived.

Following the conclusion of hostilities in 1945, the Justice Department's antitrust case was reintroduced with the result that in May 1948 the Supreme Court ruled that the majors would have to divest themselves of their exhibition chains. Thus, even as independent filmmaking had become an institutionalized mode of production toward the end of the forties, so now the big studios, which were functioning predominantly as distributors, and even the banks that were involved in the funding of these projects, demanded a greater input at all levels of production. As a result, by the mid-to-late fifties most independent productions were as conservative as their mainstream counterparts.

Notwithstanding this movement toward the traditional conservatism of Hollywood entertainment, in the independent production sector of the forties and early fifties there was a brief but intensive period of artistic creativity and technological and stylistic innovation. This was due in part to the need for product differentiation, a need that in many respects encouraged both the hybridization of genres *and* what would be belatedly recognized as auteurism (the stylistic and thematic features that can be discerned as recurring motifs throughout a given filmmaker's oeuvre). It was also determined, however, by the budgetary constraints of B-film production and the restraints on film content imposed by the production code. These factors would prove instrumental in prompting the genesis of a film noir style,[5] encouraging technological innovation, extensive location work, night-for-night shooting, and expressive camera and lighting work in films like *Stranger on the Third Floor* (Boris Ingster, 1940), *The Seventh Victim* (Mark Robson, 1943), *Phantom Lady* (Robert Siodmak, 1944), *Detour* (Edgar G. Ulmer, 1945), and *T-Men* (Anthony Mann, 1948). Recently, the classical Hollywood filmmaker Edward Dmytryk has even suggested that the regulations of the production code contributed to the visual power of film noir because it forced filmmakers to relay narrative and thematic information "deviously" (that is, in lighting, mise-en-scène, camera movement, framing, and so forth).[6] The B-film directors, became, in the words of Martin Scorsese, film "smugglers" who subverted preconditioned expectations regarding film production, style, and content.[7]

Of course, film noir was not exclusive to B-film production, and several of the early films noirs that initially prompted the post-war French critics to coin the term, such as *The Maltese Falcon, The Glass Key* (Stuart Heisler, 1942), *Double Indemnity, Laura, Murder, My Sweet, The Postman Always Rings Twice* (Tay Garnett, 1946), and *The Big Sleep* (Howard Hawks, 1946), were major studio A-picture productions that featured marquee names and were invariably adapted at great expense from best-selling novels (it is estimated, for example, that at $10,000 the screen rights alone for *The Big Sleep* cost more than the entire production of a low-budget film noir feature like PRC's *Detour*). Generally, however, the enduring attraction of classic film noir stems from its differentiation, indeed its opposition to the standard A-feature Hollywood product. This bears testament both to the differences between the A- and B-picture during the forties and, in the case of the aforementioned texts, the occasional incorporation of B-film characteristics (visual flourishes, thinly veiled sociopolitical critique) by noir filmmakers into the more lucrative A-features.

Classic film noir, as a product of the American film industry, represents an institutionally sanctioned alternative cinema to that traditionally associated with the American studios of the thirties and early forties, one that often stretches the limitations of established production policies. For example:

- Where the major studio pictures of the "Golden Era" are generically specific, the film noir, and in particular the B film noir, is often transgeneric, as in the noir gangster pictures *White Heat* (Raoul Walsh, 1949), *Kiss Tomorrow Goodbye* (Gordon Douglas, 1950), and *The Phenix City Story* (Phil Karlson, 1955) or the noir westerns *Pursued* (Raoul Walsh, 1947), *Station West* (Sidney Lanfield, 1948), and *Rancho Notorious* (Fritz Lang, 1952). *Station West,* for example, resituates the hard-boiled investigative narrative in a small-town western setting, and juxtaposes the traditional mise-en-scène of the western with the thematic motifs of film noir.
- Where classical texts conform to the exigencies of the production code, film noir frequently violates them, particularly in its treatment of violence and sexuality, as in the torture sequence and (implied) oral sex sequence of *The Big Combo* (Joseph H. Lewis, 1955).
- Where the standard Hollywood product favors narrative resolution and affirmation of the American Dream, film noir invariably offers a dark nightmare alternative to that dream, either closing on a pessimistic note, often the death of the protagonist, as in *D.O.A.,* or featuring an ending so happy that it is incongruous with all that has gone before, as in *Shadow of a Doubt* (Alfred Hitchcock, 1943).
- Finally, where most classical Hollywood films favor narrative coherence, invisibility of style, and the subordination of talent to the collective filmmaking process, film noir is frequently self-reflexive, foregrounding by means of convoluted narrative structures and expressive visual flourishes the creative processes and the individual talent that contribute to a film's production. In fact, in classic film noir

many artists and technicians found an arena for new forms of expression usually denied them by the conservative policies of mainstream film production. Screenwriters, for example, could approximate the work of novelists by introducing complex flashback/voice-over structures, narrative devices that also offered imaginative opportunities for editors; cinematographers could experiment with lighting levels, camera angles, shot lengths, and camera movement; and art directors and actors could free themselves from the constraints of "realism."

In a pattern that we shall see repeated in the case of neo-noir, however, even the qualities of difference associated with classic film noir became gradually institutionalized. Noir thrillers, detective pictures, crime melodramas, and woman's pictures became staples of both production and consumption during the forties and into the fifties. They were even parodied in such films as the comic Bob Hope vehicle *My Favorite Brunette* (Elliott Nugent, 1947) and the musical *The Band Wagon* (Vincente Minnelli, 1953). As Palmer notes in *Hollywood's Dark Cinema,* such was the popularity of the noir narrative that as the cinematic production of such texts diminished during the fifties, so a somewhat whitewashed version of film noir was increasingly visible on network television in such shows as *Dragnet, Peter Gunn, Johnny Staccato, 77 Sunset Strip, Mickey Spillane's Mike Hammer, Perry Mason,* and *The Fugitive.*[8] Contrary to the assertions of the early anglophone noir historians who identify 1958 as the end of the film noir era, the genre never actually left the American public consciousness, continuing as a popular cultural mode of entertainment on the small screen, in comic strips, in pulp-fiction (the novels of Mickey Spillane, David Goodis, Jim Thompson, and Ross Macdonald, for example), and indeed in imported European films. In the Hollywood of the fifties and early sixties, however, film noir gradually ceased to be a viable proposition for film production.

As already noted, the fifties was a period of significant change in the structure and function of the American film industry. This was the decade in which the last of the majors (MGM) was finally divorced from its theatrical interests, the number of independent production companies in operation exceeded 160 (accounting for 58 percent of all production in the United States), the policy of "runaway" production became more widespread as an increasing number of films were made either overseas or in areas of the United States other than California, and studio production policy shifted from that of the factory conveyor-belt to that of the package deal.[9] From this point onward, as Hollywood's "blockbuster mentality" took hold,[10] productions became increasingly grander in "cost, spectacle and gesture,"[11] demanding huge budgets, lavish sets, and marquee names in the lead roles. This was also a period that bore witness to irrevocable changes in the look of the standard Hollywood picture, changes once again prompted by the need for differentiation, this time from the images accessible to millions on the small television screen.

By the mid-fifties approximately half of all American film productions were employing color film stock, benefiting from a reduction in price and an improvement in the quality of stock supplied by Technicolor, whose three-strip process had been available since 1935, and Eastman Kodak, which had developed an alternative stock in 1949 that could be used with conventional cameras. Another form of technological development, which served the dual purpose of differentiating cinema from television and fulfilling the industrial commitment to grandiosity, involved the enlargement of the cinematic image itself. Cinerama, which offered a widescreen image, an image with an aspect ratio larger than the industrial standard of 1.33:1, and multidirectional sound, was introduced in late 1952 (as was the short-lived 3-D fad), but proved to be economically prohibitive and never progressed beyond the early phases of development. CinemaScope, however, which was also developed in 1952 by Twentieth Century-Fox and first exhibited theatrically in *The Robe* (Henry Koster, 1953), was a different proposition altogether. Here was a system that anamorphically compressed a widescreen image, offered stereophonic sound, and required minimal investment by exhibitors (the purchase of a wider screen and a new lens to be fitted to existing projectors). By 1954 more than ten thousand theaters had been converted to project the new system, and all the majors except RKO, which was soon to terminate production, and Paramount, which had developed its own widescreen system, Vista Vision, had films in production that employed the new process.[12]

Productions in the fifties tended toward the epic in length, spectacle, and budget, and simplicity and brightness in lighting. The combination of an elongated frame and color film stock, which now began to lose its connotations of the fantastic and to usurp black and white as the signifier of realism, rapidly became established as the industrial norm. As producers began to favor the production of expansive westerns like *The Searchers* (John Ford, 1956), colorful musicals like *South Pacific* (Joshua Logan, 1958), and exotic overseas spectacles like *El Cid* (Anthony Mann, 1961), the production of American films noirs, whose intimate, low-budget dramas had deployed both the cluttered frame of the

Academy aspect ratio and complex black and white cinematography to expressive effect, declined temporarily.[13]

Another possible reason for the demise of the theatrical film noir during this period was the closing between 1948 and 1954 of approximately three thousand small B and third-run theaters in inner-city areas, one of the consequences of demographic change that saw the car-owning middle-class population shift from city center to suburb. Nevertheless, the actual number of American theaters diminished only minimally as the cinematic tastes of a more mobile audience were accommodated by the rise of drive-in theaters (numbering approximately 3,800 by 1954). The changes in Hollywood production policies during the fifties, therefore, were governed as much by changes in exhibition policies as by a need to differentiate cinema from television, or indeed from the pre-1949 Hollywood pictures now broadcast by the television networks.

The rise of the drive-in and the demise of the double bill as an exhibition standard were direct consequences of these changes, as, more significantly, was the new policy of marketing and exhibiting films to target audiences such as the youth market, an increasingly important consumer in the wake of the post-war baby boom, and the art-house audience, whose appreciation of imported films was possibly a by-product of the cine-literacy of a generation of television-educated filmgoers.[14] In fact, such was the taste of these two distinct markets, the former for titillating and violent exploitation fare such as that produced by American International Pictures (AIP), an independent production company founded in 1954, the latter for the sophisticated films (often featuring "adult" subject matter) imported from Europe, that, in conjunction with the open defiance of several mainstream Hollywood filmmakers (the production, for example, of Otto Preminger's 1955 *The Man with the Golden Arm* or Elia Kazan's 1956 *Baby Doll*), they proved instrumental in forcing the revision of the production code in December of 1956.

By the late fifties, the mode of production, the look, and to an extent the content of Hollywood pictures, the policy of exhibition, and the homogeneity of the filmgoing audience itself had all undergone irrevocable changes in relation to those of the thirties and early forties. Nevertheless, despite attempts to diminish its power, the industry continued to be dominated by the old oligopoly. From the end of the fifties, however, even this long-standing institution began to be overhauled as the Hollywood studios entered a sustained period of diversification and conglomeration, in effect creating a cross-media culture industry that today has largely colonized most channels of entertainment in the Western world.

THE NEW HOLLYWOOD

Throughout the sixties the studios continued to pursue their policy of investing enormous sums in blockbuster pictures, in effect gambling on their potential to garner huge financial returns. Increasingly, however, such a policy was costing rather than earning money, with the studios often vainly trying to repeat a one-off commercial success with a series of imitative box-office disasters. The case of Fox in the sixties is exemplary. In 1963 the studio's *Cleopatra* (Joseph L. Mankiewicz, 1963) lost $40 million, prompting the hiring of Darryl Zanuck and his son Richard, who soon put into production *The Sound of Music* (Robert Wise, 1965) with a budget of $10 million. The film grossed $100 million, recouping the *Cleopatra* losses and earning a significant profit over and above that. The studio then tried to replicate this success with other epic musical productions like *Dr. Dolittle* (Richard Fleischer, 1967), *Star!* (Robert Wise, 1968), and *Hello, Dolly!* (Gene Kelly, 1969), all of which failed at the box office, contributing to huge financial losses in 1969 and 1970. Were it not for the commercial success of "relatively inexpensive, offbeat films" like *Butch Cassidy and the Sundance Kid* (George Roy Hill, 1969) and *M*A*S*H* (Robert Altman, 1970), which earned $46 million and $36.7 million respectively, the studio probably would have gone bankrupt.[15]

Such films marked two significant developments in the "New Hollywood" of the late sixties and early seventies. First, there was the emergence of a new wave of filmmakers during the sixties such as the directors Robert Altman, Arthur Penn, Bob Rafelson, Francis Ford Coppola, Brian DePalma, Terence Malick, Martin Scorsese, and Steven Spielberg, and the cinematographers William Fraker, Conrad Hall, Laslo Kovacs, Haskell Wexler, and Vilmos Zsigmond. These were filmmakers who entered the industry as cine-literates often having either graduated from film school (Scorsese), worked in television (Altman), or done a combination of both (Spielberg). Their filmic interests were inspired as much by European as by classical Hollywood cinema. Second, the early films of the so-called "movie brat" generation were targeted at a like-minded audience, a cine-literate baby boom generation of filmgoers who, during the late sixties, were embroiled in the rise of the counterculture and the "New Left." This was the audience that was the principal art-house film import consumer, and would prove to be responsible for the respectable commercial success of such American productions as *The Graduate* (Mike Nichols, 1967), *Bonnie and Clyde* (Arthur Penn, 1967), *2001: A Space Odyssey* (Stanley Kubrick, 1968), *Butch Cassidy and the*

Sundance Kid, Midnight Cowboy (John Schlesinger, 1969), *Easy Rider* (Dennis Hopper, 1969), *Medium Cool* (Haskell Wexler, 1969), *The Wild Bunch* (Sam Peckinpah, 1969), *M*A*S*H,* and *Woodstock* (Mike Wadleigh, 1970).

The commercial disaster of several blockbusters during the sixties prompted a period of widespread experimentation and innovation, resulting in the assimilation of European art cinema filmmaking techniques into the American mainstream cinema. Films of this period, like several of their European counterparts (the Sergio Leone–Clint Eastwood spaghetti westerns, for example), also featured unprecedented levels of violence, sexuality, and profane language, the result of a more dramatic overhaul of censorship regulations than those implemented in 1956. In 1966 the Motion Picture Association of America (MPAA) introduced the *Code of Self-Regulation,* which was "designed to keep in closer harmony with the mores, the culture, the moral sense and the expectations of our society." In light of the films that have subsequently been made under the aegis of the code, and in particular the often violent and sexually explicit neo-noirs that are of immediate interest to this study, it is worth quoting the code's "Standards for Production" at some length:

The basic dignity and value of human life shall be respected and upheld. Restraint shall be exercised in portraying the taking of life.

*   *   *

Evil, sin, crime and wrong-doing shall not be justified.

*   *   *

Special restraint shall be exercised in portraying criminal or anti-social activities in which minors participate or are involved.

*   *   *

Detailed and protracted acts of brutality, cruelty, physical violence, torture and abuse, shall not be presented.

*   *   *

Indecent exposure of the human body shall not be presented.

*   *   *

Illicit sexual relationships shall not be justified. Intimate sex scenes violating common standards of decency shall not be portrayed. Restraint and care shall be exercised in presentations dealing with sexual aberrations.

*   *   *

Obscene speech, gestures or movements shall not be presented. Undue profanity shall not be permitted.

*   *   *

Religion shall not be demeaned.

*   *   *

Words or symbols contemptuous of racial, religious or national groups, shall not be used to incite bigotry or hatred.

*   *   *

Excessive cruelty to animals shall not be portrayed and animals shall not be treated inhumanely.

In many respects the code was a concession to the fragmentation of the previously homogeneous family audience that consumed films in the thirties and forties. Indeed, one of the provisions of the new code reflects the youthfulness of the average audience in the late sixties. Identifying parents as "the arbiters of family conduct," the code now required that, first, "by advertizing, by displays at the theatre and by other means" parents should be better informed about the content of a given film in order to "choose which motion pictures their children should see," and, second, that, in cooperation with the Code Administration, producers should identify certain films as "Suggested for Mature Audiences." This identification, and ultimately, some might argue, segregation, of target audiences became institutionalized as a standard policy of film exhibition two years later when in 1968 the MPAA established a Ratings Board which functioned to rate films according to their suitability for specified age-groups.

By the late sixties the American film industry was in the midst of a transitional stage. Gone was the conveyor-belt system of production, the homogeneous audience, and the distinctive identities of the old studios themselves. As Robert Phillip Kolker has observed in his study of post-classical Hollywood cinema, *A Cinema of Loneliness,* during this period of conglomeration and diversification "the focal point of Hollywood filmmaking became diffuse, and by the end of the decade the 'product,' once controlled by a studio from inception to exhibition, was controlled and executed by different hands, from different sources, and for different ends."[16] Inevitably the long-term effect of this was a gradual movement, despite audience diversity, toward the homogeneity of product in mainstream American cinema, as the moneymen of the huge corporate entities that now controlled film production sought to avoid the kind of financial malaise that affected the industry in the mid-sixties through the early seventies (an estimated $51 million drop in average profits between the periods 1964–68 and 1969–73).[17] Nevertheless, this uncertain transitional period in the history of American cinema, as with the impact of the Consent Decree of 1940 on low-budget filmmaking, did pave the way for a brief period of innovation and experimentation, the period, that is, of the "neo-modern," which was instrumental in encouraging the genesis of American neo-noir.

In his study of neo-modern cinema, *Cinema and Modernity,* John Orr suggests that the "moment of the modern in Western cinema" was a phenomenon peculiar to the period 1958 through to 1978, and in effect represented a return to the high modernism of the late teens and early twenties that had made only the most minimal of impressions on the cinematic medium while it was still in its technical infancy.[18] From the late fifties, however, and above all in Europe, a small number of filmmakers began to experiment with the forms and conventions of cinematic representation. This twenty-year period marked the moment of the European new waves, the Hollywood renaissance, and the emergence of the self-conscious auteur, cinema's equivalent of the literary modernist. This was the period during which filmmakers like Godard, Truffaut, Antonioni, Bertolucci, Saura, Erice, Fassbinder, Herzog, Wenders, Forman, Menzel, Altman, Penn, Coppola, and Scorsese first came to prominence in Western cinema, and during which others like Bergman, Bresson, Buñuel, Fellini, and Kubrick consolidated their position within it.

It was above all the work of the young *cinéastes* of the French *nouvelle vague,* however, that proved instrumental in introducing the neo-modern to American filmmakers, prompting a reassessment of American film history and a revival of film noir in the Hollywood cinema of the late sixties. This group of francophone filmmakers included Jean-Luc Godard, François Truffaut, Claude Chabrol, Eric Rohmer, and Jacques Rivette, all of them graduates of the film journal *Cahiers du Cinéma.* As critics they had championed American cinema to the detriment of their own national film industry, developing *la politique des auteurs* by which they illustrated how filmmakers like Hawks, Hitchcock, Ray, Welles, as well as many of the B-film directors, visually and thematically imposed their own artistic visions on essentially generic material. Entering the film industry themselves, they self-consciously played with the formal means at their disposal, above all subverting the classical Hollywood filmmaking paradigm of self-effacement. They constantly alluded to films of the past and "delighted in making the viewer aware of the act of watching a film, revealing it as an artifice, something made in special ways, to be perceived in special ways."[19] The qualities that attracted such "art cinema" directors to film noir have been aptly summarized by Palmer as

> a fascination with subjectivity, exemplified by first-person narration and the representation of inner consciousness; the subversion of middle-class

values regarding law and order, family, sexual expression, material success, and poetic justice; a critical perspective on the discontents of modern urban life; a tradition of stylistic expressivity; and the thematizing of alienation and the limits of human freedom, ideas very resonant with the existential ethos of many 1960s intellectuals, especially in France.[20]

The style of the *nouvelle vague* films was replete with jump cuts, long hand-held takes, extreme close-ups, freeze-frames, and extradiegetic sound, all of which represented a radical departure from the formal paradigms of classical Hollywood cinema (establishing shots, the 180-degree rule, continuity editing). Nevertheless, many of the early *nouvelle vague* films like *A bout de souffle* (Jean-Luc Godard, 1959), *Tirez sur le pianiste* (François Truffaut, 1960), and *Alphaville* (Jean-Luc Godard, 1965) perpetuated the cinematic tradition of film noir, in particular the B films noirs of Joseph H. Lewis, André De Toth, Edgar G. Ulmer, Nicholas Ray, Robert Siodmak, and Samuel Fuller, by employing generically determined iconography and exploring traditional noir themes. Their playful allusion to classic noir texts both cinematic and literary (the ending of *A bout de souffle*, for example, invites comparison with that of *They Live By Night*, and in *Alphaville* not only does the protagonist wear the private investigator's trade mark trench coat, but at one stage he even reads Chandler's *The Big Sleep*),[21] combined with their stylistic innovation and generic transformation (*Alphaville*, for example, is a noir science-fiction hybrid) helped modernize the genre at a time when films noirs had all but ceased to be produced by American filmmakers.

In this sense the landmark film, both in terms of according the *nouvelle vague* and its subversive attitude toward "classical" cinema international recognition and in terms of reinventing film noir in the wake of the self-conscious baroqueness of *Touch of Evil* (Orson Welles, 1958), was *A bout de souffle*. Not only did Godard's film self-consciously experiment with film form, rupturing the classical paradigms of American filmmaking, but it also managed to lend a certain intellectual cachet to essentially pulp material. *A bout de souffle* juxtaposes popular cultural references to Hollywood B-films, American film personalities, and comic strips, for example, with pseudophilosophical discussions of love and death, as well as allusions to William Faulkner, Dylan Thomas, Claude Renoir, and Pablo Picasso. Additionally, the film continues classic film noir's critique of modernity (here represented by the labyrinthine Parisian urban landscape) and the middle class (in particular their sexual relations, their economic aspirations, and their intellectual pretensions).

In this sense the esthetic and ideological agenda in operation in the film is not that distant from the literary modernism of the twenties. It constitutes a fusion of high art and popular culture, and it places a thematic emphasis on the alienating effects of modernity, the breakdown of human interaction, the devaluation of romantic love, the psychological fragmentation of modern man, and a critique of capitalist society.

A bout de souffle was the film, to invoke Damico's concept of the cyclical pattern of generic evolution by which a genre experiences "periods of birth, development, flowering which presumably includes its purest examples, and either evolution into a new form or death,"[22] that signaled film noir's metamorphosis into a "new form," and it did for film noir what Sergio Leone's *A Fistful of Dollars* (1964) would do for the western. In effect, Godard's film initiated an art cinema cycle of neo-modern neo-noir productions that, although restricted to European productions like *Tirez sur le pianiste, Crimen de doble filo* (José Luis Borau, 1964), *Le Samouraï* (Jean-Pierre Melville, 1967), and *Il Conformista* (Bernardo Bertolucci, 1970) throughout most of the sixties and early seventies, would eventually include American texts like *Point Blank* (John Boorman, 1967), *Bonnie and Clyde, Klute* (Alan J. Pakula, 1971), *Play Misty for Me* (Clint Eastwood, 1971), *The Long Goodbye* (Robert Altman, 1973), *Mean Streets* (Martin Scorsese, 1973), *Badlands* (Terence Malick, 1974), *Chinatown, The Conversation* (Francis Ford Coppola, 1974), *Night Moves, Taxi Driver, New York, New York* (Martin Scorsese, 1977), and *The Driver* (Walter Hill, 1978). Such early examples of American neo-noir commodified *nouvelle vague* stylistic techniques, successfully assimilating art-house innovation into the American mainstream (as witness the editing patterns in the early sequences of *Bonnie and Clyde* and *Point Blank* or the experimentation with sound in *The Conversation*). For many young filmmakers, moreover, the French-initiated contemporary revival of film noir, in addition to serving as a vehicle for formal experimentation, would also offer a platform for sociopolitical commentary.

In fact, not only did European auteurs like Godard contribute to the thematic and stylistic revisionism of film noir, but it was, moreover, the burgeoning influence of European film theory in the United States and Great Britain that in the first place instigated the Anglo-American critical interest in the filmmakers responsible for the style and content of the best of American genre cinema, prompting the rediscovery of the work of many of the innovative B film noir filmmakers (Lewis, Ulmer, and Alton, for example), and encouraged the anglophone assimilation of the critical concept of film noir toward the end of the sixties, instituting an inquiry into the history and legacy of film noir by academics and critics that frequently paralleled that of the neo-modern filmmakers.[23] In this sense, the self-consciously auteurist American cinema of the seventies, in terms both of its artistic sensibility and the pessimistic vision it offered of American society, was the least "American" in its outlook since the influx into Hollywood of the European *émigrés* (Lang, Siodmak, Wilder, de Toth, Renoir, Curtiz) in the thirties and forties.

In 1971 Paul Schrader, one of the pioneering anglophone film noir theorists, observed:

> Hollywood's *film noir* has recently become the subject of renewed interest among movie-goers and critics. The fascination *film noir* holds for today's young film-goers and film students reflects recent trends in American cinema: American movies are again taking a look at the underside of the American character . . . As the current political mood hardens, film-goers and film-makers will find the *film noir* of the late forties increasingly attractive.[24]

In fact, by the late sixties film noir had already been subjected to a revisionist revival, with self-reflexive films like *Bonnie and Clyde* and *Point Blank* respectively investigating the traditional noir subgenres of the outlaw couple road movie, epitomized by such classic texts as *They Live By Night* and *Gun Crazy,* and the moody seeker-hero narrative, exemplified by noir thrillers like *Act of Violence* (Fred Zinnemann, 1949) and *D.O.A.* Offering paradigmatic noir narratives, these films visually refurbished film noir in color and widescreen. In terms of sexuality and violence they made explicit what could only be suggested in their classic counterparts, and, by co-opting *nouvelle vague* stylistic techniques, they introduced a degree of formal experimentation unprecedented in the traditionally conservative American mainstream cinema. Films like *Klute, Play Misty for Me, The Long Goodbye, The Conversation,* and *Taxi Driver* similarly would be founded on this formal and stylistic compromise between art-house experimentation and the conventions of American genre cinema.

As with the genres institutionally recognized during the era of classical Hollywood cinema such as the musical, western, gangster picture, and war film, film noir in the hands of the post-classical Hollywood filmmakers became both an object of generic revisionism and a tool for a more overtly political investigation of American society than had been

the case in the days of the production code. Like the revisionist musicals
Funny Girl (William Wyler, 1968), *Cabaret* (Bob Fosse, 1972), and *New
York, New York* or the westerns *The Wild Bunch, Little Big Man* (Arthur
Penn, 1970), and *McCabe and Mrs. Miller* (Robert Altman, 1971), seventies' neo-noir, and in particular the detective variant of the genre as in
Hickey & Boggs (Robert Culp, 1972), *The Long Goodbye,* and *Night
Moves,* became a popular means of illustrating "the failure of American
myths to define the nature of contemporary life."[25] These films, as neo-
noir critic Leighton Grist argues, challenged "crucial ideological assumptions embedded in the genre" and enacted a "process of formal revision and thematic demystification."[26]

Suggesting the Hollywood renaissance filmmakers' familiarity with
the history of the genre, many of the seventies' neo-noir films tend to
take as a point of departure the archetypal narratives of the original hard-
boiled novelists like Hammett, Cain, and Chandler, and the forties' A-
feature films noirs adapted from their work, such as *The Maltese Falcon,
Double Indemnity, The Big Sleep,* and *The Postman Always Rings Twice.*
At the same time, however, these revisionist texts consistently suggest
the combined influence of the classical Hollywood B-film, the European
auteur and new wave filmmakers, the second generation of hard-boiled
novelists (Thompson, Goodis, and Macdonald, for example), and in particular the fifties film noir cycle of "psychotic action and suicidal impulse," which includes *Gun Crazy* (Joseph H. Lewis, 1950), *Night and
the City* (Jules Dassin, 1950), *Pickup on South Street* (Samuel Fuller,
1953), *The Big Heat* (Fritz Lang, 1953), *The Big Combo, The Phenix City
Story, Kiss Me Deadly* (Robert Aldrich, 1955), and *Touch of Evil.*[27]
Many of the seventies neo-noir texts are not only noteworthy for a degree of formal experimentation uncharacteristic of mainstream Hollywood cinema and a similarly unprecedented level of overtly political social commentary but also for their status as self-conscious testaments to
the continuing evolution of the noir genre. Their self-consciousness may
not be as playfully overstated as that of Godard's *A bout de souffle* and
Alphaville, but it nevertheless informs our understanding of these films
as neo-modern artifacts.

The revival of film noir, however, cannot simply be attributed to the
influence of the French *nouvelle vague* on a handful of young American
filmmakers. As already noted, in the United States of the late fifties and
sixties' noir — in the form of crime fiction, television police procedural
and private detective serials, photography, and painting — remained very
much a popular cultural tradition. By the late sixties a formulaic and

commodified version of film noir was beginning to reappear in American cinemas. Like many of the forties noir A pictures such as *The Big Sleep,* these tended to be star vehicle literary adaptations like the neo-noir detective pictures *Harper* (Jack Smight, 1966) adapted from Ross Macdonald's novel *Moving Target* and starring Paul Newman, *Marlowe* (Paul Bogart, 1969) adapted from Raymond Chandler's novel *The Little Sister* and starring James Garner, and *Farewell, My Lovely* (Dick Richards, 1975) adapted from Chandler's novel of the same title and starring Robert Mitchum. By the early seventies, therefore, there was in coexistence two distinctive neo-noir traditions, the revisionist and the formulaic, the former inspired by the *nouvelle vague*'s experimental/investigative approach to film, the latter a manifestation of renewed cinematic interest in a popular narrative pattern that had temporarily been relegated to the small screen and other art forms. Both strands of neo-noir have endured into the nineties, the former becoming a staple of low-budget independent feature film production and the latter a staple of both mainstream major studio film production and low-budget straight-to-video and made-for-television production.[28]

RETRENCHMENT, FORMULARIZATION, AND INDEPENDENT VISIONS

That experimentation had been possible in the mainstream productions of the late sixties and early seventies was largely a result of the uncertainty that permeated the Hollywood studios in the aftermath of the collapse of the studio system. As the industry was restructured and stability returned in the wake of conglomeration and diversification, however, the standardized patterns of production and formularized narrative content traditionally associated with Hollywood cinema also reappeared, so bringing to a close the brief period of renaissance. In the wake of the fiscal uncertainty of the late sixties, the mid-to-late seventies was a period of retrenchment and restabilization in the American film industry, prior to a renewed spate of mergers and takeovers and the streamlining of existing conglomerates during the eighties and nineties.

As in the fifties, the output of the studios diminished during the late seventies, eighties, and nineties as Hollywood film production once again was geared toward the multimillion dollar "blockbuster mentality" epitomized by *Jaws* (Steven Spielberg, 1975), *Star Wars* (George Lucas, 1977), *Top Gun* (Tony Scott, 1986), and *Batman* (Tim Burton, 1989).[29]

In contemporary films the experiments of the late sixties filmmakers were commodified, and their innovative projects once again gave way to formulaic mainstream productions. This process has been marked by the complicity of many of the Hollywood renaissance filmmakers themselves (as witness, for example, Coppola's formularization of his *Godfather* series in the 1990 *The Godfather, Part III*). In the age of multimedia conglomeration film franchising has also become a widespread policy with films designed to reap millions of dollars not only in box-office receipts but also in network, cable, and satellite television broadcasts, video rentals and sales, and movie-related merchandising such as video games, soundtrack albums, books, and T-shirts.

The dominant tendencies of mainstream films in the post-renaissance era of the mid-seventies to the present represent a return of sorts to the ideological and stylistic (genre-based, continuity, closure) conservatism of much of the classical Hollywood cinema that prevailed prior to the industrial upheaval of the late fifties and sixties. In films like *Rocky* (John G. Avildsen, 1976), *Star Wars, Superman* (Richard Donner, 1978), *Kramer vs. Kramer* (Robert Benton, 1979), *Raiders of the Lost Ark* (Steven Spielberg, 1981), *Red Dawn* (John Milius, 1984), *Ghostbusters* (Ivan Reitman, 1984), *Rambo* (George Pan Cosmatos, 1985), and *Back to the Future* (Robert Zemeckis, 1985), we witness the reclamation of patriarchal values, the rediscovery of masculine heroism, the return of class, gender, and ethnic stereotyping, the celebration of technology, and articulations of nuclear anxiety, anti-Communism, and fear of "otherness" (xenophobia, patriotic jingoism, misogyny, homophobia). In many of these films there is a degree of formularization that far exceeds the traditional generic markers of iconography, character types, and narrative patterns. In fact, one of the tendencies of mainstream contemporary Hollywood productions is toward a cinema of serials, sequels, remakes, comic pastiche, and comic-strip adaptation, which becomes the progenitor of a seemingly endless cycle of *Star Wars, Superman, Rambo, Rocky, Police Academy, Back to the Future, Indiana Jones, Lethal Weapon, Die Hard, Batman, A Nightmare on Elm Street,* and *Friday the Thirteenth*. Such films are modeled on the concept of homogeneity of product, and they constitute a cinema in which the classic staples of plot and character are secondary to computer-generated special effects and visual pyrotechnics. In such texts style is nearly always of greater value than content.

In this sense, the increasing appeal of film noir to mainstream filmmakers during the eighties and nineties is unsurprising. The *concept* of noir, particularly as theorized by those stressing the visual qualities of the classic film noir texts, has become commodified not only by the contemporary feature film industry but also by advertising agencies, television production companies, animators, and specialists in promotional music videos. In the film noir science-fiction hybrid *Blade Runner* (Ridley Scott, 1982), for example, there is a catalog of visual and narrative "markers" that apparently are intended to signify the film's "noirishness," including low-key lighting, claustrophobic framing, imbalanced frame compositions, tilted camera angles, light filtered through venetian blinds and reflected off rain-washed streets, and costumes that invoke the forties' film noir iconography of the hard-boiled detective and the femme fatale.[30]

As Jeremy Butler has argued, the eighties commodification of the noir stylistic is further developed in the popular television series *Miami Vice* which proved to be a significant influence on the formulaic feature-length neo-noirs of recent years.[31] In *Miami Vice* stylistic effects traditionally associated with classic film noir in anglophone film criticism of the seventies and eighties (low-key lighting, cluttered frames, extreme camera angles) are juxtaposed with stylistic effects associated with the new wave filmmakers of the sixties and seventies (slow motion, freeze-frames, steadicam). The editing, moreover, is often governed by a music soundtrack showcasing contemporary chart hits (again, a legacy of seventies filmmakers like Scorsese who used popular music in films like *Mean Streets* and *New York, New York,* for example, to comment on narrative events and underscore thematic motifs), and the series often gives the impression of being an extended MTV video, with mood added by the clichéd use of smoke and the aforementioned noirish lighting tropes,[32] a hackneyed stylistic effect that pervades the contemporary noir thriller epitomized, for example, by *Deceived* (Damian Harris, 1991), *Shattered* (Wolfgang Petersen, 1991), and *Final Analysis* (Phil Joanou, 1992).

The traditional noir seeker-hero and victim-hero narratives have similarly become commodified and formularized in eighties and nineties mainstream productions.[33] This is prompted in part by recent anglophone theory *about* classic film noir, so that a film like *Body Heat* (Lawrence Kasdan, 1981), for example, can be read as both a contemporary reworking of *Double Indemnity* and an attempt to put into effect a "rudimentary working prototype" for the noir narrative similar to that defined by James Damico in 1978:

Either because he is fated to do so by chance, or because he has been hired for a job specifically associated with her, a man whose experience of life has left him sanguine and often bitter meets a not-innocent woman of similar outlook to whom he is sexually and fatally attracted. Through this attraction, either because the woman induces him to it or because it is the natural result of their relationship, the man comes to cheat, attempt to murder, or actually murder a second man to whom the woman is unhappily or unwillingly attached (generally he is her husband or lover), an act which often leads to the woman's betrayal of the protagonist, but which in any event brings about the sometimes metaphoric, but usually literal destruction of the woman, the man to whom she is attached, and frequently the protagonist himself.[34]

It is also encouraged, however, by the proven success of narrative formulae such as the one developed by screenwriter Joe Eszterhas in *Jagged Edge* (Richard Marquand, 1985), one of the key films in the eighties "yuppie nightmare" cycle, and repeated by the same writer with minor variations and to diminishing effect in *Betrayed* (Constantin Costa-Gavras, 1988), *Basic Instinct* (Paul Verhoeven, 1992), and *Jade*. Hyperbolic in tone and parodic in style, such films tend to mark the creative and technical redundancy of mainstream eighties and nineties Hollywood cinema.

This redundancy is further suggested by the proliferation of eighties and nineties remakes of classic films noirs such as *Against All Odds* (Taylor Hackford, 1984), a reworking of *Out of the Past* (Jacques Tourneur, 1947) that effectively dismantles the tightly wrought plot and intricate mise-en-scène of the original, abandoning altogether the "existential determinism" of *Out of the Past*,[35] and substituting banal rock-scored love scenes and car chases for the suggestively erotic imagery of classical Hollywood director Jacques Tourneur and cinematographer Nicholas Musuraca. Other neo-noir remakes include *Thieves Like Us* (Robert Altman, 1974), based on *They Live By Night; The Morning After* (Sidney Lumet, 1986), based on *The Blue Gardenia* (Fritz Lang, 1953); *No Way Out* (Roger Donaldson, 1987), based on *The Big Clock* (John Farrow, 1948); *The Underneath* (Steven Soderbergh, 1995), based on *Criss Cross* (Robert Siodmak, 1949); and similarly *The Big Sleep* (Michael Winner, 1978, UK; Howard Hawks, 1946), *The Postman Always Rings Twice* (Bob Rafelson, 1981; Tay Garnett, 1946), *D.O.A.* (Rocky Morton and Annabel Jankel, 1988; Rudolph Maté 1950), *The Desperate Hours* (Michael Cimino, 1990; William Wyler, 1955), *The Narrow Margin* (Peter Hyams, 1990; Richard Fleischer, 1952), *A Kiss Before Dying* (James Dearden, 1991; Gerd Oswald, 1956), *Cape Fear* (Martin Scorsese, 1991; J. Lee Thompson, 1962), *Night of the Hunter*

(David Greene, 1991; Charles Laughton, 1955), *Night and the City* (Irwin Winkler, 1992; Jules Dassin, 1950), *Detour* (Wade Williams, 1992; Edgar G. Ulmer, 1945), and *Kiss of Death* (Barbet Schroeder, 1994; Henry Hathaway, 1947). Even Godard's seminal text *A bout de souffle* has been remade as *Breathless* (Jim McBride, 1983) in a film that proved to be highly influential on contemporary neo-noir auteur Quentin Tarantino, and there currently are plans to remake both *Brute Force* (Jules Dassin, 1947) and *Kiss Me Deadly*.[36]

In the cinema of the eighties and nineties, then, film noir no longer constitutes an industrially sanctioned alternative cinema to the mainstream, as was the case in the forties and fifties, but is now a cornerstone of mainstream Hollywood production. This is not to argue that in the eighties and nineties the revisionism of the seventies auteurs has wholly given way to mainstream formularization. Indeed, there are a number of neo-noirs like *Atlantic City* (Louis Malle, 1981), *Thief* (Michael Mann, 1981), *Hammett* (Wim Wenders, 1982), *Black Widow* (Bob Rafelson, 1987), *House of Games* (David Mamet, 1987), *Sea of Love, The Two Jakes* (Jack Nicholson, 1990), *Miller's Crossing* (Joel and Ethan Coen, 1990), *Internal Affairs* (Mike Figgis, 1990), *Q & A* (Sidney Lumet, 1990), *Mortal Thoughts* (Alan Rudolph, 1991), *The Public Eye* (Howard Franklin, 1992), *Boiling Point* (James B. Harris, 1993), *Clockers, Heat,* and *Fargo* (Joel and Ethan Coen, 1996) which, funded in whole or in part by major studios, seem to depart from or challenge the formularization of noir evidenced by the majority of contemporary mainstream thrillers.[37] These are neo-noir texts which, as Grist has observed, "at least partly eschew postmodern pastiche for a more integrated, if no less self-conscious, use of generic convention, with a return to textual depth instead of just a play of surfaces."[38] Several of these films consciously play with the narrative patterns of classical film noir (*The Two Jakes, Mortal Thoughts*) and allude to the cultural origins of the genre (*Hammett, Miller's Crossing*), while others revive the thematic concerns of the seventies neo-noir texts (corruption, social injustice, dysfunctionality), bringing into play issues relating to gender roles, ethnic identity, and the sociopolitical disparities that exist between the rich and the poor.

House of Games, for example, produced by independent company Filmhaus on behalf of Orion, is the directorial debut film of playwright and screenwriter David Mamet. The film belongs to the cycle of yuppie nightmare films initiated by *After Hours,* and is formulaic in that it is structured around the archetypal film noir narrative of the middle-class protagonist's descent into an alien, subterranean world of crime and corruption. Where the film most apparently dismantles its formulaic structure, however, is in the reversal of the archetypal gender roles. This is a text in which the *female* protagonist is exploited by an enigmatic and alluring *male,* indeed a text in which none of the males who appear on screen are beyond suspicion. It is, moreover, a film that like the neo-modern neo-noirs of the seventies self-consciously investigates the generic traditions it invokes (its emphasis on psychoanalysis, its Hop-perish mise-en-scène, its voyeurism, its foregrounding of role-playing), and unlike the formulaic films of the era ends on a note of ambiguity (is the death of Joe Mantegna's Mike simply a fantasy projection of Lind-say Crouse's Margaret, or is it diegetic reality?).

The majority of independently produced neo-noir productions simi-larly sustain the formal experimentation and thematic investigation of the seventies neo-modernists. Despite the conservatism of mainstream cinema since the late seventies, American independent cinema has been particularly buoyant in recent years, frequently leading the way in the American market with films like *She's Gotta Have It* (Spike Lee, 1986), *sex, lies and videotape* (Steven Soderbergh, 1989), and *Reservoir Dogs,* only to see their innovative projects imitated and formularized in the Hollywood mainstream.[39] The revival of the independent sector in the late eighties, led in part by the critical and commercial success of the award-winning *sex, lies and videotape,*[40] has resulted in the establish-ment of a number of new production companies like Castle Rock, Mira-max, Morgan Creek, and New Line; the emergence of a second genera-tion of cine-literate filmmakers that includes the Coen Brothers, Spike Lee, Jim Jarmusch, Gus Van Sant, Hal Hartley, Richard Linklater, Kevin Smith, Allison Anders, Robert Rodriguez, and Quentin Tarantino; and the consolidation of a regular cinephile audience in the art houses and on the film festival circuit, where directors rather than stars remain the ma-jor box-office attraction. Frequently the work produced in this sector is technically innovative, intensely personal, and often uncompromising in its representation of violence and sexuality.

In independently produced neo-noirs like *Union City* (Mark Reichert, 1980), *A Flash of Green* (Victor Nuñez, 1984), *Blood Simple, Man-hunter* (Michael Mann, 1986), *Slamdance* (Wayne Wang, 1987), *Cop* (James B. Harris, 1988), *Cat Chaser* (Abel Ferrara, 1989), *Kill Me Again* (John Dahl, 1989), *The Kill-Off* (Maggie Greenwald, 1990), *The Grifters* (Stephen Frears, 1990), *Reservoir Dogs, Guncrazy* (Tamra Davis, 1992), *Deep Cover* (Bill Duke, 1992), *One False Move, Pulp Fiction, The Last Seduction* (John Dahl, 1994), *Romeo is Bleeding, The Usual Suspects,* and *Things To Do In Denver When You're Dead,* as with the classic B film noir, filmmakers have been forced to turn "economic necessity into stylistic virtue."[41] In the tradition of the early works of the French *nouvelle vague* and the American "movie brats" these films represent a self-conscious celebration of the cinematic medium itself. It is, moreover, in such violent, lurid works that the true pulp qualities of the original films noirs appear to have been recaptured. *Guncrazy,* for example, offers a nineties hybrid of the classic film noir road movies *They Live By Night* and *Gun Crazy* and the seventies neo-noir *Badlands.* Its protagonist is a sexually abused high school girl Anita (Drew Barrymore) who murders her absent prostitute mother's boyfriend with whom she shares a trailer and marries an impotent, gun-obsessed ex-con Howard (James Le Gros) to whom she has been writing in prison. When Howard murders the young men who have repeatedly abused Anita, the two take to the road on a crime spree.

As with the work of contemporary crime novelists like Elmore Leonard, James Ellroy, Carl Hiaasen, Walter Mosley, and James Lee Burke, these independent texts flaunt the filmmakers' knowledge of a cultural heritage that extends beyond the cinema into the realms of television (*Dragnet* and *Johnny Staccato*), the visual arts (the paintings of Edward Hopper and the photography of Weegee),[42] and hard-boiled fiction (James M. Cain, Cornell Woolrich, Jim Thompson, et al.). In an interview given at the time of the release of *Blood Simple,* for example, discussing the film's relation to classic film noir, Joel Coen observed, "We tried to emulate the *source* that those movies came from rather than the movies themselves."[43] The return to the literary origins of the genre is a phenomenon that has permeated peripheral mainstream and independent neo-noir throughout the eighties and nineties, culminating in Quentin Tarantino's 1994 film *Pulp Fiction.* Films like *Blood Simple, Guncrazy,* and *One False Move,* then, meditate on and constitute a revision of that cultural heritage while simultaneously, in the tradition of both classic film noir and seventies neo-noir, bringing into play contemporary concerns that relate to the social and cultural realities of living in the United States today. It is to the political and sociocultural contextualization of the evolution of film noir that we now turn.

America Noir

2 political paranoia, social malaise

Fundamental to an understanding of noir in both its classic and neo-noir manifestations is a sense of how the genre captures the notion of the American Dream gone wrong. As J. P. Telotte puts it, film noir

> generally focuses on urban crime and corruption, and on sudden up-wellings of violence in a culture whose fabric seems to be unraveling. Because of these typical concerns, the *film noir* seems fundamentally *about* violations: vice, corruption, unrestrained desire, and, most fundamental of all, abrogation of the American dream's most basic promises—of hope, prosperity, and safety from persecution.[1]

The genre, then, points to the fallacy of economic expectations about the United States as a land of opportunity and reveals the impossibility of social equality in contemporary society. Noir tends to chronicle social rifts, on the one hand highlighting the increasing power of the wealthy at the expense of the poor, and on the other thematizing male paranoia regarding female autonomy. More recently the genre has also begun to chronicle racial and ethnic divisions, foregrounding how such issues relate to inner-city malaise and widespread economic deprivation in the United States today.

In many respects film noir is a genre of and about fragmentation, not only stylistically (the disruptive effects of lighting, mise-en-scène, and editing) and structurally (the employment of flashbacks and voice-overs) but also thematically (the dissolution of community and family, the psychological fragmentation of the protagonist). Typically, whether following the fortunes of the apparently incorruptible Chandlerian protagonist as in *The Big Sleep* and *Farewell, My Lovely,* the inveterate narcissist as in *Kiss Me Deadly* and *Badlands,* or the psychologically unstable sociopath as in *Gun Crazy* and *Taxi Driver,* the noir narrative is in effect an exploration of the personal identity crises of its protagonists. The surface nature of such crises varies from film to film, but they are frequently underpinned by issues relating to the uneven distribution of wealth and the allure of financial gain. In noir wealth rather than birth tends to demarcate class differences. There are those who have immense fortunes and those who are poverty-stricken, but very few who inhabit the middle ground. Such social divisions are indicated in the film noir by the fact that, first, members of ethnic minorities who have access to vast fortunes, particularly Italian-Americans and Jews, are typically presented as gangsters; second, rich women are nearly always gold-digging femmes fatales often married to men who are several years older; and third, the rich, whether male or female, are frequently characterized either as sexually "deviant" (homosexual, bisexual, or simply excessive in their sexual habits), politically corrupt, or a combination of both.

What classic film noir did was bring to the fore those issues—crime, violence, individualism, greed—that formed the subtexts of the pre-production code thirties films like the gangster pictures *The Public Enemy* (William A. Wellman, 1931) and *Scarface* (Howard Hawks, 1932) and the backstage musicals *Gold Diggers of 1933* (Mervyn LeRoy, 1933) and *42nd Street* (Lloyd Bacon, 1933), drawing also from the class and sexual politics of the late thirties and early forties screwball comedies of filmmakers like Preston Sturges, Howard Hawks, and Frank Capra. In the late forties, the heyday of classic film noir, such concerns suggested how the events and social injustices of America's immediate past (the Prohibition and Depression years) still impinged on the present.[2] As the genre developed through the forties and on into the fifties, shaped in part by the social realities of contemporary America, the depiction of a fragmented and increasingly violent society became more pronounced still.

Indeed, as suggested by urban theorist Mike Davis in his study of Los Angeles, *City of Quartz*,[3] and illustrated by contemporary crime fiction writer James Ellroy in his "L.A. Quartet" (*The Black Dahlia, The Big Nowhere, L.A. Confidential,* and *White Jazz*) and his "Underworld U.S.A. Trilogy" (of which only *American Tabloid* has been published to date), the political and sociocultural history of the United States in the twentieth century often approximates that of a noir narrative. It is unsurprising, therefore, that it has proven to be such a powerful determinant in helping shape the evolution of the noir genre in both its literary and its cinematic manifestations. The impact of economic depression, U.S. involvement in overseas military campaigns and the concomitant psychological dislocations that result from protracted exposure both physically and through the media to warfare, the eruption of violence (assassination attempts, terrorist acts, riots) on American soil, civil rights campaigns by both ethnic minorities and women, the ever-present threat of nuclear destruction, and repeated revelations of mismanagement and corruption in the highest echelons of government are motifs that run through both the recent history of the United States and the noir genre.

DEPRESSION AND WAR

After her triumphant intervention in the First World War, the United States emerged as one of the most powerful military and trading nations in the world. The twenties proved to be an immensely prosperous period, with economic production nearly doubling between 1921 and 1929. In October of 1929, however, the bottom fell out of the Wall Street stock market. The Great Crash, as it subsequently came to be known, had an immediate impact on the nation's economy, with a sharp rise in unemployment and a dramatic drop in the Gross National Product. As the Depression (an era that forms the backdrop to films noirs as diverse as *Detour, The Postman Always Rings Twice, They Live by Night, Bonnie and Clyde, They Shoot Horses Don't They?* [Sydney Pollack, 1969], *Thieves Like Us, Chinatown,* and *Last Man Standing* [Walter Hill, 1996]) set in, bankruptcies multiplied, housing fell into a state of disrepair or remained unoccupied, and, while thousands took to the road in search of work and food, crops were destroyed because farmers could not afford the cost of transportation. Invariably it was members of the lower middle and working classes who were worst hit, thus reaffirming the great divide that separated them from the wealthy ruling class who had been the principal beneficiaries of the prosperous twenties. Class struggle was hardly a new phenomenon, however. Like the discrimination against immigrants, African-Americans, and Communists, it pre-dated the industrial expansion of the twenties. As reflected in the gangster pictures, social problem films, backstage musicals, and even comedies of the period, this was an era of class and economic aspirations, dreams gone awry, individualism, greed, and criminality. Such motifs would be co-opted by the noir genre, the legacy of the Depression still impinging on noir productions in the late forties, as witness *They Live by Night.*

In November 1932 Franklin D. Roosevelt was elected president of the United States. In the first one hundred days after his March 1933 inauguration ceremony the Roosevelt administration put into effect the

New Deal program. This introduced a number of policies designed to strengthen the powers of the federal government and instigate economic recovery. Acts were introduced to avert the collapse of America's banking system, to create jobs for men aged eighteen to twenty-five, to help state and city authorities care for the unemployed, to introduce codes of fair business competition, to oversee the construction of public facilities (including schools and roads), to control the production of crops, and to help farmers refinance mortgages. Such policies, however, represented little more than a kickstart to the New Deal. Further measures such as the National Housing Act (1934) and the Social Security Act (1935) were introduced with the aim of furthering gradual economic recovery and social reform. By 1940 economic recovery was underway, unemployment was down to 14 percent, and Roosevelt's attention was now focused on the conflicts in Europe and the Far East.

Between 1935 and 1937 the United States legislated three neutrality acts designed to avoid a repetition of events that had resulted in the nation's participation in the First World War. By late 1940, however, as German armed forces swept across Europe, the U.S. isolationist policy loosened as the American people were made to realize that supplying of arms to Allied nations like Britain could prove vital to the security of the United States itself. By only supplying arms, not men, it was believed that American bloodshed would still be avoided. The defense budget was increased fivefold by Congress and the United States began a massive program of military and industrial mobilization, the direct consequence of which was the revival of the industrial sector, a drop in unemployment, and a dissipation of the social unrest that had marked the thirties.

By the time the United States was finally forced into full participation in the war, following the Japanese bombing of Pearl Harbor in December 1941, an economic boom was in full swing. The military and industrial requirements made full employment a realistic possibility, the nation was self-sufficient incurring no international debts nor suffering the bombardments and deprivations inflicted upon the European Allies, and the government's economic resources were rapidly multiplying. During the conflicts, as the ideology of national unity took hold, there was a notable change in gender and, to a lesser extent, ethnic roles in American society as huge numbers of women and African-Americans became involved in the war effort.

The entry of so many women into the workforce during this era has been of particular interest to feminist noir critics. Sylvia Harvey, for example, has argued that the "underlying sense of horror and uncertainty in film noir may be seen, in part, as an indirect response to this forcible assault on traditional family structures and the traditional and conservative values they embodied."[4] Women, it has been argued, were feared and resented by returning war veterans for having achieved economic independence during the war years, for being reluctant to return to their pre-war roles, and for occupying jobs that the men wanted, hence the proliferation of strong and threatening femme fatale figures like Mrs. Grayle (Claire Trevor) in *Murder, My Sweet* and the occasional masculinization of businesswomen figures like Mildred (Joan Crawford) in *Mildred Pierce* (Michael Curtiz, 1945) in the film noir narratives of this era.

Certainly employment was an area of some concern in post-war America. In the first ten days of peace, approximately two million people were made redundant, compelling the Democratic administration under new President Harry Truman to introduce the Full Employment Bill, which was part of a wider program designed to reconvert the U.S. economy to peacetime conditions as smoothly as possible. This was greatly modified, however, by the Republican-dominated Congress and was passed as the Employment Act. Similarly, attempts to control prices were rejected by Congress, the result of which was an 18 percent rise in the cost of living in the aftermath of the war.

As American industry and society reaccustomed itself to peace and the demand for labor declined, the fragile concept of national unity crumbled and old class, racial, and sexual prejudices were reasserted, manifesting themselves in a variety of forms. Distribution of wealth, for example, again became an issue as the unions, seeking to gain a share of corporate wartime profits for laborers and wage increases that would compensate for the rising costs of living, began a program of industrial action in 1945 and 1946 that affected the mining, steel, automobile, petroleum, railroad, and film industries. The Republican midterm election triumph of 1946, however, which had seen them gain a majority in Congress, quickly curbed the power of the unions in 1947, when the Taft-Hartley Bill was introduced despite a presidential veto.

The issue of civil rights also forced itself onto the political agenda in the aftermath of the war as African-Americans began to campaign for equality in the face of racial discrimination, segregation, and violent suppression, particularly in the southern states. In response, the Truman administration introduced legislation that outlawed lynching, abolished the poll tax, and sought to desegregate the armed forces. Nevertheless, classic films noirs that directly confronted the question of racial and ethnic differences remained few in number, although as William Luhr has noted, several films noirs and hard-boiled novels of this period, such as *The Maltese Falcon* (the Hammett novel *and* the Huston film), did thematize the "erosive effects of the foreign upon the American norm."[5] Of course, ethnic stereotyping was common (Italian-Americans as gangsters, Irish-Americans as policemen), and there was the occasional film that did thematize racial tensions such as *Crossfire* (Edward Dmytryk, 1947) which tackled the issue of anti-Semitism, and *No Way Out* (Joseph L. Mankiewicz, 1950) and *Odds Against Tomorrow* (Robert Wise, 1959) which featured African-American stars Sidney Poitier and Harry Belafonte respectively.

In general, however, forties noir tended to conflate WASPish values with the concept of "Americanness," so establishing a paradigm by which to be foreign or to belong to an ethnic minority was to be "other" and therefore threatening. Such ethnic paranoia was poignantly exploited by Welles, for example, in *Touch of Evil*, in which an American border town becomes the seedy playground of Mexican criminals. In fact, the "foreignness" of the modern industrialized city in these films, in which the (usually) WASP protagonist traverses an urban landscape populated by Irish, Italian, and Hispanic Catholics, East European Jews, and African-Americans, was a recurrent motif informed in part by the late forties and fifties migration of the WASP American from the urban center to the suburb. The alienating qualities of the city are further augmented for the film noir protagonist both by the ease with which the criminal and the femme fatale move through its less than accommodating environs and by the violence with which he is invariably confronted during his urban journeys.[6] This is well illustrated in *The Maltese Falcon* when Archer (Jerome Cowan) is murdered while tailing Brigid O'Shaughnessy (Mary Astor) through the city at night.[7]

Another social problem frequently explored by such forties films noirs as *The Blue Dahlia* (George Marshall, 1946), *Dead Reckoning* (John Cromwell, 1947), and *Crossfire* was the rehabilitation of the returning war veteran. As Paul Schrader puts it, in these films, in which disillusionment with post-war society is rife, the "war continues, but now the antagonism turns with new viciousness towards American society itself."[8] The source of the ex-servicemen's discontent is invariably psychological, suggesting the difficulty of abandoning wartime behavioral patterns and readapting to pre-service social roles. The war veteran (who resurfaces in the post-Vietnam films of the seventies and eighties) is not, however, the only character to suffer in forties and fifties noir. In fact, Richard Maltby argues in "The Politics of the Maladjusted Text" that the archetypal noir protagonist—whether detective, serviceman, petty criminal, or nondescript middle-class citizen—is "afflicted with one or another form of compulsive behavior, psychosis, identity crisis, guilt complex, amnesia or general paranoia."[9] Invariably such protagonists are male, although *Phantom Lady,* which features an *investigative* female protagonist, and noir women's pictures like *Caught* (Max Ophüls, 1949) and *The Reckless Moment* (Max Ophüls, 1949), which feature a victim-heroine, represent notable exceptions to this general rule (there are many more exceptions in the post-feminist neo-noirs of the eighties and nineties). Plagued by the fragmentary impulses associated with schizophrenia, narcissism, and psychosis during their journeys through the noir underworld, these figures are usually irreparably damaged, both physically and psychologically, by their contact with such an alien universe. The narrative of *D.O.A.,* in which the fatally poisoned protagonist Frank Bigelow (Edmond O'Brien), a public accountant, voluntarily enters the noir underworld in order to find his murderers, is exemplary in this respect.

COLD WAR HYSTERIA

Having intervened decisively in Europe and Asia during the war, the late forties was to see the United States intensifying its involvement in international affairs. This period was notable for the U.S. membership in the International Court of Justice, its foundation of the National Security Council and Central Intelligence Agency (CIA), and its attempts to revitalize the economies and defenses of European and Latin American nations (the Marshall Plan and the Organization of American States respectively). This heightened activity in the security and economic affairs of other nations was underpinned by two national preoccupations that were to overshadow the politics and culture of the United States throughout much of the fifties and sixties, namely, the spread of Communism (suggested, for example, by the presence in New York of a Communist spy ring in Samuel Fuller's 1953 film noir classic *Pickup on South Street*) and the threat of a nuclear holocaust (poignantly expressed in the nihilistic ending of Robert Aldrich's 1955 detective noir *Kiss Me Deadly*).[10] Such preoccupations were shaped in part by U.S. employment of the atomic bomb in 1945, which destroyed the Japanese cities of Hiroshima and Nagasaki, and by the Soviet Union's detonation of their own bomb in 1949 and the subsequent escalation of the cold war. They also reflected the anxiety caused in the United States by the Soviets' powerful hold on Eastern Europe, and the 1949 founding of the Chinese Peoples Republic under the leadership of Mao Tse-tung.

With involvement in the creation of the Atomic Energy Commission in 1946, the Berlin airlift of 1948–49, and the 1949 founding of the North Atlantic Treaty Organization (NATO), the United States entered the arms race and initiated a policy of stockpiling both conventional and nuclear weapons. Already frosty relations with the Communist nations were further compounded in 1950 when the United States interceded on behalf of South Korea in the Korean War. After initial military successes, American forces suffered a number of setbacks following the alignment of Communist Chinese forces with the North Koreans. The result was a stalemate from which the Americans did not extricate themselves until a new government was formed under President Dwight D. Eisenhower in 1953. At home the economic repercussions of U.S. involvement in this war were profound and caused yet another substantial increase in both military expenditure and the cost of living, which once again prompted a wave of industrial action.

The Korean War intensified concerns in the United States regarding the spread of Communism. This had previously manifested itself in the hysterical right-wing Communist "witch-hunts" that had rocked the motion picture industry during the previous decade and now resurfaced as the anti-Communists focused their attention on American politics in the fifties. In fact, during the late forties several members of the Communist Party had been prosecuted, members of the government had been subjected to interviews by loyalty boards, and a number of prominent figures in the motion picture industry had been interviewed by the House Committee on Un-American Activities (HUAC) and subsequently blacklisted or in a few cases imprisoned (this period in American film history was explored in Irwin Winkler's 1991 film *Guilty by Suspicion*). In 1950 a new act was passed that served to establish the Subversive Activities Control Board and was designed to monitor the activities of Communists in the United States and prevent the immigration of any member of a Communist organization.

It was, however, the activities of Communist witch-hunter Senator Joseph McCarthy that proved to be the most telling of this era. McCarthy's unsubstantiated assertions of Communist infiltration into the Department of State in the early fifties did little to inspire confidence in a government that was already under pressure over U.S. involvement in the Korean War, the poor state of the economy, and revelations of corruption within the Truman administration. McCarthy instigated a number of often quite arbitrary investigations into the activities of other government agencies, but it was his 1954 attempt to investigate the U.S. Army that proved to be his undoing. McCarthy himself was investigated by the Senate and censured for his methods and abuse of persons in positions of authority. His witch-hunt campaigns, however, left an indelible mark on the fifties offering an aspect of Republicanism that differed considerably from that represented by the new President and former war hero Eisenhower.

Paranoia about political and corporate corruption informed the narratives of many of the films noirs of the late forties and early fifties. A general mistrust of institutions and bureaucracy was suggested in the numerous films, such as *I Walk Alone* (Byron Haskin, 1948), *The Big Clock, Force of Evil* (Abraham Polonsky, 1948), *All the King's Men* (Robert Rossen, 1949), *Ace in the Hole* (Billy Wilder, 1951), *The Big Heat, The Big Combo, The Phenix City Story,* and *Party Girl* (Nicholas Ray, 1958), that were concerned with the syndication of organized crime and the corruption of public figures. In *The Phenix City Story,* for example, a young lawyer returns home from the war to find that his hometown is wracked by political corruption, and that the prominent citizens are all in thrall to the power of a mobster based in the city's seedy gambling district. The film dwells on the moral degradation and violence of the modern world. Usually, these films return to the motif of the corrupt city that prevailed in the early noir detective pictures, illustrating the pervasive effects of financial and political corruption in contemporary society.

Eisenhower's presidential victory late in 1952 signaled the end of twenty years of Democratic control of the White House. His policies, despite his hands-off approach and delegation of authority to both his business-oriented cabinet and local government, complemented in many respects the legislative programs of Roosevelt's New Deal and Truman's Fair Deal. His two terms in office coincided with a period of relative affluence and stable home policy. Unemployment, for example, averaged only 4.5 percent throughout much of the decade. Despite a brief recession in the mid-fifties and a crisis in agriculture, the Eisenhower administration was successful in its attempts to balance the budget. The decade of the fifties saw reduced federal spending, low taxation, and the rise of the automobile, home ownership, the suburbs, and television. It was also a period witness to a rising standard of living and rampant consumerism. By the end of the decade film noir had all but disappeared from U.S. theaters, reflecting not only the aforementioned shifts in exhibition policy by the major studios and diversification of the once homogeneous audience, but a less tumultuous period in the nation's sociocultural and political history.

Social grievances were still numerous. General discontent with the government, as opposed to the popular president himself, was evidenced, for example, when the Democrats regained control of both houses of Congress in the mid-fifties. It was further compounded in the late fifties, after Eisenhower's reelection, by evidence of financial corruption in the government, a brief recession, and a gradual rise in unemployment levels. A particularly contentious issue throughout Eisenhower's two terms in office was the civil rights campaign. The Eisenhower administration sought to widen the policy of desegregation in the government, the armed forces, the schools, and transportation. Throughout the decade African-Americans campaigned for racial equality in both the courts and the public arena, organizing marches and sit-ins. In 1957 Congress passed the Civil Rights Act, which established a civil rights commission. Such policies, unsurprisingly, proved unpopular with white voters in the South and resulted in violent clashes between blacks and whites, prompting Eisenhower on one occasion to send federal troops to help African-American students attend Central High School in Little Rock, Arkansas, in September 1957.

As Schrader observes in "Notes on *Film Noir*," in the fifties noir took another turn. Although the genre had all but disappeared from American screens by the end of the decade, the early-to-mid fifties represented the height of the classic film noir period of "psychotic action and suicidal impulse."[11] This was a period during which films like *The Asphalt Jungle* (John Huston, 1950), *In a Lonely Place* (Nicholas Ray, 1950), *Strangers on a Train* (Alfred Hitchcock, 1951), *Detective Story* (William Wyler, 1951), *The Big Heat, Pickup on South Street, The Big Combo, Kiss Me Deadly,* and *Touch of Evil* marginalized the figure of the femme fatale and brought to the fore the male psychopath (Humphrey Bogart's Dix Steele in *In a Lonely Place*), the homme fatal (Robert Walker's Bruno Anthony in *Strangers on a Train*), the corporate gangster (Richard Conte's Mr. Brown in *The Big Combo*), and the corrupt public official (Orson Welles's Hank Quinlan in *Touch of Evil*). Surreptitiously these films articulated the fears of American society about masculine violence (fostered by the nation's participation in two recent wars), corporate and political corruption, Communist infiltration, and the threat of nuclear holocaust. Their style, moreover, was often overtly expressionist, underpinning their thematization of existential angst, paranoiac fear of "otherness" (ethnicity, sexuality, gender, politics), psychic fragmentation, and crisis of identity.

As noir productions diminished, however, with Hollywood production methods shifting to accommodate the new technologies (widescreen and color) and the increasingly pervasive "blockbuster mentality," it was left to problem pictures like *On the Waterfront* (Elia Kazan, 1954), *The Wild One* (Laslo Benedek, 1954), *East of Eden* (Elia Kazan, 1955), *The Blackboard Jungle* (Richard Brooks, 1955), and *Rebel Without a Cause* (Nicholas Ray, 1955), frequently directed by filmmakers who had hitherto worked in film noir, to articulate social concerns. Similarly it became the province of science-fiction films like *The Day the Earth Stood Still* (Robert Wise, 1951), *Them!* (Gordon Douglas, 1954), *Invasion of the Body Snatchers* (Don Siegel, 1956), *Forbidden Planet* (Fred M. Wilcox, 1956) and *The Incredible Shrinking Man* (Jack Arnold, 1957) to metaphorically invoke cold war anxiety. Despite a period of prolonged sociocultural upheaval in the post-Eisenhower years and an intensification of cold war rivalry that brought the nation to the brink of a third world war and the very real possibility of nuclear annihilation, it was not until the late sixties, in the wake of political assassinations, race riots, and U.S. involvement in another protracted overseas military campaign that the cinema-going public would once again see a "dark mirror" held up to American society in the Hollywood renaissance filmmakers' revival of film noir.

REVOLUTION AND COUNTERREVOLUTION

The sixties and early seventies proved to be one of the most turbulent periods in recent American history. The issue of civil rights, for example, continued to command attention, and in the sixties was the cause célèbre of both African-American and women's rights campaigners, both movements reflective of a more widespread social mobilization that saw the emergence of the New Left and the counterculture. There were profound economic problems, a legacy of the apparently affluent Eisenhower years during which the introduction of the credit card and the policy of hire purchase had seen consumer indebtedness rise to $196 billion by 1960. In foreign policy, the 1961 plot to overthrow Fidel Castro in Cuba resulted in the Bay of Pigs debacle, a source of acute embarrassment for the new president, John F. Kennedy. The threat of full-scale nuclear warfare with the Soviet Union was only narrowly avoided with the resolution of the Cuban missile crisis late in 1962. There were, however, three significant events that defined the era and made a lasting impression on America's self-image and popular culture: (1) the assassination of President Kennedy in Dallas on 22 November 1963; (2) the protracted U.S. involvement and ultimate defeat in the Vietnam War; and (3) the revelation of governmental corruption and the subsequent resignation of President Richard Nixon in the Watergate scandal.

The enduring legacy of these events is well illustrated by the treatment of Kennedy's assassination in recent years. Both Oliver Stone's political intrigue thriller *JFK* (1991) and crime fiction writer James Ellroy's novel *American Tabloid* (1995), for example, nearly thirty years after the event, seek to reaffirm complex conspiracy theories that were prompted by Kennedy's death. John Mackenzie's neo-noir *Ruby* (1992), on the other hand, focuses on the underworld figure Jack Ruby who himself murdered Lee Harvey Oswald, the reputed assassin of the president. The assassination, the murder of Oswald, and the televised funeral of the president, compounded by the findings of the Warren Commission, traumatized American society and helped fuel speculation about an assassination plot, a governmental conspiracy, and a coverup. In September 1964, the commission, the first of a number of high-profile investigations in recent U.S. political history, ruled that Lee Harvey Oswald was the sole assassin of the president, despite ballistic evidence that suggested there may have been more than one gunman.

Conspiracy theories were further strengthened by the controversy that surrounded Abraham Zapruder's home-movie footage of the president's death. This was purchased by *Life* magazine executives who chose to publish a number of stills from the footage but opted to keep the film itself out of the public domain. When the Zapruder footage was finally broadcast on American network television in the mid-seventies, it was the first time that the American public had been shown images of Kennedy's head exploding with the impact of the second bullet, again suggestive of a second gunman shooting from a location different from that supposedly occupied by Oswald. The cultural and sociopolitical implications of the broadcast are reflected, for example, by the fact that the footage is discussed by two characters in Arthur Penn's 1975 film *Night Moves,* as is the footage of the murder of the president's brother Robert Kennedy in 1968. Both assassinations serve as a historical frame of reference for *The Parallax View* (Alan J. Pakula, 1974) and the legacy of John's assassination is fundamental to the psychological makeup of the protagonist in *In the Line of Fire* (Wolfgang Petersen, 1993).

The violence of the event itself, in conjunction with the political paranoia prompted by rumors of a coverup and the revelation of both patriarchal vulnerability (Kennedy's death) *and* patriarchal corruption (the suggestion of an assassination plot), set the tone for the following years. Little more than a decade after Kennedy's death the United States had witnessed the assassinations of other prominent public figures such as the black civil rights activists Malcolm X (1965) and Martin Luther King (1968), urban race riots such as those in Harlem in 1964 and Watts in 1965, the televised barbarities of the Vietnam War, and the revelation of political corruption in the upper echelons of the Nixon administration.

The second of the era's major events to leave an enduring legacy in American popular culture, as witness *The Deer Hunter* (Michael Cimino, 1978), *Platoon* (Oliver Stone, 1986), and *Full Metal Jacket* (Stanley Kubrick, 1987), was U.S. involvement in the military conflict in Vietnam. The war began to escalate in August 1964, when two American destroyers were attacked in the Gulf of Tonkin. With the support of the Senate, President Lyndon B. Johnson ordered the active involvement of American jets, authorizing the bombing of military targets in North Vietnam. Throughout 1965 the number of American military personnel in the Vietnam area was gradually augmented so that by the end of the year there were some 200,000 troops on active duty in South Vietnam. By 1968 there were in excess of half a million troops, and late in 1967 it was revealed by the Pentagon that thus far, in addition to the financial cost ($25 billion per annum), the war had cost 15,058 deaths and 109,527 wounded.

At home thousands mobilized to protest against American involvement in the war, infuriated not only by the financial and human cost of the war but also by the revelation of war atrocities committed by American troops (the My Lai incident of 1968, for example). Public dissatisfaction with Johnson's handling of the conflict ultimately resulted in his suspension of bombing in North Vietnam and his noncandidacy for the 1968 presidential elections. Protests escalated as the war continued, and in 1970 four students were killed by the National Guard at Kent State University in Ohio during demonstrations against U.S. action in Cambodia that had been authorized by the new Republican president, Richard Nixon. Dissatisfaction with the Vietnam situation was further compounded in 1971 with the publication of the Pentagon Papers, which served to further undermine public confidence in the conduct of government, both Republican and Democrat.

Despite the violence that marked many of the key social, cultural, and political events of the decade, the sixties were witness to the most sustained period of social reform since the early years of the Roosevelt administration. By 1968, when the Republicans eventually regained control of the White House, the Democrats, under the Roosevelt protégé Johnson, had managed to implement measures that, according to political historian Ian Derbyshire, "extended the role of the Federal government in economic and social affairs and established a more comprehensive welfare state."[12] Johnson's implementation of what he called the Great Society program encompassed the introduction of the Economic Opportunity Act (1964), the Civil Rights Act (1964), the Voting Rights Act (1965), the Housing and Urban Development Act (1965), the Elementary and Secondary Education Act (1965), and Medicare (1966). Nevertheless, as the urban ghetto riots of 1964–68 well demonstrate, the benefits of Johnson's Great Society were not enjoyed by all.

Despite the strides taken with the legislation of the mid-sixties, economic and social inequality remained rife as unemployment rose and women and African-Americans continued to campaign for equal rights. Civil unrest also began to manifest itself in demonstrations directed against U.S. involvement in the Vietnam War. In many respects the late sixties in the United States were all about mobilization, not simply in military terms but also in terms of the gathering momentum of social movements responding to "the issues of civil rights, poverty, feminism, and militarism."[13] This was the era of youthful rebellion, the National Organization for Women (NOW), black militant protest, counterculture, and antiwar sentiment. By the end of the decade, however, a conservative backlash had swept Richard Nixon and the New Right to power.

The American cinema of this era, particularly the work of young filmmakers just breaking into the industry, in many respects helped provide a platform for previously repressed minority voices and reflected the cultural and sociopolitical concerns of the various countercultural, youth, black, and, to a much lesser extent, feminist movements.[14] They suggested the turbulence of American society in the late sixties, foregrounding the social divide that existed between generations (*The Graduate*, for example), classes (*Midnight Cowboy*), and ethnic groups (*Sweet Sweetback's Baadass Song,* Melvin Van Peebles, 1971), and offered a vision of the United States that demythologized the representation of the nation and its people offered by classical Hollywood cinema. As Ryan and Kellner observe in *Camera Politica,* collectively the renaissance pictures of the late sixties and seventies (*The Graduate, Bonnie and Clyde, Midnight Cowboy, M*A*S*H*) repetitively returned to the central image of the individual rebelling against "conservative authority and social conformity" and invariably featured representations of the "Establishment"

> as a set of outdated conservative values, of the police as an enemy rather than a friend, of the patriarchal family as an institution for the oppression of women, of the liberal ideal of consensus as a cloak for white racial domination, of the government as the slave of economic interests, especially war industry interests, of foreign policy as a form of neoimperialism, of Third World liberation struggles as heroic, of the value of subjective experiences related to mysticism and drugs, of the importance of the preservation of nature, of sexuality as a rich terrain of possibility rather than as an evil to be repressed, and of capitalism as a form of enslavement instead of a realm of freedom.[15]

Generally speaking, film noir was co-opted by the liberal filmmakers of the Hollywood renaissance as witness *Bonnie and Clyde, Klute, The Conversation, The Parallax View, Night Moves, Three Days of the Condor* (Sydney Pollack, 1975), and *All the President's Men* (Alan J. Pakula, 1976), films that thematized dysfunctionality and patriarchal corruption, and succeeded in commodifying the left-wing politics and generically revisionist art cinema experimentation of the *nouvelle vague* for consumption by a mass mainstream Hollywood market. Such contemporary neo-noirs offered an ideological alternative to the conventionally generic right-wing police procedural and vigilante films like *Dirty Harry* (Don Siegel, 1971), *The French Connection* (William Friedkin, 1971), and *Death Wish* (Michael Winner, 1974), which reaffirmed both the patriarchal values and the regressive mythology of the Right.

The new Republican president, Richard Nixon, came to power in 1968 proposing a New Federalism, a program designed to restore social stability and limit the power of the federal government, and promising to withdraw troops from Vietnam. Nixon's major political triumphs lay in his handling of foreign affairs. He withdrew a substantial number of troops from Vietnam early in his term in office and subsequently signed a 1973 cease-fire agreement that facilitated the withdrawal of all troops. He also succeeded, with the assistance of secretary of state Henry Kissinger, in thawing U.S. relations with Communist China, initiating Strategic Arms Limitation Talks (SALT) with the Soviet Union, and resolving the Yom Kippur War in the Middle East. Nixon's downfall, however, was prompted by the revelation of a series of government and corporate irregular activities, foremost among which was the Watergate scandal.

This, after the assassination of John F. Kennedy and the Vietnam War, represents the third of contemporary America's psychological scars.

The arrest of five men employed by the Committee for the Re-election of the President (CREEP) in the offices of the Democratic National Committee at the Watergate complex in Washington on 17 June 1972 ultimately unearthed an illegal espionage campaign that incriminated several of the most powerful men in Washington. These included former attorney general John Mitchell, White House staffers John Dean, H. R. Haldeman, and John Erlichman, and the president himself.[16] Between the day of the arrests and the opening of the Senate Select Committee hearings on presidential activities in May 1973, public interest in the Watergate scandal gradually mounted. In April 1973, following a series of resignations and sackings from the government, a full-scale investigation into the break-in was initiated by Archibald Cox. It soon became apparent that not only were prominent public figures behind the break-in but that they had attempted to cover up their involvement by paying off the burglars with CREEP funds. In July it was revealed that the president had automatically recorded all conversations held in the Oval Office. Cox subpoenaed eight tapes, which, despite district and appeal court rulings to the contrary, Nixon refused to surrender on the grounds that they were relevant to national security. At Nixon's urging Cox was finally discharged from office as part of the infamous Saturday Night Massacre of 20 October, which also saw another spate of prominent resignations from the government. When Nixon finally relinquished the tapes, it was discovered that a number of relevant conversations were missing and that one tape in particular featured an 18½-minute gap, the result of repeated erasures. In the following months a number of additional tapes were subpoenaed that revealed Nixon's involvement in the political shenanigans of his reelection campaign of 1972 and the subsequent coverup attempts. In July 1974 the House Judiciary Committee moved in favor of the president's impeachment, and on 9 August Nixon became the first president in the history of the United States to resign from office. Further revelations of political corruption in the Nixon administration that came to light in the months following his resignation did little to restore public faith in the United States or its government.

Espionage and patriarchal corruption had been a mainstay of many neo-noir productions, such as *Klute, The Conversation,* and *Chinatown,* made throughout the period of Nixon's term in office. The Watergate scandal, however, triggered a new cycle of neo-noir films, including *The Parallax View, Three Days of the Condor,* and *All the President's Men,*

which thematized the American public's political paranoia in the aftermath of Nixon's incrimination and articulated their discontent with both
the government and corporate America. These films also gave expression, in light of the controversy over Nixon's recorded conversations, to
mounting unease regarding technological development (the surveillance
equipment of *Klute* and *The Conversation,* the high-tech offices of the
Washington Post in *All the President's Men*). Just as the automobile and
the firearm formed part of the iconography of the thirties gangster picture (and all subsequent crime films), so dehumanized modes of communication (computers, fax machines, answering machines) and surveillance (phone taps, zoom lenses, camcorders) increasingly began to
form part of the iconography of the contemporary neo-noir in the wake
of this brief political paranoia cycle, as witness such eighties and nineties
texts as *Blow Out* (Brian DePalma, 1981), *Blade Runner, Manhunter, No
Way Out, Shattered,* and *Strange Days.*

Collectively the seventies political paranoia films, as Leighton Grist
has observed, present "a claustrophobic/paranoiac world of threat and
mistrust, within which their protagonists seek, but usually fail, to expose
the corruption within an all-powerful, oppressive economic or political
organization."[17] As with the liberal films of the late sixties and early seventies, such films offered a demythologized vision of the United States
to the cinema-going public, a dark nightmare universe in which political corruption, abuse of power, covert operations, assassinations, and
coverups were the norm. The historical reality of the Kennedy assassinations, Watergate, and the 1975 congressional investigation of CIA operations lent potency to their fictional narratives. Indeed, generally
speaking, many of the social realities of the United States in the early-
to-mid seventies were not that distant from those represented in the neo-
noir texts of this era.

By the time hostilities had ceased in the Second World War, the
United States had established itself as the strongest economic and military power on the globe. But by the end of the seventies, this was patently
no longer the case. As political historians Robert Garson and Christopher
Bailey note, "The limits of American military and economic power were
clear for all to see. The armies of the United States were being humbled
in the jungles of south-east Asia, its monopoly of atomic weapons had
long disappeared, and its economic prominence was being challenged by
Japan and West Germany."[18] The Watergate scandal, rising crime and
unemployment, and economic stagflation, which had been further compounded by the OPEC embargo on oil shipments to the United States and

the subsequent rise in oil prices, only served to further compound these issues. A sense of impotence and directionlessness seemed to take hold in the mid-to-late seventies, manifesting itself both in the political activity of the Gerald Ford and Jimmy Carter administrations and in the popular culture of the era epitomized, for example, by the rambling narrative of *Nashville* (Robert Altman, 1975), an ironic tribute to the nation's bicentennial celebrations.

Abroad, the United States witnessed the final humiliation in the Vietnam saga as Communist forces finally secured victory in April 1975. At home, Ford's brief term in office was marked by an unprecedented series of presidential vetoes indicating his administration's inability to find solutions for unemployment, inflation, and the energy crisis. There was little improvement under Carter, whose economic policy was at best haphazard and whose questionable leadership qualities were exposed in the handling of the Iranian hostage crisis in Tehran. In April 1980 the apparent powerlessness of the administration was illustrated when Carter sanctioned a rescue mission that proved to be an abortive fiasco. It was not until January 1981, after President Ronald Reagan had been sworn in, that the last of the hostages were finally released. Concurrently, relations with the Soviet Union deteriorated following their invasion of Afghanistan in 1979. In response, Carter refused to sign the SALT II treaty and ordered trade restrictions and a boycott of the Moscow Olympic Games in 1980, once again provoking anxiety in American society about the escalation of the cold war and the concomitant threat of global nuclear destruction.

In the films noirs, and indeed in the romans noirs of the mid-to-late seventies (the work of Ross Macdonald, Elmore Leonard, and Edward Bunker, for example), there was clear evidence of a return to the thematic concerns of the late forties and fifties texts, which themselves had suggested the malaise of American society in the post-war era. In general, the vision of contemporary America offered by seventies neo-noir was darker, more cynical, and more downbeat than its classical Hollywood cinema counterpart. As the authors of "*Films Noir* and Their Remade Versions" put it,

At the core of noir film is expression of the existential dilemma which posits that man is alone in a chaotic and uncaring universe, and must therefore create a meaning and purpose in life, which is ultimately an act of faith. Healthy societies can greatly aid an individual in accomplishing this, but when there is malaise about the rightness and nurturing ability of one's society, then alienation, fearfulness, obsession, and anxiety creep deep into the psyche.[19]

Such issues become the driving force behind the narratives of seventies and early eighties neo-noir texts like *Night Moves, Taxi Driver, The Driver,* and *Cutter's Way* (Ivan Passer, 1981).

In these films America is once again presented as a place of corporate crime, patriarchal corruption, masculine dysfunctionality, and urban violence; the central characters are embroiled in a crisis of identity that will never be resolved; and the sanctified institution of the nuclear family is distorted beyond recognition: mothers are either absent or totally corrupt, fathers are rendered impotent, and children have dropped out of society, seeking solace in counterculture. As Ryan and Kellner observe, ultimately such films are "distinguished by a sense of pessimism devoid of even the individual triumphs that the traditional noir detective enjoyed."[20] In *Cutter's Way,* for example, despite events being played out against a background of communal celebration, the principal characters Alex Cutter (John Heard), Richard Bone (Jeff Bridges), and Maureen Cutter (Lisa Eichhorn) are each tainted by the loneliness, lack of direction, paranoia, cynicism, impotence, and fear of post-assassination, post-Vietnam, post-Watergate American society. Even when his friends Alex, a disabled and bitter war veteran, and Maureen, his alcoholic wife, die as a consequence of Cutter and Bone's attempts to implicate powerful businessman J. J. Cord (Stephen Elliott) in a murder investigation, Bone is unable to assume the heroic mantle toward which Alex has been pushing him. When Cord is shot in the film's final frame, it is the lifeless finger of Alex Cutter rather than his own that Bone holds to the trigger.

NEO-CONSERVATISM AND INDIVIDUALISM

Ronald Reagan entered the White House on the back of a resurgent right-wing movement that espoused capitalism, individualism, entrepreneurialism, anti-Communism, and military might. In Reagan's two terms in office, as the economy and defense remained two of the most pressing issues on the political agenda, the society that had been shaped by the Democratic New Deal and Great Society programs of the thirties and sixties was effectively dismantled. In effect, the Reagan and Bush years were distinguished by a gradual freezing of the socioeconomic gains of African-Americans and women, who both had campaigned so vigorously for their civil rights during the previous two decades; by the not-unrelated widening of the economic and class divide in American society; by the promotion of individualism, selfishness, and greed, underpinned by Reaganomics and the get-rich-quick mentality that saw the rise (and fall) of the yuppie; by imperialist American intervention overseas that was intended to recapture the myth of American military might that had prevailed before the Vietnam debacle (a status tentatively regained in the wake of the U.S. military involvement in the Gulf War in 1991, but subsequently undermined by events in Somalia); and by the widespread propagation of a patriarchal ideology that sought to revive the notion of (white) male supremacy.

Where seventies texts diminished the importance of the figure of the femme fatale and tended to thematize political paranoia, distrust founded on the inability to communicate, and masculine dysfunctionality, in the often formulaic films noirs of the eighties and nineties there is now a hyperbolic, some would argue postmodern, return to classic noir types that in many respects can be read as a commentary on the neo-conservative values of the Reagan administration. In the neo-noir of the eighties and nineties, the America depicted on screen is one populated by ineffective law enforcers, impotent private investigators, homicidal maniacs, and petty thieves, a society in which the criminal element is equally at home in the daylight and night worlds, in the urban jungle and on the open road. In the era of the yuppie and of AIDS, femmes fatales and hommes fatals are more individualistic, corrupt, and violent than in the past. Greed, both economic and sexual, invariably results in an extended personal nightmare from which there is often no escape, as in *Body Heat, Fatal Attraction* (Adrian Lyne, 1987), *Bad Influence* (Curtis Hanson, 1990), *Basic Instinct,* and *Romeo is Bleeding.*

The nightmare, moreover, extends into suburbia and middle America. In films like *Blue Velvet* (David Lynch, 1986), *Something Wild* (Jonathan Demme, 1986), *The Hot Spot* (Dennis Hopper, 1990), *Wild at Heart* (David Lynch, 1990), *Guncrazy,* and *One False Move,* it is no longer simply a case of the intrusion of a malevolent urban force into a rural setting as in classic film noir (*Out of the Past, Act of Violence,* and *Ace in the Hole,* for example).[21] Now all of American society is implicated in the dark visions these films offer. In *Blue Velvet,* for example, the young middle-class protagonist Jeffrey Beaumont (Kyle MacLachlan) is drawn into the noir underworld of both small-town America and his own imagination. His encounters with the archetypal figures who populate this world (the torch singer, the psychopath, the corrupt police officer) reveal a sordid community of criminal activity (drug dealing, kidnapping), sexual perversion (voyeurism, sadomasochism, incest), masculine violence, misogyny, and patriarchal corruption. The corruption he discovers, the film seems to suggest, is simply an extension of the world he knows; it simmers just below the surface of "respectable" society.

Blue Velvet forms part of the yuppie nightmare cycle, a neo-noir sub-genre that also includes *After Hours, Jagged Edge, Something Wild, House of Games,* and *Bad Influence.* Collectively these films serve up an interesting indictment of neo-conservative individualism and the not unrelated get-rich-quick mentality that underpinned the economic policy of the Reagan-Bush administrations. In *Bad Influence,* for example, the protagonist Michael Boll (James Spader) is a successful young market analyst anxious about his future career and impending marriage into a wealthy family. After an apparently chance encounter with the mysterious Alex (Rob Lowe), Michael is drawn into a nocturnal underworld of uninhibited sexuality, criminality, and, ultimately, violence. Again, as in *Blue Velvet,* the film emphasizes the darkness that lurks below the surface of the apparently ordered world ("You didn't do anything that wasn't in you already," Alex tells Michael in their final confrontation), and it equates the desire for financial gain with corruption and perversion. In this sense the psychopathic kidnapper/blackmailer Frank (Dennis Hopper) in *Blue Velvet* and the homme fatal Alex in *Bad Influence* are the doubles of Jeffrey and Michael respectively, projections of what they will become if they remain in thrall to their egotistical desires.

Eighties and nineties neo-noir also marks the rediscovery of the strong independent woman. The return of the femme fatale serves to reintroduce in the post-censorship era the sexual component of film noir that was either missing or perverted (incest and rape in *Chinatown,* for example) in the films of the seventies. It also illustrates the relative autonomy of women in the United States today.[22] The contemporary femme fatale is infinitely more evil and dangerous than her classic noir counterpart. She is more intelligent, more devious, and she self-consciously uses her sexuality not simply as a commodity but as a weapon (as witness the actions of the female protagonist in *Basic Instinct,* who kills her victims during sexual intercourse).[23] Patriarchal society frequently fails to either punish or rehabilitate her, as in *Body Heat, The Hot Spot, Basic Instinct,* and *The Last Seduction.* Another figure, one developed by crime fiction writers like Marcia Muller, Sara Paretsky, and Sue Grafton, that has emerged in the neo-noirs of the eighties and nineties is the female investigator, as in *Black Widow, Impulse* (Sondra

Locke, 1990), *Blue Steel* (Kathryn Bigelow, 1990), *V. I. Warshawski* (Jeff Kanew, 1991), and *Silence of the Lambs* (Jonathan Demme, 1991). Frequently she is presented as a solitary figure defiantly making her way through a man's world.[24]

The case of Bob Rafelson's 1987 film *Black Widow* is of particular interest as it juxtaposes the figure of the female investigator with that of the femme fatale, and either marginalizes or relegates to the position of victim the male characters. In a sense, the film documents the investigative protagonist Alex Barnes's (Debra Winger) gradual reconciliation of her femininity with her traditionally (in cinematic terms at least) male job as a Justice Department researcher. At the start of the film, Alex is virtually indistinguishable from the men with whom she works. Her investigation of and eventual relationship with the femme fatale Catherine (Theresa Russell), however, with its suggestive lesbian undertones, ultimately serves to feminize her. At the end of the film she has become like Catherine, both dressing like her and employing an elaborate ruse to ensnare her prey in the same way that Catherine has trapped the various wealthy men she marries and then kills. As Marina Heung observes in her *Film Quarterly* review of the film, *Black Widow* "is no different from its predecessors in exploiting full-blown the iconography of the femme fatale based as it is on the fetishism of the female body and the mythology of woman's unbridled sexuality and her willingness to use it to control men."[25] Where it differs is in placing a woman in the traditional male position of investigator/voyeur whose fascination with another woman "is turned back into an awareness of what she herself lacks."[26]

More by accident than design—further evidence, if any were required, of the fumbling nature of America's patriarchs (in both politics and in fiction) during the seventies and eighties—the U.S. economy entered a sustained period of growth during Reagan's period in office that saw an increase in the gross national product, a decrease in interest rates, and a reduction in unemployment, a situation paradoxically catalyzed by the massive federal deficit. In many respects the long-term effects of Reagan's economic policies were not that dissimilar to those of Eisenhower which, similarly founded on immense debt (albeit consumer as opposed to government borrowing), had ultimately served to usher in a sustained period of economic recession in the sixties. Reagan's policies, designed to encourage economic growth, maintain low rates of inflation, and decrease the number of unemployed, had the immediate effect of making a privileged minority very wealthy (the yuppie phenomenon). With a view to the long term, however, they laid the foundations for yet another lengthy economic slump. By 1986, as a result of foreign invest-ment and an overvalued dollar that made it difficult to export American goods, the United States had become the world's largest debtor nation. The nation's economic problems were further exacerbated when, on 19 October 1987, or "Black Monday," the stock market suffered its largest single-day loss in history. In response, Reagan introduced an economic package that brought a temporary respite to the nation's budget deficit crisis, but a major economic recession occurred when he left office.

As the United States began to reassert itself as an economic power in the first term of the Reagan administration, there was a simultaneous move to recapture the military status of the past, one that had been so se-verely damaged by the Vietnam debacle. On assuming office, the Rea-gan administration distanced itself from the humanitarian foreign policy of the Carter years and opted for a more militarist-interventionist policy. In the early eighties the United States sent peace-keeping forces to Lebanon, but these were withdrawn in 1984 following heavy casualties. In 1983 Reagan ordered the invasion of Marxist Grenada, ostensibly to rescue American medical students, and in 1986 he authorized the bomb-ing of Libya as retribution for terrorist activities. Elsewhere a number of often covert operations were undertaken in Latin America, Africa, and Asia. Unsurprisingly, the neo-conservatives' ascension to office also ushered in a "new cold war era" and saw the United States adopt a more hard-line approach in its relations with the Soviet Union than had been the case under Nixon, Ford, and Carter. The beginnings of this new cold war initiated an arms build-up at home and saw the development of the Strategic Defense Initiative, or Star Wars program.

As relations with the Soviet Union appeared to deteriorate in the early and mid-eighties, as in the classic noir texts of the late forties and early fifties, a sense of nuclear anxiety seemed to shape the thematic content of a number of Hollywood texts. In their dystopic vision of post-apocalyptic Los Angeles, for example, the film noir science-fiction hy-brids *Blade Runner* and *The Terminator* (James Cameron, 1984) give ex-pression to fears of a violent technocratic future. *No Way Out,* on the other hand, a remake of the classic film noir *The Big Clock,* combines a thematic interest in technophobia with a paranoid narrative of Soviet es-pionage that is reminiscent of the classic film noir texts of the McCarthy era. Such films promote the neo-noir iconography of communication and surveillance and, more poignantly, of destruction (the weaponry, in par-ticular, of the science-fiction films), perhaps additionally reflecting the contemporary economic boom in the U.S. military-industrial complex and the meteoric rise of the microelectronics industry in California's Silicon Valley.

A by-product of the Reagan administration's militarist, anti-Communist stance was its interventionist policy in third world affairs. Of great concern to both the American public and Congress during the early years of the Reagan administration, therefore, was the government's increasing involvement in the affairs of the Central American nations Nicaragua and El Salvador, which some perceived could lead to a repeat of the Vietnam situation. By 1984 the Reagan administration's efforts to stop the spread of Communism in Central America by supporting the Contra rebels in Nicaragua and the government in El Salvador had been checked by Congress. Congress agreed to only limited support for the government in El Salvador and, with the Boland Amendment (1984), prohibited the further supply of military aid to the Contra rebels in Nicaragua. Nevertheless, the administration continued to support the rebels in a number of ways. The CIA, for example, remained active in the region, and the White House encouraged private citizens to make financial contributions to the Contra cause. It was another scheme, however, designed by Lieutenant Colonel Oliver North, a member of the National Security Council, that was to trigger a political scandal when it was unearthed in late 1986. As with the sixties political assassinations and the seventies Watergate scandal, the media furor and public interest aroused by this controversial affair, in conjunction with those surrounding the U.S. invasion of Panama and the arrest of General Noriega under the Bush administration, were to inform the narratives of patriarchal corruption and political intrigue of the late eighties and early nineties, as witness *No Way Out, The Two Jakes, Shattered, Deep Cover,* and *White Sands* (Roger Donaldson, 1992). The latter two films, in particular *Deep Cover* with its diplomatically protected Latin American drug barons and overt references to Noriega and *White Sands* with its corrupt intelligence services officers and illicit arms deals, draw strongly from the legacy of these affairs.

North's idea was to sell arms to the Iranians (1) to help secure the release of American hostages held by Islamic fundamentalists in Beirut and (2) to help raise funds that could be used to finance the Contras. Once the story broke in the American media, Reagan was quick to distance himself from North's activities and set up the Tower Commission to investigate the scandal. Like Watergate, the Iran-Contra affair resulted in the resignation of key figures in the administration, including John Poindexter, Reagan's national security adviser, and Donald Regan, the White House chief of staff. Although few believed that the president had no knowledge of the arms-to-Iran policy, Poindexter's testimony to the Senate and House "Irangate" select committee in July 1987, in which he assumed full responsibility for the policy, together with North's illegal shredding of government documents, effectively brought the investigation to a close. Poindexter and North were convicted (although both convictions were subsequently overturned), and the Reagan administration was censured for its lack of control over the activities of the National Security Council.

The most telling legacy of the Reagan era—by which is meant not only the eight years of the Ronald Reagan's two terms in office, but also the period of the George Bush and Bill Clinton administrations, for it is the impact of Reagan's social and economic policies that have endured beyond his own presidency, his political ideals today embodied in the figure of the right-wing Speaker of the House Newt Gingrich—has been the debunking of the concept of the American Dream. The promotion of economic aspiration and entrepreneurialism, for example, have seen the benefits reaped by the few and an ever-widening chasm materialize between the wealthy and the poor, laying bare the fallacy of any belief in the dream's ideal of social equality. The Reagan years, despite the isolated political triumphs of the likes of Geraldine Ferraro and Jesse Jackson, were marked by a slackening of the gains in social status achieved by women (heretofore an increasingly dynamic presence in the business sector; the legalization of abortion) and African-Americans (improved academic performance; a growth in the black middle-class) during the previous two decades. The Equal Rights Amendment, which had been approved by Congress in 1972 and was subsequently passed to the states for ratification, was finally defeated in 1982, thus making problematic the issues of pay equity, sexual discrimination, child care, and abortion. The employment in the industrial sector of cheap, nonunionized foreign labor, in particular the rapidly increasing numbers of Hispanic and Southeast Asian immigrants, had a devastating impact on the inner-city African-American populace. By the end of the decade it was estimated that the average African-American family's median income was less than three-fifths that of a white family. The already deteriorating state of the urban black ghettos was further compounded, therefore, by increasing levels of poverty and black-on-black violence, itself a consequence of the related issues of gang warfare and the burgeoning drug problem. Indeed, the myth of the "kinder, gentler nation" that was promoted by the Bush administration was brutally illustrated when one of the worst riots in the history of the United States erupted in Los Angeles in April

1992 in response to the acquittal of four white policemen whose savage beating of a black motorist, Rodney King, had been recorded on video (as with *JFK*'s incorporation of the Zapruder footage, this latest testament to the violence of American society was co-opted by Spike Lee in his 1992 noirish bio-pic *Malcolm X*). The riot cost fifty-eight lives and some $750 million in damages.

A significant development in the neo-noirs of the early nineties has been the exploration of ethnicity. It is those neo-noirs produced by African-American filmmakers during the early-to-mid nineties, films such as *A Rage in Harlem* (Bill Duke, 1991), *Deep Cover, One False Move, Juice* (Ernest Dickerson, 1992), *Menace II Society* (Albert and Allen Hughes, 1993), *Panther* (Mario Van Peebles, 1995), *Clockers,* and *Dead Presidents* (Albert and Allen Hughes, 1995), that most clearly reflect the realities of contemporary American society, foregrounding problems related to inner-city malaise, gang violence, poverty, crime, and drugs. Many of these examples of "*noir* by *noirs*" draw from their own culturally specific agenda.[27] Their points of reference are less the classical Hollywood films noirs of the forties and fifties than the "blaxploitation" films of the seventies (and indeed Scorsese's Italian-American films of the same era), the novels of African-American writers like Chester Himes (*A Rage in Harlem*) and, more recently, Walter Mosley (*Devil in a Blue Dress*), and the music of rappers like Public Enemy, Ice T, Ice Cube, and Snoop Doggy Dog. Many of these African-American films explore the violence of everyday life in the nation's urban ghettos, highlighting either through the absence (*Boyz N the Hood,* John Singleton, 1991) or indifference (*Clockers*) of white America the social divide, both economic and ethnic, that exists in contemporary American society.

Such films demonstrate that in the United States of the eighties and nineties the American Dream of economic success and social equality is more elusive than ever before. The America inherited by the Democratic Clinton administration and portrayed in the contemporary film noir is one wracked by economic decline, racial tension, inner-city poverty, drug wars, and violent crime. It is characterized by an ever-widening gap, both social and monetary, between the wealthy and the poor, and it is increasingly marked by a wave of militancy among whites (as witness the Waco and Oklahoma City bomb incidents of 1994 and 1995 respectively) and blacks (as witness the October 1995 march on Washington of African-American males led by the Nation of Islam leader Louis Farrakhan). The inherent racism of American society was clearly reflected in the opposing reactions of whites and blacks regarding the acquittal of former football star O. J. Simpson in a double murder case. In this society all dreams have been put on hold as its citizens have been forced to adapt to a social system in which only the fittest survive.

As was the case in the years that followed the end of the Second World War, the collapse of the Communist bloc in Eastern Europe, symbolized by the dismantling of the Berlin Wall, the downgrading of the U.S. nuclear armament program, and the final death throes of the cold war itself, have once again prompted American filmmakers to focus their attention on the problems at the heart of their own society. In the postmodern era, epitomized by a new president, Bill Clinton, whose first term in office has often seemed a pastiche of the previous decades (his media-friendly image à la John F. Kennedy, the Whitewater controversy à la Watergate and Irangate, his involvement in the volatile politics of the Middle East à la Richard Nixon, the early indecision in home affairs and foreign policy à la Jimmy Carter, and so on), film noir has returned, in cyclical fashion, as an appropriate tool for social critique. At its best, neo-noir turns its dark mirror on the social injustice, violence, and greed that still prevail in American society, ultimately illustrating the futility of American Dream.

The Legacy of Film Noir

Seventies Revisionism

3

This study opened with a quotation from the French philosopher and cultural theorist Jacques Derrida: "What are we doing when, to practice a 'genre,' we quote a genre, represent it, stage it, expose its *generic law,* analyze it practically? Are we still practicing the genre?" In the case of film noir—or any genre, literary or cinematic—the response to this can be unequivocally affirmative. Of course "we are still practicing the genre." It is just that the genre itself has changed, evolving directly in relation to an industrial, political, and sociocultural context that is forever in a state of flux. It is for this reason that contemporary noir remakes and formulaic endeavors to "recapture" or "reproduce" classic film noir, while not in themselves worthless, are generally far less interesting than the work of filmmakers like Martin Scorsese (himself guilty of a stylized, disappointing remake in *Cape Fear*), Arthur Penn, Alan Rudolph, the Coen Brothers, and Quentin Tarantino who put their own peculiar spin on the noir tradition. Such filmmakers are not usually interested in "reproduction" (by which is meant the essentially redundant recycling of hackneyed stylistic clichés and formulaic narratives as opposed to the recreation of period settings and events, an exercise that in such films as *Chinatown, The Two Jakes,* and *Miller's Crossing* often suggests the parallels between the past and the present, indeed the cyclical nature of history), but in taking the genre as a point of departure, weaving its themes and (occasionally) its stylistic effects into essentially personal narratives. Today the viewer also brings to the movie theater so much more historical and cultural baggage than in the past: classic film noir tapped into the anxieties of the Depression, Second World War, and cold war eras, and to that must now be added the legacy of political assassinations, Vietnam, Watergate, Irangate, a more recent economic recession, the Gulf War, and so on. There is also, of course, the question now of the television-fueled cine-literacy of the average filmgoer and an awareness of what "noir" actually is.

In the part I of this study, "From Film Noir to Neo-noir," we have contextualized the evolution of film noir in relation to the recent histories of both American filmmaking practices and American society itself, exploring how industrial transformation and temporally specific social, political, and cultural considerations have affected the style and content of the genre. In part II of our exploration of the noir phenomenon, we shall consider in more detail the period of the post-classical Hollywood neo-noir. In this section we will examine how the noir films of the seventies, eighties, and nineties speak to and of the era by intersecting with dominant cultural tendencies and exploiting the collective anxieties of contemporary American society. We will explore how these films have developed and have transformed a generic tradition that has exerted its influence on Western popular culture for more than half a century.

In each of the three chapters, which are divided by decade, an introductory section exploring general cultural tendencies during the era and the continuing evolution and transformation of the noir genre will be followed by detailed analyses of three representative neo-noir texts of, respectively, the seventies (*Chinatown, Night Moves,* and *Taxi Driver*), the eighties (*After Hours, Blood Simple,* and *Sea of Love*), and the nineties (*Reservoir Dogs, Romeo is Bleeding,* and *One False Move*). These textual analyses will foreground, in particular, the enduring principals of artistic creativity and technical virtuosity that have been traditionally associated with film noir, the genre's ongoing investigation of masculinity, neo-noir's continuing exploration of the darker side of the collective American psyche, and the not-unrelated issue of the self-consciously mythic structure of many of the films under consideration. Toward the end of the present chapter and throughout chapters 4 and 5, the importance of Martin Scorsese's neo-noir work to the subsequent evolution and history of the noir genre will be explored.

The evolution of film noir, like history itself, is marked by both repetition and gradual transformation. Indeed, the sixties' revival of film noir in many respects mirrors its forties creation, illustrating significantly more than simply the cyclical nature of "audience popularity and *need*."[1] In the late thirties and forties the genesis and development of film noir had been informed by an uncertain sociopolitical climate (depression, war, unemployment, nuclear anxiety, and so forth), significant change within the infrastructure of the film industry itself (development of the

B-film and of independent production, divestiture, changes in exhibition policy), and the influence of *émigré* filmmakers, in particular Europeans from Germany, Austria, Hungary, and France, who introduced alternative stylistic systems (German Expressionism and French Poetic Realism, for example) into the American film industry. As we have already observed, the period of the late sixties and early-to-mid seventies, witness to the emergence of the American neo-noir, was similarly characterized by sociopolitical uncertainty (the rise of the New Left, the counterculture, feminism, racial tension, political assassination, war, government scandal, unemployment, and economic stagflation), tumultuous change within the industry (the collapse of the studio system, conglomeration and diversification, the emergence of new creative and technical talent, the development of new technologies, the fragmentation of the once homogeneous audience, the overhaul of the production code), and the influence on a new generation of American filmmakers of an alternative European style of cinema (the *nouvelle vague,* the concepts of auteurism and art cinema). The result in both cases was the creation of some of the most stylistically experimental, formally adventurous, self-consciously political, cynical, and pessimistic work to be produced under the aegis of Hollywood cinema.

The revival of American film noir, which in effect dates from the release of *Harper* in 1966, and its transformation in the hands of the neo-modernist filmmakers of the Hollywood renaissance in such films as *Bonnie and Clyde, Klute, The Long Goodbye, Mean Streets,* and *The Conversation,* however, is also informed by a growing awareness (in industrial, critical, and academic circles at least) of the concept of "film noir." Indeed, an essentially diffuse idea of what actually constituted film noir permeated anglophone film culture during this era. To a degree, the films of the late sixties and early seventies can be perceived, in their self-consciously inquisitive and deconstructive investigation of the genre, as cinematic counterparts to the noir-related publications that appeared in film journals throughout the renaissance period.

Of course, the late sixties and seventies neo-noirs were also shaped in part by an artistic and political agenda inherited from the French *nouvelle vague,* which the Hollywood renaissance filmmakers adapted and commodified for consumption by an American audience. In effect, they introduced into American genre cinema an unprecedented degree of stylistic experimentation and overt sociopolitical critique. Their films, in general, were formally iconoclastic, generically revisionist, self-referential, even at times playful in their celebration of the potential of the cinematic medium.

At the same time, however, their neo-noirs were unswerving in their exploration of the darker side of contemporary American society, reflecting an era overshadowed by political assassination, the Warren Commission, Vietnam, Watergate, economic depression, and the struggles associated with the civil rights movement, feminism, and the counterculture. The darkness of their mood and the cynicism of their tone is reflected in the thematization of patriarchal corruption (*The Long Goodbye* and *All the President's Men,* for example), masculine violence (*Badlands* and *Taxi Driver*), male anxiety regarding female autonomy (*Klute* and *Play Misty for Me*), alienation (*Point Blank* and *Taxi Driver*), the dysfunctionality of family and community (*Chinatown* and *Night Moves*), and paranoia regarding corporate and political power (*The Conversation* and *The Parallax View*).

Many of these revisionist seventies neo-noirs take the figure of the forties male private investigator, but place him in the context of the fifties noir of "psychotic action and suicidal impulse." Here, often at the expense of his own psychological stability as in *The Conversation, Chinatown,* and *Night Moves,* he is likely to uncover rampant social and political corruption that stems from the abuse of corporate and/or governmental power by figures of authority, as witness the political paranoia cycle of films which includes *The Parallax View, Three Days of the Condor,* and *All the President's Men.* Indeed, the vision of patriarchal American society offered in the seventies neo-noir is generally cynical and pessimistic. Films like *Klute, The Conversation, The Parallax View, Chinatown,* and *Night Moves,* for example, foreground both patriarchal corruption and masculine impotence (lack of knowledge, hence lack of power),[2] whereas others, like *Point Blank, The Long Goodbye, Mean Streets, Badlands,* and *Taxi Driver,* suggest the violent decline of contemporary patriarchal civilization. Such texts suggest a sustained interest in questions of knowledge and fragmentation characteristic of the modernist/neo-modern agenda of post-fifties Western (particularly European) cinema. In *The Conversation,* for example, the modernist formal experimentation of the film is complemented by the equally modernist concept of the investigative protagonist's gradual psychic dissolution, which is prompted by both his paranoia and his sense of inadequacy and failure.

In this respect, the figure of the investigative protagonist in films like *The Conversation, The Parallax View, Chinatown,* and *Night Moves* invokes, in the specifically American context of the seventies neo-noir, both the numerous investigations that were a feature of American politics in the sixties and seventies (from the mid-sixties' Warren Commission to the mid-seventies' inquiry into CIA operations) and, in broader esthetic terms, the notion of the epistemological quest that is such a dominant motif in modernist fiction (from Eliot's *The Waste Land* and Joyce's *Ulysses* to Bellow's *Henderson the Rain King* and Pynchon's *The Crying of Lot 49*). Similarly the figure of the psychopath, an archetype who has appeared with increasing frequency throughout the neo-noir era, in films like *Klute, Play Misty for Me, Badlands,* and *Taxi Driver,* is suggestive of contemporary violence (assassinations, race riots, Vietnam) and the equally modernist concept of the identity crisis and psychological fragmentation of modern man (from Picasso's cubist paintings to Bergman's 1966 film *Persona*). Frequently, moreover, in investigative films like *Klute* the psychopath constitutes an extension of the protagonist's own identity, an external projection of his darker self.

As with classic film noir, in the neo-noirs of the sixties and seventies there exists in the characterization of the ineffective investigator, the psychotic law enforcer, the corrupt politician, the embittered war veteran, and the unstable sociopath an ongoing concern with the deviancy of the male. Indeed, where the classic films noirs of the forties were founded on male-female relations, with the woman serving as the locus of male psychological dislocation and sexual dysfunction, the seventies neo-noir tends to follow the fifties texts by concentrating more overtly on masculinity and the corruption of patriarchy. In the seventies film noir the classic noir figure of the femme fatale tends to be marginalized. In such texts the female protagonist frequently becomes either the male's partner in crime, as in the outlaw road movies *Bonnie and Clyde* and *Badlands,* or the actual/potential victim of male violence, as in the seeker-hero films *Klute* and *Chinatown*. There are, naturally, exceptions to this general rule. *Play Misty for Me,* for example, features one of the first neo-noir female psychopaths, a figure that would play a prominent role in the neo-noir texts of the eighties and nineties (indeed, *Fatal Attraction* could almost be considered a remake of Eastwood's film); *The Conversation* includes both a duplicitous sexual woman and a young woman involved in a plot to murder her father; and period productions like *Farewell, My Lovely* and *Goodnight, My Love* (Peter Hyams, 1972) feature the archetypal figure of the femme fatale, but more as a means of cultivating nostalgia for the old films in their colorized revisionism of the noir genre than as a form of expressing misogynist anxiety (although this still clearly remains a contributory factor, as witness the portrayal of the sadistic lesbian brothel madam in *Farewell, My Lovely*).

Despite the marginalization of the erotic woman in the seventies neo-noir, sexual activity is still integral to the contemporary noir narrative, and its representation in the wake of the late sixties censorship revisions is far more explicit than it had been in the past (the nudity and shared beds of *Bonnie and Clyde* or *Mean Streets,* for example, the discussion of sexual activity in *Klute,* the prostitution of minors in *Taxi Driver,* and so forth). Its significance in the majority of seventies neo-noirs, however, is often only tangential to the central issue of patriarchal corruption. In the seventies neo-noir this usually manifests itself in physical violence, which is portrayed with even greater explicitness than sexual activity in contemporary American cinema (the slow motion massacre of Faye Dunaway's Bonnie and Warren Beatty's Clyde, the mindless destruction of a woman's face in *The Long Goodbye,* the nose-slicing scene in *Chinatown,* the bloody carnage of *Taxi Driver*). This violence, however, is itself frequently a by-product of sexual anxiety (the protagonist in *Taxi Driver*), perversion (the incestuous father in *Chinatown*), or male impotence (Clyde in *Bonnie and Clyde*), prompting John Orr to observe of contemporary neo-noirs that "the element of horror in all these films comes from the systematic perversions of eros which the male protagonist uncovers."[3]

The conflation of sex and violence, the displacement of Eros by Thanatos, is a recurrent motif in the seventies neo-noir. In *Klute,* for example, the female protagonist Bree Daniels (Jane Fonda), an unemployed actress who earns a living as a prostitute in New York City, is the recipient of threatening phone calls from a former, physically abusive, client. As the narrative develops, Bree becomes tentatively involved with a small-town Pennsylvania police detective, the male protagonist John Klute (Donald Sutherland). This narrative strand is, however, only secondary to the film's revelation of masculinity in crisis. Klute is in New York looking for leads that may help him in his search for missing friend Tom Gruneman (Robert Milli). His investigation ultimately incriminates another small-town friend, Peter Cable (Charles Ciotti), who, it transpires, is the mystery caller and the murderer of Gruneman and two prostitutes. Cable is motivated by misogynist contempt, achieving sexual gratification by inflicting violence on women. The text implies parallels between Cable and Klute both in their voyeuristic connection to Bree Daniels and their reaction to the "moral decadence and sexual alienation of city life."[4] In conjunction with the film's rather ambiguous ending (has Bree really entered into a serious relationship with Klute or is she simply fulfilling the fantasy desires of another client?), this would appear to suggest the pervasiveness of patriarchal corruption and the hopelessness of any future relationship between Klute and Bree.

The narratives of *Chinatown, Night Moves,* and *Taxi Driver,* the three films of immediate interest to us in the present chapter, are equally, if not more, despairing. They have been chosen for their reflection of/intersection with the dominant cultural anxieties of the seventies, for their thematization of patriarchal corruption and social dysfunction, for their status as modern-day fables exploring the dangers of wealth and power, the debasement of love, and the violent fragmentation of society, and, above all, for their revisionism and reinvention of the noir genre, their thematic and stylistic overhaul of one of the "most enduring" of American film genres.[5]

CHINATOWN

Plot Summary

Drought-stricken Los Angeles, 1937. Private investigator J. J. (Jake) Gittes (Jack Nicholson), a specialist in divorce work, is hired to investigate the fidelity of L.A. Water and Power chief engineer Hollis Mulwray (Darrell Zwerling) by a woman masquerading as his wife, Evelyn. Gittes and his colleagues follow Mulwray until they discover a secret liaison with a young woman. The story is headline news the following day, and Gittes is served with a writ by the authentic Evelyn Mulwray (Faye Dunaway). However, when Mulwray's body is discovered drowned in a local reservoir, Gittes suspects foul play and is hired by Evelyn to find his murderer. Prior to his death, Mulwray had been vehemently opposed to the construction of a new dam in the San Fernando Valley. Following up this lead and a tip from the Evelyn Mulwray impersonator, Ida Sessions (Diane Ladd), Gittes unearths a corrupt scheme masterminded by Noah Cross (John Huston), Evelyn's father and Mulwray's former business partner: The drought has been fabricated by diverting water away from the L.A. region, and land in the San Fernando Valley, which will benefit from the construction of the proposed dam, is being fraudulently purchased on Cross's behalf. Simultaneously, Gittes becomes romantically involved with Evelyn. He learns that the young woman whom he saw with Mulwray is in fact Evelyn's daughter and sister, the progeny of her rape by Cross as a teenager. Gittes determines to help Evelyn and Katherine (Belinda Palmer) escape to Mexico, enlisting the help of a former client Curly (Burt Young). They are intercepted, however, at their rendezvous in Chinatown by Gittes's former police colleagues Escobar (Perry Lopez) and Loach (Dick Bakalayan), while Jake is himself escorted at gunpoint by Cross and his henchman Mulvihill (Roy Jensen). As Evelyn attempts to escape with Katherine, she is killed by Loach, leaving Cross to triumphantly reclaim his daughter/granddaughter and continue his ecological rape of the L.A. landscape.

Analysis

As a self-consciously revisionist text, *Chinatown* addresses itself to a cine-literate audience. Indeed, in its simultaneous evocation and revision of a generic tradition, it demands the complicity of the viewer. This is a characteristic feature of American cinema of the late sixties and early seventies. As Pam Cook has observed,

> One of the characteristics of New Hollywood that marks it off from classic Hollywood is that it's produced and consumed by knowledgeable intellectuals. It sells itself on the basis of its reflexivity, calling up classic Hollywood in order to differentiate itself from it. The "modernity" of New Hollywood lies in the way it plays on the known conventions of past Hollywood to displace it, while retaining the pleasures of homage to the past.[6]

Chinatown, in its attention to period detail in dialogue and mise-en-scène, endeavors to cultivate a nostalgic attitude toward classic film noir in keeping with, say, Dick Richard's *Farewell, My Lovely,* while simultaneously offering the noir-literate viewer the deconstructive revisionism/demythologization of Robert Altman's contemporary adaptation of *The Long Goodbye.* Not only does the film demand a more expansive canvas (Panavision, color film stock) than that of classic film noir, but it also self-consciously foregrounds the mythological paradigms that underpin the genre, and playfully alludes to classic film noir (the casting of John Huston, for example).[7] The film's worldview, however, is firmly grounded in the seventies of the film's production rather than the thirties of its period re-creation, informed, that is, by the cynicism of the Watergate era rather than the pessimism of the Depression.

  In simplistic revisionist terms, like other contemporary noir detective films such as *Harper, Marlowe, Goodnight, My Love, The Long Goodbye, The Yakuza* (Sydney Pollack, 1975), *Farewell, My Lovely, Night Moves, The Drowning Pool* (Stuart Rosenberg, 1975), and *The Late Show* (Robert Benton, 1977), *Chinatown* invokes the generic tradition of the hard-boiled detective narrative that it then proceeds to investigate and unravel. Traditionally such a narrative concerns a private investigator's quest to solve an enigma—a journey founded on the acquisition of knowledge. It has as its protagonist a financially constrained lower-middle-class man of character and integrity who (in many cases) once held an official role (a police officer or attorney, for example) in society, but now finds himself an outsider in both respectable society and the criminal milieu. The initial hiring of the private investigator, frequently under false pretenses, sets in motion "an effect of movement, intrigue, cross-purposes, and the gradual elucidation of character."[8] His increasingly violent quest through the wasteland of the modern city, which is marked by an accumulation of corpses, ultimately lays bare a corrupt society in which the rich and powerful are in league with the criminal underworld, a revelation that ironically serves to underpin the protagonist's own moral integrity. Having traversed the "mean streets" of the hard-boiled universe, then, the detective manages to resurface with honor and integrity intact, having brought his principal antagonist to justice (often by his own hand), even if such action ultimately "holds out no real hope for a restoration of order and justice" in the community at large.[9]

Many seventies' neo-noirs pay homage to this narrative tradition, but find no place in their contemporary narratives for the romanticism and idealism that prevailed in such classic noir texts as *The Maltese Falcon,* *Murder, My Sweet,* and *The Big Sleep,* nor indeed for the glimmer of optimism offered by the meting out of justice to the arch criminal. More so than in the past, in the majority of modern noir detective films the private investigator finds himself implicated in both the crimes he investigates and the widespread corruption and social malaise he encounters. He too has become a man of inertia and impotence, readily manipulated by those in positions of wealth and power, and easily outwitted by those who live outside the realm of the law. Jake Gittes, the protagonist of *Chinatown,* is such a man. The fact that he specializes in "matrimonial work," for example, brings his own integrity into question. This is no Sam Spade or Philip Marlowe. Gittes's clothing, car, office furnishings, and ability to employ assistants—his associates Walsh (Joe Mantell) and Duffy (Bruce Glover), and his secretary Sophie (Nandu Hinds)—distinguishes him from his classic noir counterparts, suggesting that, despite originally humble origins as a Chinatown-based police officer, he now enjoys economic success and upward mobility, a status never really attained by the protagonists of the classic hard-boiled texts. In the figure of Jake Gittes, then, we witness the traditional and romanticized Chandlerian notion of the private investigator being gradually usurped by a "reinterpreted" concept of that figure more in keeping with the prevailing cynicism of the seventies. By the time of *Night Moves* few vestiges of the traditional investigative figure remain.

Despite the modernization of the investigative figure in *Chinatown,* Gittes is nevertheless an archetypal protagonist of film noir. Like the protagonists of such classic noir texts as *The Dark Corner* (Henry Hathaway, 1946), *Out of the Past,* and *Act of Violence,* Jake Gittes is a man haunted by his past, tormented by his former inadequacy (in this case, his inability to prevent the woman he loved from being hurt when he was a police officer based in Chinatown). Burdened by this past he has become a powerless man of inaction. When his investigation into the death of Hollis Mulwray leads him back into the world of physical violence and unspeakable evil that he associates with his past life in Chinatown, not only does it leave him physically and symbolically scarred (his bandaged nose), but it also underscores his powerlessness (and by implication that of the common man in his struggle with the rich and corrupt) as his actions "leave the basic source of corruption untouched."[10] By the end of the film, Gittes has solved, or rather had spelled out for him, the enigma posed by Mulwray's death. But, as in the past, his investigation has damaged those most dear to him. Unlike his classic counterparts, moreover, he is unable to bring the archcriminal to justice, but is instead a manacled spectator to the slaughter of Evelyn Mulwray and Noah Cross's reclamation of his daughter/granddaughter Katherine. In the sequel to *Chinatown, The Two Jakes,* it is this former inability to save Evelyn, his regrets about what might have been had they had a chance to develop their relationship, and his guilt about losing touch with Katherine that both torments and motivates Gittes in his handling of the Berman-Bodine case. Gittes's new adventure becomes a psychological/mythical voyage toward full health as he is presented with an opportunity to put his inner demons to rest.

In many respects, the hard-boiled narrative is little more than a modernization of the mythic hero adventure (and by extension the psychological quest for an integrated identity). Indeed, John Cawelti has argued that "the creation of the hard-boiled pattern involved a shift in the underlying archetype of the detective story from the pattern of mystery to that of heroic adventure."[11] In *Chinatown,* however, this pattern is ironically invoked to illustrate how Jake Gittes's quest is a consummate failure, in both a mythical and a psychological sense. The contemporary urban detective here fails both to overcome his evil adversary Noah Cross and to attain a sense of psychological stability, and thus fails to regenerate his barren, drought-stricken homeland (echoes here of Arthurian legend by way of Eliot's *The Waste Land,* including the motifs of "the sterile kingdom, the dying king and the drowned man beneath it").[12] The result is fragmentation, both of society (the ever-present divisions between the wealthy and the poor)[13] and of Gittes's psyche.

The purpose of the film's allusive references to the Oedipus myth (most obviously the incest motif, but also the eye motif) are, therefore, twofold.[14] As the man who solved the Sphinx's riddle, Oedipus stands as one of the first great detectives in Western mythology, heroically succeeding in saving the city of Thebes, whereas Jake Gittes fails miserably in his attempt to keep Los Angeles free of the clutches of the monstrous Noah Cross. On the other hand, Oedipus is the figure who killed his father and married his mother and, by so doing, brought a plague on his kingdom, just as in *Chinatown* it is Noah Cross who has murdered one of the city's founding fathers and violated both his daughter and the land over which he presides. The eye motif, as it relates both to the Oedipal myth and to the detective narrative, requires further elaboration.

The detective's livelihood depends on his ability to "see," both in a literal sense, observing the actions of the people he investigates, and in a metaphorical sense, assimilating information and interpreting clues in order, ultimately, to solve the enigma that has been the reason for his quest (not unlike Tiresias the blind seer at the center of both the Oedipus myth and *The Waste Land*). In *Chinatown,* the opening sequences emphasize the detective's gaze and—a suggestion here of Gittes's personal inadequacy—his dependency on such mechanical aids to human vision as binoculars, cameras, and zoom lenses that assist him in his accumulation of knowledge. The film, however, as in the Oedipus myth (the blindness of Tiresias, the metaphorical and ultimately literal blindness of Oedipus), proliferates with images of flawed vision: Gittes's broken sunglasses, the flaw in Evelyn's iris, the black eye of Curly's adulterous wife, and the fatal mutilation of Evelyn's eye in the film's final sequence. These images, together with the slicing of Gittes's nose, point to the dulling of the detective's senses, his subsequent difficulty in solving the enigma, and his ultimate impotence. Like the club-footed Oedipus, he can do nothing to stop the inexorable forces of fate that have prompted the corruption of the patriarchal order.

To an extent, *Chinatown*'s water and power plot, the most overt manifestation of *widespread* patriarchal corruption in the film, resembles that of a western, another genre with mythical resonances that has much in common with the hard-boiled detective narrative (a quest structure, the loner hero, the final shoot-out). A contemporaneous western such as *Once Upon a Time in the West* (Sergio Leone, 1969), for example, similarly documents the violent decline of patriarchal civilization in direct proportion to the advent of modernity on the western frontier. In both cases, in their pioneering efforts to impose modernity and civilization on the natural wilderness, in the form of the railroad in *Once Upon a Time in the West* and the proposed Alto Vallejo dam and reservoir in *Chinatown,* the patriarch has resorted to violence and political corruption.[15] Furthermore, given the basis of *Chinatown*'s water scandal plot in historical reality (the 1906 "Rape of Owens Valley" masterminded by the head of the water and power department William Mulholland),[16] the film's numerous western allusions (the loner hero's journey from the city into the wilderness, for example, or the sheriff's horsemen who practice at Cross's Albacore Club) remind the viewer of a not-too-distant past in turn-of-the-century California when the founding fathers of Los Angeles were laying the foundations for one of the western frontier's first modern cities.

Chinatown ironically invokes the hero adventure (the Oedipus myth, the western) and employs historical allusion to comment on the present. Indeed, the tone and mood of the seventies are captured in its portrayal of public despair (voiced by the various farmers in the film) at the corruption of government institutions, here epitomized by the figures of the oily civil servant Ross Yelburton (John Hillerman), the slovenly former sheriff Mulvihill, and, ultimately, the powerful landowner Noah Cross. The last, the irony of whose biblically derived name is presumably intended to underscore the perversion of patriarchy, is a composite figure of the Los Angeles founding fathers involved in the Owens Valley scandal. He is politically corrupt, morally reprehensible, and, like Cable in *Klute,* he has allowed his evil to manifest itself in physical and sexual violence (the drowning of Hollis, the rape of his teenage daughter). His is a quest for power in which, as he observes to Gittes, he is prepared and able to do anything. In keeping with the tone of such contemporaneous texts as *The Conversation, The Parallax View,* and *Three Days of the Condor,* at the end of the film this figure remains untouchable and all-powerful, while the detective is left once again to reflect on his own inadequacies.

In Arthur Penn's *Night Moves,* produced a year after *Chinatown,* the detective proves similarly inept in unraveling the enigma of patriarchal corruption. Its mood, however, is significantly darker than the former film. In *Chinatown,* Noah Cross is like a malignant tumor, the removal of which may possibly lead to a healthy recovery. Gittes, however, fails in his quest and society is doomed. In *Night Moves,* the cancer has spread and the condition is terminal; corruption does not stem from one dominant figure like Cross, but manifests itself in a multiplicity of forms. Wherever the detective turns in the latter film, be it in work, in play, or at home, he encounters a society founded on moral degradation, alienation, greed, corruption, and emotional emptiness. If *Chinatown* constitutes a rearticulation of the motifs that permeated Eliot's narrative poem *The Waste Land,* then *Night Moves* represents the contemporary counterpart to his *Hollow Men.*

NIGHT MOVES

Plot Summary

Los Angeles-based private investigator Harry Moseby (Gene Hackman), who suffers from a compulsive "need to know," is hired by has-been movie star Arlene Iverson (Janet Ward) to find her runaway daughter Delly Grastner (Melanie Griffith). Moseby follows her trail to a movie-set location in New Mexico where Delly has had a relationship with stunt man Marv Ellman (Anthony Costello), one of her mother's former lovers. Moseby finds the promiscuous Delly at the cabin of her stepfather Tom Iverson (John Crawford) in the Florida Keys. Her initial reluctance to return home is overcome when she, Moseby, and Paula (Jennifer Warren), Iverson's partner, discover the sunken wreck of an airplane and the decomposed remains of its pilot. Moseby enjoys a night of adultery with Paula before returning to Los Angeles to his alienated wife Ellen (Susan Clark). He determines to give up investigating, prompted in part by the sourness of Delly's reconciliation with her avaricious mother and in part by the need to rescue his marriage—his wife is having an affair with the crippled Marty Heller (Harris Yulin). He is, however, once again drawn into the plot when he learns of Delly's death in a car accident involving the stunt man Joey Ziegler (Edward Binns), whom he had befriended on his visit to the New Mexico set. Moseby repeatedly watches footage of Delly's death, then confronts the mechanic Quentin (James Woods), who also features in an amateur documentary film of the stunt. Almost by accident Moseby has uncovered a smuggling ring specializing in pre-Columbian art involving Iverson, Paula, and the stunt men from the film set. He returns to the Florida Keys to confront Iverson. There he discovers Quentin's body, and, after a fight with Iverson, he and Paula set out to recover the latest smuggled artifact from the ocean. When they reach their destination, they are attacked from the sky. Injured, Moseby can only watch helplessly as Paula is killed and Ziegler, Iverson's smuggling partner, drowns in his crashed aircraft.

Analysis

Like *Chinatown*, Arthur Penn's *Night Moves* is full of references to the hard-boiled detective tradition (Marty Heller, arguing with Moseby, even invokes the figure of Hammett/Bogart's Sam Spade: "Go on Harry, sock me—the way Sam Spade would") and to classical mythology (to the extent that an allusive biblical name—Delilah—and the motifs of incest and the drowning man reappear). As with most of Penn's films of the fifties, sixties, and seventies (certainly from the 1958 *The Left-Handed Gun* to the 1976 *The Missouri Breaks*), *Night Moves* is a film that seeks to revise genre by means of generic demythologization.[17] Lacking, however, the nostalgic qualities of *Chinatown*'s period setting, the vision of American society offered in *Night Moves* is, if anything, bleaker than *Chinatown*'s because it is manifestly closer to the experiences of the contemporary viewer. As with Penn's oeuvre in general, the film requires that it be understood "as a meditation on/investigation of aspects of the U.S.A., its history, peoples and myths,"[18] and it is unremitting in exposing the anachronism, in the context of the present communal disintegration, of the values and traditions espoused by American mythology, particularly in the form of classical Hollywood genres. In a recent interview Penn outlined his intentions in the film:

> It was the period after all those assassinations, you know? That depleted one's optimism: the ability to feel that tomorrow is going to be better was definitely gone. I thought that's what this movie is about. Then also, I thought, gee, detective films have always been so clever, the detective always figured it out at the end. What happens if he himself is psychologically blocked in an area that keeps him from being able to perceive what the central event is all about?[19]

Harry Moseby's quest extends beyond the urban confines of Los Angeles and takes him across the breadth of the nation. Like Jake Gittes's quest through Southern California, it exposes a society riddled with corruption. The America he traverses is dominated by middle-aged men, the wealthy, and the crippled (broken limbs, crutches, walking sticks, alcoholism, intellectual impotence). In this fragmented post-Vietnam society it is the privilege of the older generation (often infirm in a physical and/or psychological sense) to outlive the young: Marv, Delly, Quentin, and Paula, for example, all die, but are survived by Harry, Ellen, Marty, Arlene, and (presumably) Tom. Of the older generation only Joey Ziegler dies on screen. What is more, in the dysfunctional society depicted in *Night Moves,* the once sacrosanct institution of the nuclear family has all but disintegrated, replaced by barren marriages (Harry and Ellen), divorce (Tom and Arlene), adulterous affairs (Ellen and Marty), promiscuity (Delly and Arlene), incest (Tom and Delly), and unknown parentage (Harry's story of his quest to find his father). *Night Moves,* like many of the neo-noirs of the late sixties and early seventies that exploited the censorship revisions of 1966, gives expression to what was already latent in the classic noir texts, making explicit the moral turpitude that could only be hinted at in the classic films.

In *Night Moves,* as in, say, *Point Blank, The Conversation,* and *Taxi Driver,* the paranoia of the forties and fifties texts, their articulation of fear regarding female autonomy, ethnicity, nuclear holocaust, and, above all, Communist infiltration of the United States, has been reformulated. The protagonist's paranoia here stems in part from his fear of contact with other people, his inability to cope with human interaction, and in part from his investigative work, which over time has revealed to him an essentially corrupt and uncaring society. His is a world of solitude, psychic fragmentation, violence, and the debasement of love. Even the brief period of human warmth and intimacy enjoyed by *Chinatown*'s Jake Gittes and Evelyn Mulwray has no place in this film. Moseby's one night with the former prostitute Paula lacks feeling and is subsequently revealed as a calculated ploy to enable Iverson to investigate the wreckage of Marv's airplane, much in the same way that Harry Caul's night with Meredith (Elizabeth MacRae) in *The Conversation* is a ruse intended to enable the theft of his recordings, while the reconciliation with his wife Ellen is quickly compromised by Moseby's return to Florida.

Night Moves is a detective narrative in which every character, the protagonist included, is implicated in the sordidness of the world his investigation exposes. Moseby's investigative quest appears to lead in ever-widening concentric circles without ever really reaching a point of resolution. The search for the missing Delly leads to the discovery of the smuggling ring which, in turn, lays bare a world in which every character who appears on screen is potentially corrupt. Nick (Kenneth Mars), for example, who originally pushes the Delly Grastner job Harry's way, is a collector of the artifacts that Iverson and Ziegler smuggle, and even Harry's wife Ellen works in an antique store where such artifacts could be legitimately sold.[20] So cynical and pessimistic is the film's vision of contemporary American society that it is unable even to offer characters of moderate integrity like Sheriff Calder (Marlon Brando) and his wife Ruby (Angie Dickinson), who withstand the maelstrom of violence, hatred, and corruption in Penn's 1966 film *The Chase.*

More so than in *Chinatown,* the world through which the detective travels, and indeed to which he belongs, is one of widespread inertia and wholesale failure. When his wife asks who is winning the football game he is watching on television, for example, Moseby can only respond, "Nobody, one side's just losing slower than the other." This pessimistic outlook extends to Moseby's professional activities (despite a past moment of glory on the football field). Hackman's detective, as with his earlier Harry Caul in Coppola's *The Conversation,* has none of the assurance and self-confidence of Bogart's Sam Spade (in Huston's *The Maltese Falcon*) or Philip Marlowe (in Hawks's *The Big Sleep*),[21] but rather is a man weighed down by the anxieties of the modern world, which themselves are only intensified by his investigation. Unlike Sam Spade, Moseby is consistently deceived by the characters he encounters and never enjoys the position of superior knowledge that was Spade's prerogative. His look, moreover, to which the viewer is bound, rather than indicating a position of power derived from knowledge, suggests only lack of control and ineptitude (ironically the boat in which he flounders as Paula and Ziegler die is even named "Point of View"). Shot in the leg in the climactic sequence, therefore, Moseby is ultimately a man of impotence, like the crippled Marty Heller and the plaster-encased Joey Ziegler.

Moseby's investigation leads him not in a linear direction, progressing from one clue to another, but in circles, like the boat in which he finds himself alone in the final frames of the film. By his own admission, the only time he has ever followed clues in a linear fashion was in the search for his father, who abandoned his mother when he was a child. Even then he was unable to take his search to a natural conclusion, preferring to watch his father from a distance rather than talk to him. It is Moseby's curse to be a curious man ("one of those intent-on-the-truth types," as Paula puts it) who is so utterly incapable of action. In a brief but incisive piece on the film, Eileen McGarry writes that the "traditional detective derived his power not just from the ability to track one clue to the next but from the insight that enabled him to see the larger picture, to justify the sordidness of his search by creating meaning out of mystery. In this sense, Harry is impotent."[22] Moseby is like the past chess master (hence the linguistic pun of the film's title) he speaks of to Paula, who, opting for one move, failed to see the strategy that would have resulted in his victory. As a detective, he simply goes through the motions resigned to the fact that in the contemporary environment of moral ambiguity it has become virtually impossible to differentiate good from evil. Ultimately, with a plot that has no resolution, *Night Moves* becomes an extended critique of the deglamorized role of the contemporary detective: "People ask you to do boring trivial sordid things and you do them," Ellen exclaims; "Somebody says go find my daughter and you go find her. Somebody says spy on somebody else, you go do that. That's what you're all about," Quentin observes; "Do you ask these questions because you want to know the answer or is it just something you think a detective should do?" Paula asks, and later states, "You're asking the wrong questions." "I didn't solve anything," acknowledges Moseby, "just fell in on top of it."

Not unlike Philip Marlowe in *Marlowe* and *The Long Goodbye* (James Garner and Elliott Gould respectively), whose moral values and traditionality are anachronistically contrasted with the youth culture of sixties/seventies Californian society, Moseby is a man who has become detached from the modern world. Frequently, like a figure in an Edward Hopper painting, he is isolated in the frame: he sits alone in his office, at home watching television, entombed in his car (the phrase is carefully chosen, given the vehicular deaths of Delly, Marv, and Joey), or in the dark empty spaces of the Florida Keys; he is framed in doorways and windows, and observed through mosquito screens and the glass bottom of a boat. His alienation, however, stems from his own inertia, distrust of others, and inability to communicate. At one point he even comments to his wife, "I can't work up much enthusiasm for talking." As in *The Conversation, All the President's Men, Blow Out,* and to a lesser extent *Chinatown,* human interaction has been displaced by interaction with technology as witness Moseby's answering machine, the computers mentioned by Nick in his recorded message, the tape recording Moseby listens to in his car (which coldly details the violent breakdown of Arlene's relationship with Tom Iverson), and the films of Delly's death (themselves anticipated in overt references by Paula and Moseby to the footage of the Kennedy assassinations).

Night Moves's greatest, and darkest, departure from the noir detective tradition of old, however, is that it cannot offer any resolution to its convoluted and ambiguous plot. Like *The Hollow Men,* it ends not so much with a bang as with a whimper. As such, *Night Moves* is not only the darkest of Arthur Penn's films, it is also one of the bleakest and most despairing of the neo-noir era, a definitive reflection on the dysfunctionality of

American society in the period of Vietnam and Watergate. In fact, so corrosive is its cynicism that even the apparent liberations offered by counterculture and the seventies emancipation of women are here turned into further potential images of horror: "She's pretty liberated, isn't she?" observes Harry of Delly, prompting Paula to respond, "When we all get liberated like Delly there'll be fighting in the streets."[23] *Night Moves,* then, stands as a testament to the directionlessness and stagnation of mid-seventies America, a society coming to terms with humiliation in the Far East, economic turmoil, political scandal (Nixon's resignation), and political paranoia (JFK conspiracy theories fueled by the first televised screening of the Zapruder footage), and, even as the Republicans were on the verge of being removed from office, the failure of liberalism as manifested in the faltering decline of the various countercultural movements initiated in the late sixties. These are issues that resurface in Martin Scorsese's *Taxi Driver,* which similarly seems to be infused with the collective pessimism of the American people in the wake of political scandal, war, and economic deprivation. It too offers up a protagonist who traverses a twilight world of hollow men. This is a man like Harry Moseby who ultimately seeks to give meaning to an otherwise pointless existence, "a man who wouldn't take it anymore." Where Harry's existential quest lies (he believes at least) in solving the enigma behind Delly's death, however, in *Taxi Driver* the protagonist, like Albert Camus's *L'Étranger,* finds a sense of identity through the perpetration of violence. The result in both films, nevertheless, is the same. They end on a note of emptiness and desolation; the hollow men prevail.

TAXI DRIVER

Plot Summary

Ex-Marine Travis Bickle (Robert De Niro) takes a job as a New York City taxi driver working the night shift. In his own words he is "God's lonely man" alienated from society, unable to sleep, and disgusted by the seedy urban environment he traverses. Travis is attracted to and, during the day, spies on Betsy (Cybill Shepherd), a campaign worker for presidential candidate Senator Charles Palantine (Leonard Harris). Summoning up his courage, he approaches her and arranges a date. On their second meeting, however, Travis offends Betsy when he takes her to see a pornographic movie. Betsy's rejection of him, in conjunction with an encounter with a violent and bigoted taxi passenger (Martin Scorsese) who spies on his adulterous wife, prompts further psychological dislocation. Travis buys firearms and begins to put himself through a rigorous program of physical exercise. By chance he is in a convenience store during a holdup and kills the gunman. Concurrently he befriends a twelve-year-old prostitute, Easy/Iris (Jodie Foster). Travis's revulsion and anger is fueled by Iris's situation and her relationship with her pimp Sport (Harvey Keitel). He determines to follow through on his plan to assassinate Senator Palantine, but is foiled by Secret Service agents at a political rally in Columbus Circle. Instead Travis violently takes out his disgust with society on Sport and his underworld colleagues, and is himself injured. His actions, which result in reuniting Iris with her family, are celebrated in the media. Physically rehabilitated, Travis once again encounters Betsy. Although his manner implies indifference, there is a suggestion that he remains psychologically unstable.

Analysis

Taxi Driver does not so much demythologize a generic tradition, as is the case with both *Chinatown* and *Night Moves* and their revisionism of the noir detective film, as reinvent it in a context more suited to the sociopolitical realities of mid-seventies America. It is informed by an understanding of the political paranoia, economic deprivation, inner-city decay, racism, and violence of the seventies (Travis Bickle is, in a sense, a composite figure of the era's most notorious political assassins and psychopaths from Lee Harvey Oswald to Charles Manson). Yet this is also an intensely personal film, shaped by the idiosyncrasies of director Martin Scorsese, bearing testament to his cine-literacy, erudition, ethnicity, and religion. Scorsese's friend, British filmmaker Michael Powell, once wrote that if "originality and truth are your aim, cultivate your own back garden."[24] Thus our understanding of the *Taxi Driver* we see on screen (as opposed to the one penned by the Dutch-American Calvinist Paul Schrader) is inextricably bound with the legacy of Scorsese's upbringing as a movie-obsessed Italian-American Catholic on the Lower East Side of New York City. This is American neo-noir descended from the fifties B film noir of "psychotic action and suicidal impulse," but by way of the French *nouvelle vague,* John Cassavetes's documentary realism, the metacinematic fantasies of Federico Fellini, and Michael Powell and Emeric Pressburger's Technicolor expressionism, a film that simultaneously captures the essence of life in the contemporary metropolis and reworks the Christ narrative.

In fact, the intersection of Martin Scorsese in the history of film noir has proven to be hugely influential on the subsequent evolution and diversification of neo-noir during the eighties and nineties, particularly in relation to the new generation of filmmakers working on the periphery of the mainstream and in the independent sector. Since the seventies and early eighties, when the bulk of his neo-noir films were produced, the "Scorsese factor" has been in evidence in the frenetic style of low-budget independent projects like *Blood Simple* and *El Mariachi* (Robert Rodriguez, 1993). It can be perceived in the exploration of masculine sexual identity in films like *Sea of Love* and *Romeo is Bleeding*. It overshadows the male criminal milieu of films like *Reservoir Dogs* and *Laws of Gravity* (Nick Gomez, 1992), and it is in evidence in the numerous contemporary noir projects in which Scorsese has served as producer or executive producer, including *The Grifters, Mad Dog and Glory* (John McNaughton, 1992), *Night and the City, Clockers,* and *Search and Destroy* (David Salle, 1995). In effect Scorsese's neo-noir oeuvre serves as both a benchmark and a point of reference to a generation of filmmakers, including Spike Lee, the Coen Brothers, and Kathryn Bigelow, interested in fusing art-house esthetics with mainstream generic structures, in employing visual pyrotechnics as a means of conveying narrative content, and in exploring the darker side of the collective American psyche, foregrounding above all the irrationality and violence of masculinity.

Scorsese's neo-noir work as a filmmaker has seen him direct, produce, and write noir material, not to mention encourage the work of others, most notably neo-noir screenwriter Richard Price (*Night and the City, Sea of Love, Mad Dog and Glory, Kiss of Death, Clockers*). Scorsese has also been involved in promoting the industrial and public awareness of the noir tradition. This he has achieved by sponsoring the restoration and subsequent transfer to video of classic film noir texts, like *Force of Evil, A Double Life* (George Cukor, 1948), and the noir-western hybrid *Pursued,* and by contributing to the documentary *The Film Noir Story* in which, in addition to discussing classic film noir, he offers commentary on his intentions in *Mean Streets* in relation to its placement in the history of the genre.[25] He also dedicates a significant section of his American film history documentary *A Century of Cinema: A Personal Journey with Martin Scorsese through American Movies* to an examination of classic film noir and its subsequent revival.[26]

Like the classic film noir texts he admires, the thematic focus of Scorsese's own neo-noir films of the seventies, eighties, and nineties —

Mean Streets, Taxi Driver, New York, New York, Raging Bull, After Hours, Cape Fear, and *Casino*—is on the personal, the microcosmic, although nearly always with broader social implications. Habitually Scorsese's films return to the motifs of alienation, claustrophobia, disillusionment, and the threat of urban violence. Scorsese's neo-noirs are intimate psychological dramas that emphasize the violence, moral degradation, dysfunctionality, and inhospitality of the modern world. Above all else, they sustain classic film noir's investigation of masculinity, placing particular emphasis on the crisis of identity prompted by male sexual anxiety. In keeping with the stylistic traditions of the noir genre, such concerns are expressed visually rather than through dialogue. In Scorsese's neo-noirs style is always in service of content and is only rarely a substitute for it.

As with the classic noir texts of the B-film auteurs, Scorsese's neo-noirs draw from and occasionally combine aspects of gangster noir, paranoid noir, and criminal procedural noir (the subcategories of the genre that were most prevalent during the classic film noir cycle's period of "psychotic action and suicidal impulse") with other generic traditions, such as black comedy in *After Hours,* the musical in *New York, New York,* the horror film in *Cape Fear,* the gangster picture in *Casino,* and the western in *Taxi Driver.* What is more, Scorsesean neo-noir tends to sustain classic film noir's disorienting juxtaposition of documentary realism and expressionism. His films combine method acting, expressionist mise-en-scène, frenetic camera movement, experimental editing, and popular music, with the pulp narratives of B film noir. Stylistically, Scorsese shares the penchant of the financially constrained classic noir filmmakers for "moulding seemingly contradictory elements into a uniform style."[27] *New York, New York,* for example, has an especially palimpsest-like quality bearing the imprint not only of the classical Hollywood cinema, to which it pays homage, but also of expressionist, European new wave, and New York independent filmmaking techniques.[28]

In addition to its own stylistic diversity, *Taxi Driver,* like other neo-noir texts by Scorsese and his fellow *nouvelle vague*–influenced Hollywood renaissance filmmakers, juxtaposes generic hybridization (film noir, the western, and the horror film), with allusions to high art and references to popular culture (Dostoyevsky's *Notes from Underground,* Sartre's *Nausea,* Bresson's 1950 *Journal d'un curé de campagne,* Ford's 1956 *The Searchers,* Irving Lerner's 1958 *Murder By Contract,* and television soap opera). This it combines with a modernist thematic interest in the alienating qualities of the modern city, the breakdown of human interaction, the debasement of love, and the fragmentation of identity.[29] As such, *Taxi Driver* supplies a fitting conclusion to the neo-modern phase of neo-noir that began with Godard's *A bout de souffle.* Indeed, in the eighties its experimental attitude toward film noir would be largely confined to the independent sector as the mainstream reverted once again to the conventions of genre cinema.

As with *Chinatown* and *Night Moves* (and indeed the celebrated literary texts of twenties modernism), *Taxi Driver* similarly draws from the mythological structure of the hero adventure as a means of illustrating the dysfunctionality of contemporary American society. In this case, however, the failed figure of *Chinatown* and *Night Moves*'s private investigator has been usurped by that of the psychopathic vigilante/urban cowboy whose quest is for the regeneration of his beleaguered city ("Someday a real rain will come and wash all this scum off the streets"). Travis Bickle is a man whose psyche gradually fragments until finally he "communicates his response to his environment through violence."[30] Like Lee Marvin's Walker in *Point Blank* or Ryan O'Neal's eponymous protagonist in *The Driver,* Travis is, like other alienated anti-heroes of neo-noir, unable to interact with the people who surround him and feels disconnected from the place he inhabits. Travis's journey through the mean streets of New York City therefore becomes, by extension, a journey through his own troubled psyche, an impossible quest for spiritual purity and integrated identity. As Bella Taylor observes in his auteurist study of Scorsese's films, this "inability to achieve psychological resolution is a source of pain and visceral frustration which in a Scorsese film will explode into anarchic violence."[31]

Violence, of course, especially sacrificial violence, is endemic to the classical mythology and primitive ritual on which theories of the hero adventure are modeled. As Julian Rice notes in his study of *Taxi Driver,* the "idea of being cleansed in blood, from Dionysian and orphic dismemberings, through the image of Christ nailed on the Cross, is a dominating motif in Western myth and religion."[32] Indeed, since the sixteenth-century Counter-Reformation the Catholic mode of representing Christ's Passion, from which Scorsese appears to have drawn in the film's extended sequence of bloodshed, is characterized by "a pictorial language of violent sensuality, spectacle, theatricality and excess."[33] In *Taxi Driver,* as in the works of European Catholic/lapsed Catholic filmmakers (Buñuel and Aranda, for example), there is a complex relationship established between religious iconography, the concept of sacrifice, and the realities of modern massacre (war, terrorism). Writing of the post–Civil War Spanish filmmakers, Marsha Kinder comments in *Blood Cinema:*

> One of the most distinguishing characteristics of the representation of violence in Spanish cinema is the interplay between these two models of primitive sacrifice and modern massacre. While this duality is glossed over by the unifying ideology of the official Francoist cinema, the filmmakers of the opposition sought to explore Spain's paradoxical role as a dual signifier of Europe's barbaric past and dehumanized future. Thus they had to expose the aesthetic mechanisms that allowed the modern massacre to be transformed into a purifying sacrificial ritual and thereby justified. That is one of the reasons the representation had to be so brutal, graphic, and ugly, so highly fetishized and specularized.[34]

A similar agenda seems to operate in *Taxi Driver*. The "barbaric past" is embodied in the western myth invoked by the film (the allusions to *The Searchers*), a myth that has perpetually "glossed over" the realities of a policy of genocide that all but wiped out Native Americans. Subliminally, the film seems to express a desire to atone for the collective guilt of the American people for the indigenous violence manifested in terrorist acts (Travis as potential political assassin), race riots (Travis as inveterate racist), and the modern-day atrocities of the Vietnam War (Travis as a Vietnam veteran). As Bella Taylor notes, "the film peers directly at the darker corners of human existence and suggests that the urge toward violence may be an increasingly natural response in a moral universe divested of human values."[35]

Taxi Driver also explores the manifestation of violence as it relates to male-female relations. The connection between masculine violence and perverted sexuality or sexual dysfunction, a motif the film shares with such neo-noirs as *Bonnie and Clyde, Klute,* and *Chinatown,* is made explicit in the conversation of the passenger who asks Travis if he has ever seen what a .44 Magnum pistol "can do to a woman's pussy."[36] In Travis's case, moreover, the psychological dislocation prompted in part by Betsy's rejection of him, in conjunction with the mixed emotions and sexual anxiety aroused by his interaction with the adolescent prostitute Iris, eventually lead to his murderous actions toward the end of the film.[37] As in *Mean Streets* (the protagonist's dream of bloody ejaculation, for example), or *New York, New York* (the protagonist's physical abuse of his wife prior to childbirth), or *Raging Bull* (the protagonist's jealousy-fueled violence in both the boxing arena and the domestic sphere), in *Taxi Driver* "violence is seen as inseparable from desire," indeed to a degree it is "validated as an essential component of masculinity."[38] However, so excessive and self-destructive is the violence evinced by Travis, and so turbulent has been his sexual anxiety, that they essentially rupture his sense of identity. Travis becomes paranoid, obsessive, schizophrenic.

As suggested by the recurrent mirror shots in his work, Scorsese's narratives are concerned with internal struggles, especially with his male protagonists' psychic fragmentation as they endeavor to come to terms with their sexuality. His characters, from J. R. (Harvey Keitel) in *Who's That Knocking at My Door?* (1969) to Jesus (Willem Dafoe) in *The Last Temptation of Christ* (1988), from Travis Bickle in *Taxi Driver* to Max Cady (Robert De Niro) in *Cape Fear,* are torn between the dual impulses toward love and death, the spiritual and the secular, priesthood and gangsterdom, sainthood and psychosis. As Lorraine Mortimer has argued,

> these men's ideas of what it is and what it takes to be a man are inextricable from their conception of what is needed to reach God. Their model of masculinity is embedded in a strong cultural and socio-political edifice. Yet it is always threatening to dissolve, as transparent and fragile as a bubble liable to burst at a touch. It is a dualist model in which fear of women and desire for male purging and purification are fundamental.[39]

In these films, as in many classic film noir texts, the way these men relate to women is central to their psychological makeup. Like the male protagonists of the classic noir films who must choose between the nurturing domestic woman and the erotic figure of the femme fatale, it seems that for the male protagonists in Scorsese's films "femininity is two-faced, embodying both suffering passivity and monstrous destructive power."[40] Travis's attitude toward Betsy and Iris in *Taxi Driver,* for example, epitomizes the virgin-whore dichotomy that is a legacy not only of classic film noir's distinction between the good woman and the femme fatale but also of Roman Catholicism's differentiation between the Madonna (the Virgin Mary) and the whore (Mary Magdalene). In Travis's eyes Betsy metamorphoses from a vision of heaven ("She appeared like an angel out of this filthy mess") to one of hell (a place he invokes in his parting words to her in the Palantine offices), whereas Iris is transformed from a literal prostitute to a teenage "virgin" reunited with her family as a result of his actions (he is himself both a fallen man *and* a savior).[41]

One of the most fascinating aspects of Scorsese's neo-noir films is how he manages to graft an essentially Roman Catholic worldview onto the gritty narratives of film noir. Indeed, what is most striking about Scorsese's neo noirs, other than their dynamic visual style, is their revelation of an overlap between the thematic concerns of film noir and Catholic convention, particularly as they relate to the concepts of guilt and masochistic suffering. In *Taxi Driver,* for example, the voice-over extracts from Travis's diary have an element of the confessional about them (a disembodied voice laying bare his soul to an unseen listener); Travis's actions, particularly as he prepares for his final mission (the rigorous training, the shooting practice, the narcissistic ceremony before his mirror, the burning of his hand), are marked by the conventions of ritual that Scorsese himself associates with the Catholic Church; and for Travis, his murderous spree in Iris's candle-filled bedroom, a ritual sacrifice of sorts, in addition to his Christ-like masochistic desire to give up his own life in order to save her, result in a spiritual cleansing—a purification by blood-letting.[42]

For the viewer, on the other hand, Travis's beliefs and actions are a manifestation of his psychosis, signifiers of his psychological fragmentation. Travis is the archetypal existential loner hero who endlessly strives to bring an end to his crisis of identity, to give meaning to an otherwise insignificant life.[43] In this film of urban psychopathology, more so even than in the detective films *Chinatown* and *Night Moves,* the viewer is bound to this disturbed character's vision of the world. We always see the New York environment from Travis's psychologically unstable perspective. As with all Scorsese's neo-noir films, *Taxi Driver* is, ultimately, a psychological study of character.[44] As in Edvard Münch's classic expressionist painting *The Scream* (later quoted by Scorsese in his 1985 neo-noir *After Hours*),[45] all that is contained in the frame becomes an extension of Travis's troubled psyche, hence the visual stylization (the use of slow motion and jump-cut editing, the expressionism of the colors), and the one-dimensionality of many of the characters who are little more than ciphers for aspects of Travis's own personality.

In fact, Scorsese's modernization of noir expressionism, his stylistic experimentation, and his occasional employment of state-of-the-art technology frequently encourage the viewer to identify with the neuroses, obsessions, and paranoia of his troubled protagonists as they negotiate the characters' complex psychic geographies. In the 1973 film *Mean Streets,* for example, Scorsese employs expressionist visual pyrotechnics and mise-en-scène to suggest the internal conflicts of the protagonist Charlie (Harvey Keitel). In that film, the camera's incessant mobility, the disjointed editing, the frequent use of slow motion, and the saturated red lighting of the bar in which the principal characters meet, on the one hand, lend a sense of foreboding to the narrative, anticipating the eruption of violence in the film's final sequence, and, on the other, align the viewer more closely with Charlie's point of view. In this sense the documentary hand-held footage of Charlie's passage through a noir landscape of bars, tenement hallways, alleys, and cramped apartments not only establishes his environment as a menacing underworld domain, but is also suggestive of the claustrophobia and indecision he experiences in his interaction with the other characters.

Similarly, in *Raging Bull,* experimentation with camera speed serves to suture the viewer to Jake La Motta's (Robert De Niro) distorted point of view, particularly in his activities outside the boxing arena.[46] Stylistically linked to the film's fight sequences (which, in addition to fetishizing/ritualizing moments of extreme physical violence as in the final "Sugar" Ray Robinson [Johnny Anderson] bout, also include point-of-view slow motion shots), the variation in camera speed here clearly establishes Jake's unstable state of mind. By juxtaposing desire and antagonism, it foreshadows his violent domestic actions later in the film. Elsewhere in *Raging Bull* Jake's psychological instability is suggested by the manipulation of sound, editing, and the employment of steadicam photography, a device frequently employed by contemporary filmmakers to express complex psychological conditions and anticipate scenes of frenzied violence as in *Halloween* (John Carpenter, 1978) and *The Shining* (Stanley Kubrick, 1980).

In *Taxi Driver,* a film that in terms of theme and character is closely connected to both *Mean Streets* and *Raging Bull,* the conflation of what the viewer sees on screen with the protagonist's perception of the world is likewise achieved by means of camera mobility (with the taxi often serving as a dolly), variations in camera speed (as in Travis's first sighting of Betsy), and the manipulation of color (as in the climactic shootout sequence). Travis's psychic fragmentation is repeatedly indicated by mirror shots (Travis's eyes in the taxi rear-view mirror, his narcissistic "performance" before the mirror in his room), and at one stage by a shot that tracks into a glass of Alka Seltzer. His sense of alienation is neatly encapsulated in a café scene with his taxi-driving colleagues in which he is constantly isolated in his own frame or physically fragmented in the framing of others.[47] Later, as Travis speaks to Betsy on the phone, the camera abandons him altogether, moving laterally to frame an empty corridor, much in the same way that it had previously abandoned him when he first left the taxi depot after seeking employment.

Travis's sense of isolation is crucial to our understanding of his psychological makeup, since it serves as the catalyst for his later actions. Travis's characterization is, therefore, a natural progression from that of Harry Moseby. In both *Taxi Driver* and *Night Moves,* as the protagonist's interaction with other people begins to break down, there is an almost entropic trajectory toward solitude, alienation, and silence. In *Taxi Driver,* moreover, Travis's failure in human interaction sees him reduced to communicating with himself through his diary. Indeed, Travis's diary entries contrast starkly with the inarticulacy of his conversations with his taxi passengers and work colleagues, or the television-derived clichés of his occasional interaction with Betsy, Iris, and Sport. The irony of Travis's situation is that when he does communicate his feelings through violence, his actions accord him celebrity status. Society applauds the psychopath at large, even though he clearly has failed to purge his sense of alienation, moral outrage, and neurosis.

This leads us to the ambiguity of the film's ending. As in *Point Blank,* it is possibly nothing more than the mindscreen of the fatally wounded protagonist, and really seems to take us back in cyclical fashion to the itinerant psychotic character of the initial credit sequence. The film, as with *Chinatown, Night Moves,* and other texts in the Scorsesean neo-noir oeuvre, "has been building to a pure emptiness."[48] Nothing changes. American society remains a wasteland, characterized by dysfunctionality, moral degradation, corruption, violence, alienation, and impotence. In *Taxi Driver* we are not even permitted the release offered by the deaths of the protagonists in classic film noir texts like *Double Indemnity* and *D.O.A.,* but instead we are condemned to a Sisyphean cycle of repetition.

Eighties Pastiche

By the eighties, film noir was a much more rounded concept than it had been in the seventies. Academically, for example, the period of the late seventies and early eighties was witness to the publication of the first English language book-length studies of the genre, which included, for example, the British Film Institute's *Women and Film Noir* (1978), Alain Silver and Elizabeth Ward's *Film Noir: An Encyclopedic Reference to the American Style* (1979), and Foster Hirsch's *The Dark Side of the Screen: Film Noir* (1981). In the film industry itself, the term *film noir,* which had never been employed in the era of classical Hollywood cinema, was very much in currency following the revisionist work of seventies filmmakers like Martin Scorsese. Indeed, Lawrence Kasdan's 1981 neo-noir *Body Heat,* for example, was both marketed and discussed in the trade press as a contemporary film noir.[1] Paradoxically, however, as critical/analytical academic interest in the genre was sustained throughout the decade and on into the nineties, the investigative/modernist approach of the neo-modern filmmakers—although maintained to a degree in such peripheral mainstream films as *Hammett, Black Widow,* and *Sea of Love,* and in independently financed productions like *Blood Simple, Manhunter,* and *Cop*—was usurped in the mass mainstream market by a general tendency toward generic formularization as in *Body Heat, Against All Odds,* and *Fatal Attraction.* This phenomenon was symptomatic of the cultural shift from the neo-modern to the postmodern with an attendant focus on style, surface, and playfulness; a commodification, that is, of the stylistic experimentation, formal revisionism, and self-referentiality of Scorsese and his fellow Hollywood renaissance filmmakers.

In fact, where Scorsese's 1976 film *Taxi Driver* effectively signals the end of the neo-modern era of neo-noir (although a case can also be made

90

for his 1977 *New York, New York* or even his 1980 *Raging Bull*), the 1981 release of *Body Heat* similarly marks the beginnings of the post-modern era. The film, in terms of mise-en-scène, narrative, and charac-ter types, posits a return to genre and the reaffirmation of the myth of the film noir crime melodrama. As Grist observes, in "place of the reflexive interrogation and reinflection of the New Hollywood period, the generic self-consciousness of *Body Heat* is superficial, and not at all analytical."[2] *Body Heat* constitutes a reworking of the "Cain-text" overtly drawing from the literary and cinematic models offered by *The Postman Always Rings Twice* and, more specifically, *Double Indemnity*.[3] It illustrates for Grist the way in which, in the postmodern era of American cinema, rep-resentation has become "a process of quotation and combination of past styles, images, and stereotypes, an undifferentiated eclecticism within an ahistorical perceptual present."[4]

The dominant esthetic mode during this era of neo-noir, therefore, is that of pastiche. Indeed, *Body Heat,* in addition to its derivative plot, of-fers a pastiche of the iconography—fedora hat, handgun, staircase, venetian blinds, overhead fan, the female protagonist's long hair—and chiaroscuro visuals of such celebrated classic films noirs as *Double In-demnity* and *Out of the Past*. Like George Deem's painting *School of Hopper,* which "quotes" from various paintings by Edward Hopper, the eighties neo-noir is laden with intertextual references to classic films noirs and hard-boiled literature that are intended to signify the filmmak-ers' knowledge of their own cultural heritage and their desire to pay homage to their forebears. In the postmodern noirs of the eighties, tex-tual allusion has become, if anything, more self-referential than that of the seventies, serving as a marker of "noirishness" as witness *Body Heat*'s borrowings from *Double Indemnity* or the comic self-referential-ity of the partly animated neo-noir *Who Framed Roger Rabbit?* (Roger Zemeckis, 1988). In such instances, by referencing the stylistic and iconographic markers of the genre's past, these films proclaim them-selves *as* contemporary films noirs.

In the majority of cases, the eighties texts' evocation of the iconogra-phy, narrative patterns, and character types of classic film noir constitutes little more than a superficial, primarily visual re-creation of film noir rather than the dynamic thematic reinvention of the genre represented by the no less allusive texts of the sixties and seventies. The principal dif-ference is that where the neo-modernists' intertextual references served to underscore their critique of contemporary American society, in the eighties texts the frame of reference is mainly esthetic and solipsistic.

Unlike the seventies *Night Moves* and *Taxi Driver,* there is a tendency in many of the eighties (and indeed the nineties) neo-noir productions to accord more prominence to the filmmakers' interest in film history itself, and specifically in the classic texts of forties film noir, than to the sociopolitical realities of contemporary America (this is taken to an extreme in Carl Reiner's 1982 noir pastiche *Dead Men Don't Wear Plaid,* which edits together sequences from classic noir texts with contemporary footage featuring Steve Martin and Rachel Ward). Part of the pleasure derived from watching postmodern cinema is in identifying the intertextual references that litter the contemporary films. They are integral to the agenda of entertainment and playfulness.

This is not to argue, however, that there is no thematic content in eighties neo-noir. What has to be addressed is the fact that what textual depth there is to be found in many of the contemporary films is often derivative, a sort of shorthand summary of the thematic motifs of both classic film noir and seventies neo-modern noir. This is well illustrated, for example, by the case of *Kill Me Again*. The film is a self-consciously formulaic neo-noir production that is characterized by a sense of nostalgic loss that recalls the mood of *Farewell, My Lovely* and *Chinatown*. Still, it engages in a deconstructive investigation of the noir genre. Like the classic film noir *Out of the Past* to which it frequently alludes (compare, for example, the Nevadan setting, the storm-accompanied love scene, and of course the male protagonist's first sighting of the femme fatale as she emerges from the shadows ironically dressed in virginal white), *Kill Me Again* hybridizes the noir crime melodrama, detective noir, and gangster noir, it borrows from the hero adventure paradigm both in its quest narrative structure and in its archetypal characterizations, and it self-consciously opens itself to critical interpretation in terms of "*noir* as a specific style, *noir* as existential drama, and the feminist view of *noir* as an articulation of male sexual paranoia."[5]

Eighties neo-noirs (like *Kill Me Again*) reclaim the financially greedy and aggressively independent sexual woman, a figure either absent (*The Parallax View* and *All the President's Men*), psychologically handicapped (*Klute* and *Chinatown*), or infantilized (*Night Moves* and *Taxi Driver*) in many of the seventies texts. This represents one of the most significant developments in the frequently cyclical evolution of noir culture. The hyperbolic return to the screen of the femme fatale and her gradual metamorphosis throughout the eighties and nineties simultaneously suggests an increasing degree of sexual anxiety in the male protagonist and a rearticulation of misogynist fears that were manifested in the post-war years of forties film noir. In the 1981 *Body Heat,* for example, the protagonist Ned Racine (William Hurt) is an inveterate womanizer, his sexual prowess compensating for his incompetence as a lawyer. He finds in the femme fatale Matty Walker (Kathleen Turner) a woman who is comfortably his intellectual superior and whose sexual appetite is more voracious than his own. By the time of the 1994 *The Last Seduction,* however, so profound is masculine sexual anxiety that the male protagonist Mike (Peter Berg) is haunted by a past indiscretion in which he was unwittingly married to a transvestite, proving himself an easy target for the femme fatale Bridget Gregory (Linda Fiorentino).

In the eighties and nineties the fetishistic fantasy of the femme fatale, or "phallic" woman, is beginning to fragment, in a sense. The independent sexual woman is no longer an ultimately reassuring male shield from castration anxiety, in the way that the femme fatale was in forties films noirs like *Double Indemnity, Murder, My Sweet, Scarlet Street, Gilda* (Charles Vidor, 1946), *Out of the Past,* and *The Lady from Shanghai* (Orson Welles, 1947). Where in the forties the femme fatale was "a symptom of male fears about feminism,"[6] constituting a projection of the "crisis in *male* identity" that nevertheless served as a decoy, deflecting attention away from the immediate problems of masculinity in an "elaborate strategy of denial,"[7] in the contemporary neo-noir of the eighties and nineties this figure is now an affirmation of the differences between the genders. Hence, in *Basic Instinct,* the woman is shown both as "castrated" (the infamous Sharon Stone crotch shot) and, in her murderous spree with an ice pick, as "castrator." The modern femme fatale of eighties and nineties neo-noir illustrates the challenge the contemporary woman now poses to the masculine domain at work, as in Meredith Johnson's (Demi Moore) harassment of Tom Sanders (Michael Douglas) in *Disclosure* (Barry Levinson, 1994), at home, as in Peyton Flanders's (Rebecca DeMornay) terrorization of the Bartel family in *The Hand That Rocks the Cradle* (Curtis Hanson, 1992), and in bed, as in the potential coupling of sexual climax and death suggested by the figure of Catherine Tramell (Sharon Stone) in *Basic Instinct.* In neo-noir, more overtly than was the case in classic film noir, the independent woman, as an articulation of male sexual anxiety, becomes the site in which the differences between fantasy and reality are blurred, prompting a crisis of identity in the male protagonist as witness the reactions of, say, Paul Hackett (Griffin Dunne) in *After Hours* and Frank Keller (Al Pacino) in *Sea of Love* to the women they encounter during the course of their respective narratives.

In *Body Heat*, the film that reintroduced the femme fatale in the hyperbolic context that still pervades the neo-noir, the figure of the strong woman is integral to male protagonist Ned Racine's psychological makeup. Matty Walker epitomizes that type of individual her husband Edmund (Richard Crenna) claims will do "whatever's necessary" in order to gain financial security, a status to which Ned aspires. What is more, she is simultaneously a projection of Ned's most profound anxieties and fears, more "femme castratrice" (the oral sex scene, for example) than femme fatale,[8] and the expression of his most fantastical sexual desires. Frequently during the scenes in which Ned and Matty are together he assumes a submissive role, letting himself be stage-managed by Matty in their first love-making scene and in a later scene allowing her to lead him around a room by his penis. The ambiguous ending of *Body Heat* in which Racine languishes in prison, but crucially learns the real identity of Matty/Mary Ann in his last appearance on screen (thus raising the possibility of her future punishment), while she suns herself in a tropical location, lends the film a certain ideological instability. Certainly *Body Heat* seems to censure the greed of Matty, and Ned, the transgressive male, is imprisoned, albeit for the murder he did not commit. Nevertheless, through the mouthpiece of public prosecutor Peter Lowenstein (Ted Danson), who at one stage in the film expresses his personal disgust for the victim and his associates, the film fails to condemn the murder of Edmund Walker. Most intriguing of all, unlike the majority of classical Hollywood femme fatale films noirs, it fails either to castigate or to rehabilitate the femme fatale on screen, a precedent followed up in such neo-noirs as *The Hot Spot, Basic Instinct,* and *The Last Seduction,* all of which feature femme fatale figures whose various crimes go unpunished.

In this sense it is important that even in the crime melodrama, or "Cain-text," films like *The Postman Always Rings Twice* and *Body Heat* the male protagonist already considers himself as a potentially rebellious figure *before* his first encounter with the femme fatale. The male protagonist is already the site of a struggle between the desire on the one hand to conform to an "ideologically ordained position" of domesticity, stability, and identification with the dominant laws of patriarchal society and on the other to transgress and venture into the unknown.[9] In his voice-over commentary in the classic film noir *Double Indemnity,* for example, the insurance salesman Walter Neff (Fred MacMurray) confesses that his involvement with the femme fatale Phyllis Dietrichson (Barbara Stanwyck) offered him the opportunity to put into practice a scheme that he had been mulling over for some time, that is, a plan devised *prior to* his first meeting with Phyllis.

Although such male protagonists of the noir crime melodrama as Walter Neff and Ned Racine are in the end victims of the femme fatale, initially at least they are willing accomplices, often manipulated into believing that they are the masterminds behind the initial transgression (usually the murder of the woman's husband). It is only as the representatives of patriarchal authority—insurance claims investigator Barton Keyes (Edward G. Robinson) in *Double Indemnity,* for example, or police detective Oscar Grace (J. A. Preston) in *Body Heat*—begin to unravel the enigma surrounding the death of the femme fatale's husband that the male protagonist fully realizes both the manner in which he has been manipulated/incriminated by his female partner and in the potentially life-threatening dangers that now confront him in his interaction with this figure. The male protagonist, therefore, is punished for both his stupidity and his transgression, his downfall and/or death a poetic justice of sorts.

Despite the more prominent position now accorded women in many of the contemporary noirs of the eighties and nineties—not only woman as femme fatale, but also woman as victim-heroine, as in *House of Games* and *Someone to Watch Over Me* (Ridley Scott, 1987), or woman as investigative seeker-heroine, as in *Black Widow* and *Impulse*—the central motif in these films remains that of patriarchal corruption, as witness the corrupt politician and the Soviet spy in *No Way Out,* the sexually perverted blackmailer and the bank robber in *The Hot Spot,* the psychopaths in *Blue Velvet* and *Blue Steel,* the hommes fatals in *Jagged Edge* and *Bad Influence,* and the serial killers in *Manhunter* and *The Silence of the Lambs.* Indeed, as in the seventies neo-noirs, particularly Scorsese's *Taxi Driver,* which has increasingly served as an index for the stylistic representation of violence in the neo-noirs of the late eighties and the nineties, the emphasis in the recent films is primarily on the physical dimension of patriarchal corruption; that is, male sexual perversion (rape, other forms of sexual assault, incest, child molestation) and, above all, the eruption of masculine violence. Violence, either as a manifestation of psychological dislocation (the scenes of slaughter in *Manhunter,* for example) or as a product of coldly calculated brutality (the homme fatal's murder of his wife in *Jagged Edge*), remains the primary means by which noir men communicate with their environment.

Increasingly, then, as neo-noir production has escalated, particularly from the mid-eighties until its peak in the mid-nineties, it has been characterized by the gradual erosion of the fetishistic fantasy of the femme fatale, the revelation of a greater degree of irrational masculine violence, and the thematization of a deep-seated sexual paranoia among its male protagonists. In the contemporary neo-noir there is a suggestion of even deeper fissures in the male sense of identity than was the case in the classic films noirs. Contemporary eighties texts like *Raging Bull, Body Heat, Blood Simple, After Hours, Manhunter, Something Wild Blue Velvet, No Way Out, Someone to Watch Over Me, Sea of Love,* and *Kill Me Again* constantly return to the motif of masculinity in crisis. They demonstrate how patriarchy is undermined by its own pervasive corruption (as in *Blood Simple* and *No Way Out*), its inadequacies and anxieties (as in *After Hours* and *Kill Me Again*), and its paranoia (as in *Raging Bull* and *Sea of Love*). In such films the fragmentation of masculinity, the dissolution of a male sense of identity, is shown to be a universal phenomenon.

In Scorsese's *Raging Bull,* for example, as in such classic films noirs as *Body and Soul* (Robert Rossen, 1947), *Force of Evil, Champion* (Mark Robson, 1949), *The Set-Up* (Robert Wise, 1949), *Killer's Kiss* (Stanley Kubrick, 1955) — even the noirish *On the Waterfront,* which Jake La Motta invokes in his stand-up routine — it is the concept of masculinity that is most overtly subjected to investigation and critique. Like *Taxi Driver* before it, *Raging Bull* in effect documents the psychic fragmentation of its protagonist. As with most of Scorsese's male protagonists, Jake's crisis of identity stems primarily from his struggle to come to terms with his own self-image and sexuality and from his need to reconcile the dual impulses he experiences toward love and death. This struggle manifests itself initially in his excessive brutality in the boxing ring, and subsequently in his obsessive desire for his second wife Vickie, his paranoid jealousy of her contact with any other man, his delusional fantasies of infidelity, his recourse to physical violence in his personal relationships with both his wife and brother Joey (Joe Pesci), his physical degeneration as his increasing obesity erodes any markers of his former athleticism, and latterly his sexual activity with minors.

At the heart of Jake's crisis of identity is the way in which he relates to women. As Deborah Thomas has observed, film noir "is most obviously about the blockage of men's emotions and the structuring of their sexuality by conventional norms of gender (toughness, ambition) and class (respectability, middle-class marriage)."[10] Jake's own conception of masculine identity revolves around the notion of machismo. He is tormented by the very idea of inadequacy or humiliation. His loss of self-respect, signaled by his physical swelling, is directly proportionate to his mistaken belief that he is losing his wife. His violence, perversely, becomes an expression of his desire, as witness his destruction of the young boxer Tony Janiro (Kevin Mahon) for whom his wife expressed passing admiration. Jake constantly does battle with the feminine aspect of his personality, an ever-present struggle that is given expression in the boxing arena, in his stand-up comedy routines and even in his interaction with Vickie.[11] Indeed, to a degree, Jake's every action, from his rigorous training as a young boxer to his provocative antagonism of the local hoodlum Salvy, from his violent beating of Janiro to his equally violent beating of his wife and brother, is an expression of his sexual paranoia.

Jake, in this sense, is the archetypal protagonist of film noir and hard-boiled fiction. As Woody Haut observes in *Pulp Culture:*

> The twisted thoughts and actions of the paranoid can be found in the behaviour of many pulp culture protagonists. This is apparent in their convoluted logic which attempts to prove what they already believe, an obsessive pursuit of hidden meanings and clues, a rejection of alternative interpretations, a subjective view of the world, a sexual anxiety based on fears concerning women and homosexuality, and an insistence on the right to question, deliberate and eavesdrop.[12]

Like all noir protagonists, Jake is inextricably bound to his own distorted perspective of reality. His delusional fantasies prompt his own psychic fragmentation, and, as was the case with Travis Bickle at the end of *Taxi Driver,* the ambiguity of the film's ending raises doubts regarding Jake's recovery. Like Francis Dollarhyde (Tom Noonan) in Michael Mann's *Manhunter* or Eugene Hunt (Ron Silver) in Kathryn Bigelow's *Blue Steel,* or indeed Jesus in Scorsese's own *The Last Temptation of Christ,* his is the psychotic's perception of the world, "a whirling confusion, voices inside and outside the head, persecutory forces waiting to pounce, nothing making sense."[13] Scorsese's next venture into the world of neo-noir, the low-budget *After Hours,* would be similarly concerned with the study of male sexual paranoia and its promotion of psychological dislocation. Eschewing the violent masculine psychosis that is at the center of both *Taxi Driver* and *Raging Bull, After Hours* nevertheless binds the viewer to the subjective point of view of a deeply troubled male protagonist as he embarks on a nightmare voyage through his own psyche.

AFTER HOURS

Plot Summary

New York City. Following a brief coffee-shop encounter with Marcy (Rosanna Arquette), bored word processor Paul Hackett (Griffin Dunne) decides to visit her in her SoHo apartment. The night gets off to a bad start when his $20 bill is lost from a speeding taxi and he is unable to pay the fare. When Paul arrives at the apartment, Marcy is out and he finds himself commandeered to help her artist friend Kiki (Linda Fiorentino). Marcy returns, but her erratic behavior scares Paul away. When he tries to take the subway home, he finds that he does not have enough change to cover the fare rise effective from midnight. Paul takes refuge from the rain in the Terminal Bar, where the bartender Tom (John Heard) offers to give him his fare in exchange for a favor. As a sign of good faith, Paul leaves his set of keys with Tom. At Tom's apartment he is mistaken for a burglar. Paul sees two men with Kiki's sculpture and scares them away. Having returned the sculpture, he then finds that Marcy has committed suicide. Back at the bar he discovers that Tom has temporarily closed it, and he accepts the waitress Julie's (Teri Garr) offer to wait for him at her place. He returns to the bar to collect his keys and discovers that Tom is Marcy's boyfriend. Wary of offending another imbalanced woman, Paul returns to Julie, but leaves on a sour note. Again the bar is closed and he still needs to collect his keys. He returns to Tom's apartment building, where he is once again accused of being a burglar. At the Club Berlin, where he has gone to find Kiki and her boyfriend Hearst (Will Patton), Paul is attacked. After encounters with yet another eccentric woman Gail (Catherine O'Hara), a gay man, and Tom, Paul finds himself chased by a posse who believe him responsible for a series of burglaries (the disgruntled Julie has covered the neighborhood with posters of Paul). Back at the Club Berlin, Paul is helped by June (Verna Bloom) who encases him in plaster as a way of hiding him from the mob. Mistaken for the work of art purchased from Kiki and then lost, the real robbers, Pepe (Thomas Chong) and Neil (Cheech Marin), "steal" Paul. Driving away from SoHo, Paul falls out of their van and finds himself back at his office building in the city.

Analysis

To a certain degree *After Hours* is the film that signals Scorsese's own submission to dominant cultural tendencies, marking a movement away from the neo-modernism of his seventies neo-noirs such as *Taxi Driver* to the postmodernism prevalent in eighties American cinema. As Leighton Grist comments in "Moving Targets and Black Widows,"

> Both films bear the mark of Scorsese's authorship, but where *Taxi Driver* provides a reflexive investigation of representation and characterisation, as well as an expressionist development of *noir* stylisation, the generic references of *After Hours* remain at the level of pastiche. In short, the film's dark, rain-slicked city streets and enclosing framing devices (windows, fire-escapes, etc.) not to mention the generic status of its characters (Paul as a victim hero, the women as *femme fatales manquées*), are all presented as mere signifiers of "*noir*-ishness" instead of contingent, historically-informed constructs to be investigated and analysed.[14]

Additionally, in keeping with the postmodernist tradition of self-referentiality, its prioritization of an artistic frame of reference over that of external reality, *After Hours* is informed by a mode of self-reflexivity that is altogether less subtle than that of *Taxi Driver*. Where *Taxi Driver* co-opted the thematic motifs of, say, John Ford's classic western *The Searchers* as a means of commentating on and critiquing the actions of the protagonist Travis Bickle, *After Hours* is simply laden with overt in-tertextual references to the films of Alfred Hitchcock and Orson Welles, *The Wizard of Oz* (Victor Fleming, 1939), Henry Miller's *Tropic of Cancer,* Dante's *Inferno,* and the literary universe of Franz Kafka, which at times serve no further purpose other than to draw attention to the film's own status as an artifact. *After Hours* ironizes and commodifies, more-over, the whole concept of Scorsesean cinema, becoming for Bryan Bruce "a film about Scorsese, or about what 'Scorsesian' might mean; it's Scorsese's joke on his own identity as auteur."[15]

For all its postmodern, stylish veneer, *After Hours* proves to be one of the most fascinating and critically underrated texts in the Scorsesean neo-noir oeuvre. This is Scorsese at his most surreal and Buñuelesque. The film both exploits the dark comic potential of the film noir narrative and constitutes a cinematic visualization of a repetitive masculine night-mare of sexual paranoia. Paul Hackett becomes the author and protago-nist of his own *Odyssey, Inferno,* and film noir narrative, wandering through an urban landscape that is an extension of his own psychic ge-ography. Like the protagonists of such films noirs as *Scarlet Street, D.O.A., Blue Velvet,* and *Bad Influence,* Paul descends from the rela-tively safe environment of his workplace and is enveloped by an alien nighttime underworld, the traversing of which heightens his own sexual anxiety and prompts a crisis of his masculine identity as he becomes "surrounded by threats of mutilation, castration and death."[16]

In the noir tradtion, *After Hours* self-consciously invokes the concept of a mythic hero adventure, a quest for identity, integration, and rebirth. Like Scorsese's seventies neo-noirs *Mean Streets, Taxi Driver,* and *New York, New York,* however, its resolution is laden with ambiguity. Paul is "reborn" in a sense, emerging from the shell of June's sculpture, but only to face yet another day of office routine with little having been resolved from the previous night's adventure. Indeed, as with *Taxi Driver, After Hours* is characterized by a Sisyphean cycle of repetition. Not only does the film's closing sequence echo its opening sequence, but during the course of Paul's night in SoHo there is a certain symmetry about his regular visits to Kiki and Marcy's loft apartment, the Terminal Bar, Tom's apartment building, the diner, the Club Berlin, and Julie's apartment, and his various encounters with Marcy, Kiki, Tom, Julie, the taxi driver, and the burglars. The film ironizes, then, the classic noir motifs of fate or predestination and the inexorable passage of linear time (an issue that is itself foregrounded on the film's soundtrack) by indicating, through its constant repetition and slight variation of events, the cyclical, almost spiral nature of time. Paul, like Scottie (James Stewart) in Alfred Hitchcock's *Vertigo* (1958) or Oedipa Maas in Thomas Pynchon's postmodern novella *The Crying of Lot 49,* experiences a vertiginous descent through space and time toward psychic fragmentation and the dissolution of his identity.

Paul's is a paradigmatic noir journey both into an urban hades and into the darkest recesses of his own psyche.[17] His crisis of identity is heightened by his entry into the unfamiliar SoHo environs, but, as the incomplete story of childhood trauma he narrates to the comatose Kiki suggests, it has its roots in the past, indeed stems from a rekindling of the fears associated with the horrific childhood experience. In effect Paul's story echoes what psychoanalyst Sigmund Freud perceived as the key moment in children's sexual evolution when they discover their mother's lack of a penis. His story is one that relates not only his childhood trauma but his continuing castration anxiety:

Paul: You have a great body.
Kiki: Yes . . . not a lot of scars.
Paul: That's true. Never occurred to me.
Kiki: I mean some women I know are covered in them head to toe. Not me.
Paul: Scars?

Kiki: Uh huh, horrible, ugly scars. Just telling you now.

Paul: Hmm, I don't know. I know when I was a kid, I had to have my tonsils out, and after the operation they didn't have enough room for me in pediatrics so they had to put me in the burn ward. And before they wheeled me in this nurse gave me this blindfold to put on and told me never to take it off, if I did they'd have to do the operation all over again. I didn't understand what my tonsils had to do with my eyes either but . . . Anyway, that night, at least I think it was night, I reached up, untied the blindfold, and I saw . . .

Metaphorically, Paul's after hours adventure in SoHo forces him to relive the primal scene, inducing in him a degree of sexual anxiety and paranoid suspicion of femininity that is informed by a masculine fear of castration. Women, in this sense, as with the femmes fatales of classic films noirs, become for the male protagonist harbingers of death. They are creatures of the night, they bear the marks of castration in physical scars, they are associated with symbols of death (Kiki's and June's replica sculptures of Münch's skull-like *The Scream,* Marcy's tattoo, Julie's rat traps), and they all manifest varying degrees of mental instability. Paul's mounting castration anxiety is most clearly indicated, however, when he first visits the Terminal Bar. In the bathroom, he is horrified by a graffiti drawing of a shark biting a man's erect penis, suggesting a more profound level of neurosis stemming from an uncertain conception of his own masculine identity.

In keeping with the psychological motifs of such classical noir narratives as *So Dark the Night* (Joseph H. Lewis, 1946) and *Whirlpool* (Otto Preminger, 1949), Paul must come to terms with his psychosexual disorder by learning to dissociate his fear of being physically scarred by fire from his conception of femininity. His is a quest, as Bill Van Daalen has argued, to put himself through "an initiation ritual, a trial by fire for the old self so that a new, more mature one can take its place," a ritual informed by Carl Jung's conception of "an archetypal descent into hell followed by renewal," one founded on the "disintegration and reorganization of the psyche."[18] Patently Paul fails in this quest. For him, women remain associated with fire (Marcy's burn lotion and book of fire victims, Gail's desire to burn a newspaper clipping off Paul's arm), pain (Kiki's sadomasochism), and destruction (Julie's rat traps, the woman Paul witnesses murder her husband). Paul does not arrive at a moment of transcendence, nor unity, nor individuation. Rather than assimilating the various archetypal figures he encounters during his voyage through his own psychic landscape, he flees them. His identity becomes fragmented, smashed like Kiki's television set and Julie's sculpture. His return to the apparently ordered world of his office is not, therefore, a rebirth, but, as suggested by the frenetic movement of Michael Ballhaus's camera, the moment of Paul's passage into psychosis. To a certain extent, in fact, the film leaves Paul at the same point where earlier Scorsesean texts entered into the worlds of, say, Travis Bickle or Jake La Motta.

Paul's sexual anxiety is not only implied by his paranoid distrust of femininity, but is signaled by the protagonist's initial desire for the alluring blonde Marcy. As in Scorsese's earlier neo-noirs, witness Travis and Betsy in *Taxi Driver* or Jake and Vickie in *Raging Bull,* this will result in catastrophe. In Scorsese's films, relationships between the male protagonist and the woman he desires are always characterized by an entropic trajectory toward dissolution, the death instinct invariably triumphing over Eros. For Paul, however, this characteristic trait of both the noir and the Scorsesean protagonist is further compounded by his encounters with SoHo's homosexual community. Already disoriented by his interaction with the independently minded sexual women who inhabit the neighborhood, Paul's developing friendship with the bartender Tom (with whom he exchanges keys, an ironically overstated "marker" of homosexuality, as is the fact that they form a "love triangle" with Marcy), his conversation with a gay couple in the Terminal Bar that intensifies his sense of guilt regarding Marcy's suicide, his pickup by a potentially gay man, and his subsequent flight from the predominantly homosexual mob, all serve to intensify his personal crisis of masculine identity.

In a sense, then, Paul's whole sexual identity short-circuits, his personal crisis suggested by "the loss of access to customary signifiers of male power: control, aggression, sexual potency, and money, and the ability to read and decipher situations, to reason, order and account for."[19] As in the classic films noirs of the forties, moreover, in *After Hours* sexual desire also becomes conflated with finance. Paul loses his potency when his $20 bill flies from the window of his speeding taxi. Paul's narrative, therefore, is not only one defined simply in terms of sexual paranoia; it is also one underpinned by the concept of a yuppie nightmare. The upwardly mobile, financially comfortable word processor is punished for departing, albeit temporarily, the comforts of his hi-tech home and office (the implicit indictment of Reaganomics in this and other yuppie nightmare films of this mid-eighties period such as *Blue Velvet, Something Wild,* and *Fatal Attraction* is the closest many eighties texts get to the overt sociopolitical critique that characterized seventies neo-noir).

As in *Mean Streets, Taxi Driver,* and *Raging Bull,* in *After Hours* the protagonist's crisis of identity, his sense of anxiety and mounting sexual paranoia is conveyed stylistically by means of complex camera movement, jump-cut editing, and, as already noted, is here enhanced by a pastiche of classic film noir's iconographical markers of psychic torment and fragmentation—odd camera angles as in Paul's third bathroom visit (in the gay pickup's house), chiaroscuro lighting effects as in Paul's second visit to Marcy's bedroom, mirrors as in the bathrooms in the Terminal Bar and Tom's apartment, venetian blinds as in the diner, and rain-washed streets (water here, as in classic film noir, as a symbol of the unconscious). As in the earlier films, in *After Hours* style is the means by which Scorsese and his collaborators, the cinematographer Michael Ballhaus, the editor Thelma Schoonmaker, and the music director Howard Shore, explore the extreme psychic state of the film's emotionally-impaired protagonist, relaying key narrative information not through dialogue but through virtuoso camera work, mise-en-scène, lighting, editing and music.

As a low-budget independent production, *After Hours* recaptures the sense of stylistic experimentation and freneticism that characterized the classic B films noirs and Scorsese's own neo-noirs of the early-to-mid seventies. Unfettered by the demands of mainstream studio production, challenged by the financial constraints of a relatively small budget ($4.5 million), and inspired by a renewed acquaintance with European filmmaking techniques (Scorsese's new collaborator, the cinematographer Michael Ballhaus, had previously worked on a long-term basis with Rainer Werner Fassbinder, one of the leading figures in New German Cinema), in *After Hours* Scorsese gives full expression to "the tracking shot mannerisms and elaborate noirish visual effects"[20] that had characterized his seventies neo-noirs. The film sustains, moreover, Scorsese's cinematic exploration of the fusion of fantasy and reality, stylistically maintaining classic film noir's juxtaposition of realism and expressionism, alluding constantly to the fantasy adventures of Dorothy (Judy Garland) in *The Wizard of Oz,* and diegetically offering the possibility that all the narrative events may simply be a dream, the subjective mind-screen of the protagonist as he sleeps before his television. Once again, then, Scorsese refuses to spell things out, the ambiguity of his film's ending and its possible status as either fantasy or reality underpinning the anxieties and tensions that run through the film's narrative.

This fusion, or confusion, of fantasy and reality and its relation to male sexual anxiety and paranoia is a motif that also informs our understanding of the Coen Brothers' *Blood Simple*. Like *After Hours*, this film examines the fragmentation of masculine identity and the increasing breakdown of communication between the genders. Where in *After Hours* Paul simply despairs when he and Gail, one of the many SoHo women he encounters, continue to talk at cross-purposes, in *Blood Simple* the misunderstandings that result from the breakdown of meaningful human interaction lead inexorably toward violence.

BLOOD SIMPLE

Plot Summary

Texas. Ray (John Getz), a small-town bartender, helps his boss's wife, Abby (Frances McDormand), leave her husband. En route to Houston they admit to mutual desire and check into a motel. Abby has been followed by a private detective, Visser (M. Emmet Walsh), who photographs them. Enraged by Visser's revelations and subsequent confrontations with both his employee and his wife, Julian Marty (Dan Hedaya) determines to have the couple killed. He hires Visser to do the job, setting up his own alibi by going on a fishing holiday and covering the assassination expenditure by leaving a message on the answering machine of another employee, Meurice (Samm-Art Williams), accusing Ray of theft. Visser is disgusted by Marty. He breaks into Ray's house, steals Abby's handgun, and again photographs the couple in bed. This time he doctors the pictures to make it look like they have been murdered. Having been paid, he murders Marty with Abby's gun. Ray breaks into the bar to steal the money Marty owes him in wage arrears and discovers both Marty's body and Abby's gun. Believing Abby to be responsible for the murder, he endeavors to clean up after her. On the road he discovers that Marty is not yet dead and is forced to bury him alive. His attempts to communicate his actions to Abby are greeted by bewilderment, and the two become distrustful of one another. Meanwhile, Visser realizes that Marty has retained the photographic evidence of the fake murder in his safe. Unable to retrieve this evidence, Visser kills Ray in Abby's apartment and then is himself killed by Abby who believes him to be her husband seeking vengeance for her infidelity.

Analysis

Blood Simple, produced a year before *After Hours* on a much smaller budget, signals the genesis of a cycle of very low-budget, independently produced eighties and nineties neo-noirs. *A Flash of Green, The Kill-Off, Reservoir Dogs, One False Move,* and *The Usual Suspects,* for example, succeed in juxtaposing the visceral pleasures of American pulp-fiction and B film noir with the thematic concerns of the seventies neo-modernists. To a degree, these films constitute a revival of the neo-modernist neo-noir projects of filmmakers like Martin Scorsese, Robert Altman, Arthur Penn, and Francis Ford Coppola, although with a greater (it could be argued, postmodernist) emphasis now placed on self-referentiality, playfulness and "entertainment."

Like both *After Hours* and *Taxi Driver,* the style of the Coen Brothers' *Blood Simple,* while exemplifying the frenetic stylistic innovation of low-budget filmmaking (the employment of "shakicam," for example), is based on an eclectic mix of post-*nouvelle vague* film noir and the low-budget horror film (*Taxi Driver'*s evocation of the western is also revived here in *Blood Simple'*s rural Texan locations and in the "corrupt sheriff" figure of Visser). Nevertheless, like Kasdan's groundbreaking postmodernist text *Body Heat,* the film also evidences a stylish veneer (expressionist chiaroscuro visuals, a traditional noir iconography and mise-en-scène), one-dimensional characterizations, and a self-consciously formulaic narrative pattern, albeit with certain innovative twists. Such qualities have prompted certain critics to unfairly dismiss *Blood Simple* as "a film-school thesis on noir," little more than "an inventive exercise in genre deconstruction."[21] However, like *The Long Goodbye, Chinatown,* and *Night Moves,* which investigated and demythologized the generic tradition of the noir detective narrative, so *Blood Simple* does in fact represent a similar exploration of the noir Cain-text narrative.

The Cain-text, which supplied a paradigmatic model for the classic film noir crime melodrama, as in *Double Indemnity, The Woman in the Window* (Fritz Lang, 1944), *Scarlet Street, The Postman Always Rings Twice, The Lady from Shanghai, The Pitfall* (André de Toth, 1948), *Criss Cross,* and *The File on Thelma Jordan* (Robert Siodmak, 1949), and which similarly provides a model for many of the films of the eighties and nineties, revolves around a narrative of financial greed and sexual desire, in which, generally speaking, a (relatively) respectable man's encounter with an alluring woman results in a series of transgressions. As Krutnik puts it, such texts "begin with the eruption of desire at the sight of the female, an eruption that displaces the hero and locks him within a trajectory of transgression—most often through the crimes of adultery and murder."[22] The Cain-text represents yet another manifestation of the post-Freudian Oedipal narrative structure (the usually young man challenging/killing/usurping the elder patriarchal figure in order to gain access to the object of his desire). Despite the centrality of the alluring femme fatale figure in this particular variant of the noir narrative, however, as in the hard-boiled detective texts, it is the issue of masculinity and the challenge to/dissolution of masculine identity that is most closely scrutinized in the noir crime melodrama (as Krutnik puts it, such films "are crucially concerned with a testing of masculinity in relation to the law").[23] Once again, the world in which the male protagonist lives and the one-dimensional characters with whom he interacts become extensions of his own psyche, expressions of subconscious anxieties and desires, projections of previously repressed fantasies.

The Coen Brothers' film *Blood Simple*, nevertheless, complicates this archetypal narrative pattern by hybridizing the Cain-text narrative with that of Dashiell Hammett's Continental Op stories. The film's title in fact is borrowed from a passage in Hammett's first novel, *The Red Harvest*, in which the protagonist complains that his immersion in the violent political shenanigans of the city Personville has rendered him "blood-simple." This fusion of Cain and Hammett—whose private detective, unlike Chandler's Marlowe, was already a flawed figure given to the excessive use of force, sexual temptation, and alcoholic self-indulgence—in the sociopolitical context of mid-eighties America, produces a wholly reprehensible investigative figure ("Gimme a call whenever you want to cut my head off," Visser says to Julian Marty, "I can always crawl around without it"). In this sense the knight errant private investigator of the forties (Marlowe in *The Big Sleep*, for example), having already evolved into the ineffective loner of the seventies (Moseby in *Night Moves*), has now been usurped in *Blood Simple* by the sociopath of the eighties, a figure who stems from rather than ventures into the noir underworld. The Coen Brothers' film suggests an awareness of the continuing evolution of both hard-boiled crime fiction and film noir, its originality lying not in its narrative content, which is almost wholly derivative, but in the humor and stylistic verve it brings to the genre.[24] In their subsequent neo-noir, the 1990 *Miller's Crossing*, the Coen Brothers would return to the literary origins of the genre, drawing once again from the influence of Dashiell Hammett.[25]

Like the seventies neo-noirs discussed in the previous chapter, *Blood Simple* thematizes the corruption of patriarchy and the disintegration of communal interaction. Each of the relationships (that of husband and wife, the adulterous lovers, the bar owner and the detective, the two bartenders, even the hispanic landlady and her brother-in-law) is tainted by deception, guilt, suspicion, and loneliness. In fact, *Blood Simple*, as with the Coens' subsequent neo-noirs *Miller's Crossing, Barton Fink* (1991), and *Fargo,* is in essence about the notion of "humans forever misinterpreting each other's actions" and failing to achieve any form of meaningful communication with one another.[26] This is a motif that, as J. P. Telotte has argued, is one of the characteristic features of the noir genre:

> Such missed connections, though, are common in the *noir* world, as are communications that have quite the opposite of their intention, distancing people all the more from each other rather than bringing them together, reinforcing a sense of otherness instead of community. The *noir* world, consequently, always seems pulled in two contrary directions, to talk and to silence, toward community—like the war-era community of common cause and united will—and toward the isolation of a universal otherness—another war legacy, along with the widespread feelings of disillusionment and alienation . . . Through a thematic focus on discourse, these films show how fundamentally our communications, even the movies themselves, carry a certain estranging force, one that renders all discourse precarious and every effort at human communication a risky wager against misunderstanding and alienation.[27]

"We don't seem to be communicating," Marty observes to a customer to whom he is making lecherous advances. "Look, you want to hustle me? I don't want to be hustled. It's as simple as that. Now that I've *communicated,* why don't you get lost?" she responds. This inability to communicate and the resultant alienation, which is a condition of the modern experience, is anticipated in Visser's voice-over which serves as a prologue to the film's principal narrative:

> The world is full of complainers. But the fact is nothing comes with a guarantee. I don't care if you're the Pope of Rome, President of the United States, or Man of the Year, something can all go wrong. And go ahead, you know, complain, tell your problems to your neighbor, ask for help, and watch him fly. Now in Russia they got it mapped out so that everyone pulls for everyone else. That's the theory anyway. But what I know about is Texas, and down here you're on your own.

The relationship between husband (Marty) and wife (Abby), moreover, is marked by violence. "He gave me a little pearl-handled .38 for our first anniversary," Abby tells Ray. In the only scene in which the two characters appear together, having been physically assaulted by Marty, Abby breaks his finger and kicks him in the testicles (the recurrent motif of masculine impotence, further evidenced by their childless marriage and by Marty "firing blanks" in his attempt to kill Ray).

Intriguingly, in a significant departure from the narrative patterns of both classic film noir and post-sixties neo-noir, *Blood Simple* fails to offer a figure with which the viewer can identify. In classic films noirs like *Double Indemnity, Detour,* and *The Postman Always Rings Twice,* or contemporary neo-noirs like *Point Blank, Taxi Driver,* and *Body Heat,* for example, the viewer is sutured to the point of view of the flawed male protagonist. The viewer experiences nearly all the narrative events from his perspective. In films that offer a voice-over narration and/or flashback structure, the viewer also has access to the protagonist's own reconstruction of those events. In *Blood Simple,* however, the fragmentation of community, the collapse of human interaction, and the psychological dislocations that the various characters experience as a result of their actions manifest themselves in a *Rashomon*-esque proliferation of points of view. Narrative events are variously presented from the contradictory perspectives of Visser, Marty, Ray, and Abby, with the minor character Meurice as a disinterested spectator. Nonetheless, this multiple-point-of-view structure serves to accentuate a recurrent noir motif, namely, the discrepancy that exists between reality and illusion, suggested by the "murder" of Ray and Abby, Visser's doctored photographs, the "theft" of Marty's money, his "death" by shooting, and Abby's dream of his resurrection.

The ironic resurrection points to *Blood Simple*'s own exploitation of mythology, a motif once again in keeping with the neo-modernist agenda of the seventies neo-noirs and anticipated in Marty and Visser's early exchange about messengers in ancient Greece. The models here are the Fisher King myth of Arthurian legend (Parsifal encounters the King of the Grail as a fisherman), the Greek myth of Dionysus, and the Egyptian myth of Osiris. Each myth is concerned with concepts of fragmentation and regeneration. Indeed, the myths of both Dionysus and Osiris symbolize the annual vegetation life cycle of growth, decay, and renewed growth. In the myth of Osiris, for example, the god-king is sealed in a sarcophagus by his brother, resurrected by his sister-wife, then once again killed by his brother, who cuts his body into fourteen pieces and then scatters them. All the pieces are eventually recovered except his genitals, which are eaten by a fish. The remains are buried in numerous graves in several different nations.[28] The Dionysian myth similarly involves a violent death by dismemberment and resurrection. Integral to the myths of both Osiris and Dionysus, moreover, is the notion of a journey into the underworld. As James G. Frazer comments in *The Golden Bough:* "Deities of vegetation, who are believed to pass a certain portion of each year underground, naturally come to be regarded as gods of the lower world or of the dead. Both Dionysus and Osiris were so conceived."[29] As in Arthurian legend, these myths carry connotations both of regeneration and of death (Gods both of fertility and of the dead).

The ironic evocation of these myths in *Blood Simple* serves to underpin the motifs of dissolution, decay, impotence, and violence. As already noted, the encounter between Marty and Abby illustrates his impotence, and in the breaking of his finger offers a dismemberment of sorts; Marty, the figure of impotence, is sent fishing by Visser;[30] the fish Marty catches (symbol of fertility in that a fish ate the genitals of Osiris and in that they come from water, itself a potential symbol of regeneration) are left to rot in Marty's office (water in the sense of dissolution rather than regeneration); Marty is buried alive, and as a figure of impotence can offer no hope of regeneration; and Visser, a figure from the underworld, brings death to Marty (almost) and to Ray.

The mythical resonances in *Blood Simple,* particularly in their application to the figures of Visser and Marty (and to a lesser extent Ray), are further illustrative of the motif of patriarchal corruption. The principal male figures are characterized as both impotent and violent, and their actions are governed by their own psychological fragmentation, their anxieties, obsessions, paranoia, and neuroses.[31] Like the investigative figure Hank Quinlan (Orson Welles) in *Touch of Evil,* Visser's corruption is further suggested by his sweaty obesity.[32] His physical and professional filth counterpoints Marty's anality, itself a manifestation of neurotic obsession. Ray, moreover, is tainted by both Visser's filth and Marty's anality as he endeavors to clean up the office and dispose of his boss's body. Even as he thinks he is protecting the woman he loves, he becomes complicit in the corruption of the other male figures, his clothing and car physically stained by Marty's blood.

As was the case with *Body Heat, Blood Simple* also illustrates the durability of the contemporary woman. She survives masculine violence and "the male culture of distrust,"[33] even meeting violence with violence in her physical confrontations with both Marty and Visser. What is more, the handgun, a penis substitute of sorts (as is the knife that she uses to stab Visser), which at some stage of the narrative is in the possession of each of the four major characters, ends up in her hands. As with *Body Heat* or *After Hours,* there is a certain ambiguity about the ending of *Blood Simple.* Abby's shooting of Visser can be read as a moment of regeneration, given the death of the last corrupt patriarch, the symbolic qualities of the water droplet (purifying/regenerative), and Abby's possession of the penis-gun. It can also be interpreted as a moment of impotence/ death, given the necessity of female union with a male to promote regeneration, water as a symbol of dissolution, and the gun as a tool of destruction. In this sense, therefore, *Blood Simple* simultaneously depicts, in the eradication of patriarchal corruption, the fulfillment of the liberal dream of the seventies and, in woman's usurpation of phallic power, the fulfillment of eighties neo-conservatism's worst nightmare.

It would appear that, as in Scorsese's *After Hours,* the characterization of Abby in *Blood Simple* ultimately exploits prevalent male anxieties about female autonomy and self-sufficiency. Woman, as the root cause of masculine paranoia in the film, the catalyst for the male protagonists' distrust of one another, and the perpetrator of the last act of violence in the film, like Marcy, Kiki, Julie, Gail, and June in *After Hours,* becomes associated with death, physical pain, and destruction. It is Abby's violent dream of Marty's resurrection, which visually and verbally foreshadows the events that lead to the film's nihilistic conclusion. It is with her gun, with the exception of Ray, that each of the male protagonists is shot. These motifs resurface in Harold Becker's 1989 neo-noir *Sea of Love,* a film that similarly exploits male sexual anxieties and explores the culture of distrust that surrounds the independent sexual woman. As in *After Hours,* in *Sea of Love,* written by frequent Scorsese collaborator Richard Price, desire leads inevitably to male paranoia and psychic fragmentation.

SEA OF LOVE

Plot Summary

New York City. To the sound of an old record ("Sea of Love" performed by Phil Phillips with the Twilights) a man simulates sexual intercourse and is then shot in the back of the head. The homicide investigation is assigned to detective Frank Keller (Al Pacino), a lonely, heavy-drinking divorcé, who is in the midst of a midlife crisis after twenty years on the force. Frank is soon partnered by Sherman Touhey (John Goodman), a Queens-based detective involved in a similar case. The detectives, working on the assumption that the killer is a woman, discover that the two victims both placed verse messages in the same edition of a singles magazine. They endeavor to warn a third man who has placed a similar message, but, fearful of his wife's reaction, he shuns their advice and is the next victim of the mystery murderer. Frank and Sherman persuade their superiors to authorize them to place their own advertisement in order to trap the killer. Alternating the roles of "lonely heart" and waiter at a local restaurant, the two men manage to acquire the fingerprints of all but one of the women who respond to their message. By chance Frank encounters this woman, Helen Cruger (Ellen Barkin), on the street. Despite his suspicions, Frank enters into a relationship with Helen that becomes increasingly obsessive. Already strained by his drunken revelations that their first meeting was part of a police operation (she has already learned that he is not a printer as he claimed), their relationship finally deteriorates into violence when he becomes convinced that Helen is in fact the killer. Frank is then attacked by and kills the real murderer, Helen's former husband Terry (Michael Rooker), a cable repairman who has been stalking his wife and killing her male friends. Some time later, the now sober Frank forces a reconciliation with Helen, who, it seems, is willing to forgive both the subterfuge and the violence.

Analysis

Thematically connected to both *After Hours* and *Blood Simple* and sharing their penchant for iconographical pastiche, *Sea of Love,* produced for Universal by Martin Bregman, nevertheless offers a stylistic contrast to the two low-budget independent productions. This is eighties mainstream Hollywood genre cinema. It is structurally formulaic and stylistically conservative, a film noir star vehicle in the tradition of such classic forties texts as *The Big Sleep* and *The Postman Always Rings Twice.* Indeed, like many of the A-feature films noirs of the forties and fifties, *Sea of Love* tends to commodify the stylistic experimentation of the low-budget independent productions and wrap up the traditional noir thematic motifs in a more consumer friendly "entertainment" package, albeit with the trappings of physical violence, sexual explicitness, and profanity that are now deemed acceptable in the post–production code era. For all its conformity to contemporary studio production values, however, there is in *Sea of Love* a degree of tension that stems (1) from the discrepancies that exist between screenwriter Richard Price's original conception of the film and his subsequent need to repackage the screenplay in a more studio-friendly manner,[34] and (2) from the film's exploitation of widespread and by 1989 (the year of the film's release) firmly entrenched cultural anxieties. As was the case with *Fatal Attraction,* although the term is never employed, *Sea of Love* speaks of and to a nation's newly discovered preoccupation with AIDS, exploiting the inherent homophobia and misogyny of a patriarchal society and playing on the traditional noir motif of the victim-hero's "proclivity for love with an improper stranger."[35]

As with Scorsese's neo-noirs, in particular *Taxi Driver,* the opening sequences of which are echoed in *Sea of Love*'s credit sequence, the film is essentially a psychological study of character, a voyage into the psyche of an existentially troubled male protagonist who feels alienated from his environment. Frank Keller, like the drug courier John LeTour (Willem Dafoe) in *Light Sleeper* (Paul Schrader, 1991), is a Travis Bickle in his forties, a man subjected to the anxieties of a midlife crisis, who is torn between a simultaneous desire for and fear of human interaction. As Frank observes in a self-critical conversation with his former wife Denise (Lorraine Bracco),[36] he is tormented by a sense of mortality that is a result of his having reached the NYPD retirement age after twenty years in the force, of his sexual anxiety, and of his solitude:

> I'm staring down a gun barrel yesterday—you know what I'm thinking? Not how am I going to get this wacko to drop the gun, I'm thinking I don't love nobody, nobody loves me, I got no wife, no kids, no nothing. These are my exact thoughts . . . The twenty year thing is kicking my ass. I don't know what . . . And I'm not a kid anymore you know—I'm gonna die someday. This job is the job, it's not gonna change, I'm not gonna quit, so this is it. I've gotta love somebody, or something. I've gotta *fall in love.* Because, I'm telling you, otherwise it's too straight a drive to the toll booth.

Frank's investigation of a series of apparently sex-related murder cases, like Paul Hackett's attempts to return home from SoHo in *After Hours* or Travis Bickle's mission to liberate Iris in *Taxi Driver,* becomes a journey of self-discovery, an identity quest that will result either in psychic dissolution or in "rebirth."

Like another of Scorsese's protagonists, Jake La Motta in *Raging Bull,* Frank is a figure who lacks self-respect. An insomniac, he torments himself by ringing Denise at "unsociable" hours. He embarrasses himself in his interaction with his former wife's new husband and his own work colleague Gruber (Richard Jenkins), and, like his father before him, he has become an alcoholic. As with the protagonist of the earlier film, he appears to pursue his own dissolution, masochistically seeking physical punishment in his provocation of Gruber, suicidally confronting the Middle Eastern bodyguard he encounters opposite the original murder site, and willingly becoming involved with Helen, a woman he still believes could be the murder suspect. Frank's desire is inseparable, then, from his death wish, as illustrated by his willing submission to the mercy of a woman he suspects to be a femme fatale.

Before his involvement with Helen, Frank's already fragmented sense of identity is signaled through the motif of role-playing or performance. When we first meet him as he participates in a police operation to round up a number of wanted felons, Frank masquerades as a former New York Yankees baseball star. Later, as Frank and Sherman Touhey put into operation their plan to capture the sex killer, he assumes the identity of a printer and further screens his real self by using his mother's poem rather than his own to serve as bait. Although Helen sees through his latter ploy, she is deceived by his subterfuge regarding his identity and social status. Until their reconciliation at the film's end, Frank continues to complicate this issue, constantly blurring the boundary between reality and fiction by revealing half-truths about himself to Helen.

Once Frank and Helen have established a relationship, the film becomes as much about Frank's ability to accept who and what he is, to achieve psychic integration, and to return to Helen a complete person as about the identification and apprehension of the real killer. As he negotiates his own psychic landscape, moreover, Frank has to overcome the hurdle of his own sexual anxiety and paranoia, his distrust of meaningful interaction between the genders, and the obsessive desire that Helen arouses in him, the instinct for "animal attraction." As with Scorsese's neo-noir protagonists, the success or otherwise of Frank's psychic journey is largely dependent on his ability to reshape his identity, to achieve a degree of harmony between the masculine and feminine aspects of his personality, and to balance the compelling attractions of the life (Eros) and death (Thanatos) principles.

The real murderer, Helen's former husband Terry, may therefore be perceived as Frank's double, a dark shadow figure who embodies Frank's repressed anxieties and prejudices, in the same way that, say, Bruno Anthony does for Guy Haines (Farley Granger) in *Strangers on a Train* or Max Cady (Robert Mitchum) does for Sam Bowden (Gregory Peck) in the original *Cape Fear*. In effect, as Nickolas Pappas has observed, Terry gives expression to both Frank's jealousy-fueled misogyny and his latent homosexuality. Terry becomes a projection of all that is dark in Frank, the latter's comradely banter with Sherman (*Sherman:* "Could you go for a babe with a dick?" *Frank:* "Depends on her personality") after a former policeman's wife has verbally abused him, crudely anticipated by the joke about anal sex that Terry tells to his co-workers, Frank's antagonism toward Gruber perversely mirrored by Terry's murderous slaughter of his former wife's male friends, and Frank's homophilia darkly echoed by Terry's reenactment of his wife's love scenes with his male victims. Pappas elaborates the analogy:

> Both Terry and Frank, in short, are shown to prefer male company—which by itself means nothing, except that the scenes in which they turn to other men are exactly those in which, according to what they say about themselves, female companionship is what they want. Frank is certainly more civilized than Terry, but that is not the issue: what matters is that both make what ought to be scenes between themselves and women into scenes between themselves and other men.[37]

This motif of psychological dislocation prompted by sexual anxiety does, however, extend beyond Frank and his double Terry. The police community to which Frank belongs is revealed to be almost exclusively male and characterized by a paranoid distrust of femininity, as witness the gathering in Frank's apartment as he and his colleagues attempt to compose verse to trap a murder suspect they are convinced is female. Theirs is a closed community of male bonding that Frank gradually shuns as he becomes more involved with Helen. He refuses, for example, an opportunity to go drinking with his friends, and toward the end of the film he remarks on Sherman's excessive embraces. The height of Frank's crisis of sexual identity, moreover, is signaled after he has drunkenly failed in his attempt to ask Helen to live with him and has let slip that their original meeting was part of a police operation. Returning home, Frank finds that Sherman, to whom he has given his apartment keys (once again, an action that is symbolically laden with homoerotic undertones), has been making love to another of the potential suspects, Gina Gallagher (Christine Estabrook), in his bed.

That Helen then reappears at this moment, appearing out of the shadows smoking a cigarette and carrying a copy of the record "Sea of Love," the two elements that Frank associates with the killer, signals, to invoke once again our analogy with the mythic hero adventure, Frank's approach to "the inmost cave,"[38] his arrival at the darkest region of his own psyche. Frank's actions during this scene and the subsequent encounter with the killer Terry will determine whether he submits to his psychosexual malaise and the attendant fragmentation of his identity, or whether he is able to recognize and come to terms with the darkness he carries within himself and reconstruct his identity, both socially and sexually. His violence, like that of, say, Mike Hammer (Ralph Meeker) in

Kiss Me Deadly or Travis Bickle in *Taxi Driver,* during his interaction with both Helen and Terry in these two sequences suggests a submission to the death wish, characterized by the mood of "psychotic action and suicidal impulse" that was a feature of fifties film noir and seventies neo-noir. The tacked-on ending, therefore, in which Frank, sometime after the conclusion of the investigation, reintroduces himself to Helen, having now reclaimed his sense of identity, lends the film a degree of textual tension reminiscent of many of the production code and studio-compromised films noirs of the forties and fifties, such as *The Blue Dahlia* and *The Big Sleep.*[39] In effect, *Sea of Love*'s narrative, up to the point of the climactic confrontation between Frank and Terry, appears to suggest Frank's trajectory toward psychosis, and the film's upbeat ending therefore sits uncomfortably with all that has gone before.

There is about the film's conclusion, moreover, a quality that is both sinisterly regressive and grudgingly progressive. On the one hand, the reconciliation between Frank and Helen is underpinned by the need to reestablish the status quo in the patriarchal order by reassimilating the transgressive and independent sexual woman that echoes the conclusion of classic noir texts like *Gilda* or contemporary neo-noirs like *Blue Velvet.* On the other hand, there is an acknowledgment that it is patriarchy that is at fault. In this sense the film critiques embedded cultural assumptions in patriarchal society, suggesting an inherent fear and distrust of "otherness." As Orr puts it, the "distrust here, so crucial to all noir narratives, is a crucial failure of perception on Pacino's part alone." He elaborates: "the film plays on the classic expectation of the form, the lure of the woman as dark and treacherous, and then undercuts it."[40] *Sea of Love,* then, ultimately works to debunk the masculine conception of the femme fatale. Helen is revealed to be both autonomous and self-sufficient (she is both a single parent and a shop manager), her desire an expression of sexual pleasure rather than a portent of impending violence, a woman who gets by in spite of the "male culture of distrust," and it is therefore not Helen but Frank, conditioned by his own sexual anxiety and emotionally impaired by years of contact with social malaise and moral degradation as a New York City detective (as witness his "cops' eyes" speech to Helen), who poses the greatest threat to his own sense of masculine order. Like many of the contemporary films noirs of the seventies, eighties, and nineties, *Sea of Love* examines the crisis of identity of modern man, suggesting, like *Taxi Driver* before it, the dangers of masculinity's entropic trajectory toward alienation and psychosis.

Nineties Irony

5

The early nineties have been witness to the consolidation of film noir's status as one of the mainstays of contemporary American genre cinema. The years 1990–95 marked one of the most prolific periods in film noir history, comparable in quantity (if not necessarily quality) to the heyday of the genre in the late forties, which saw the production of such classic texts as *The House on 92nd Street* (Henry Hathaway, 1945), *The Dark Corner, The Blue Dahlia, Gilda, The Big Sleep, The Strange Love of Martha Ivers, Born to Kill* (Robert Wise, 1947), *Crossfire, Body and Soul, Kiss of Death, Out of the Past, T-Men, The Lady from Shanghai, Cry of the City* (Robert Siodmak, 1948), *Force of Evil, Act of Violence,* and *They Live by Night.* Similarly, nineties neo-noir has been noteworthy for its diversity, appealing in equal measure to the visual/action-oriented filmmakers of the Hollywood mainstream (Tony Scott, Paul Verhoeven, and Wolfgang Petersen, for example) and the more dialogue/plot-oriented young filmmakers of the independent sector (John Dahl, Quentin Tarantino, and Bryan Singer). The wideranging appeal of the genre, moreover, has contributed to the genesis and/or revival of a number of film noir subgenres such as the noir road movie, as in *Guncrazy, True Romance* (Tony Scott, 1993), and *A Boy Called Hate* (Mitch Marcus, 1995); the serial-killer film, as in *Silence of the Lambs, Kalifornia* (Dominic Sena, 1993), and *Seven;* the private investigator noir, as in *The Two Jakes, The Last Boy Scout* (Tony Scott, 1991), and *Mulholland Falls* (Lee Tamahori, 1995); the police procedural noir, as in *Internal Affairs, Q & A,* and *Deep Cover;* the heist film, as in *Reservoir Dogs, The Usual Suspects,* and *Heat;* the yuppie nightmare film, as in *Bad Influence, Cape Fear,* and *Unlawful Entry* (Jonathan Kaplan, 1992); the African-American noir, as in *A Rage in Harlem, One False Move,* and *Devil in a Blue Dress;* the futuristic techno-noir, as in *Terminator 2:*

Judgment Day (James Cameron, 1991), *Johnny Mnemonic* (Robert Longo, 1995), and *Strange Days;* the femme fatale film noir, as in *Basic Instinct, The Last Seduction,* and *Normal Life* (John McNaughton, 1996); and a mini-cycle of films inspired by the newly popular writings of crime novelist Jim Thompson as in *The Kill-Off, The Grifters,* and *After Dark, My Sweet* (James Foley, 1990).

Where seventies neo-noir — which in itself constituted an investigation and critique of the noir form — was characterized by a thematic revival of the latter-day films noirs of the fifties, and eighties' neo-noir tended toward a visual pastiche of what was perceived as a classic noir style, nineties neo-noir offers an eclectic mix of all that has gone before, a self-consciously ironic palimpsest informed by knowledge of the history of the film noir genre from its inception in the forties to its revival in the sixties and continuing evolution through the seventies and eighties. The trajectory from neo-modern noir to postmodern noir, signaled by the production of *Body Heat* and developed throughout the eighties, is complete. In fact, many of the nineties texts either engage with contemporary social realities by referencing the cinematic past, as in *Deep Cover*'s deployment of a formulaic narrative of a police detective's infiltration of the noir underworld as a means of illustrating the contemporary nineties drug problem and inner-city malaise, or they are so wholly self-referential that they frequently have little, if any, foundation in external reality, as in *Final Analysis*'s recycling of Hitchcockian clichés.

The postmodern neo-noirs of the nineties are more overtly allusive and more playful in their intertextual references than the films of the eighties. These films constantly proclaim their status as contemporary films noirs by alluding to classic texts of the forties and fifties (*Bad Influence*'s reworking of the plot of *Strangers on a Train*) and occasionally "quoting" from the neo-noirs of the sixties and seventies (*Clockers*'s brief homage to *Taxi Driver*). As with much eighties neo-noir, many of the nineties films, in particular the big-budget major studio productions, also indulge in an extended pastiche of the visual style and iconography of the classic texts, as witness the chiaroscuro, venetian-blind lighting effects of, say, *Shattered* and *Final Analysis*. Additionally, in a further development of the cyclical evolution of film noir, a number of nineties neo-noirs such as *The Two Jakes, After Dark, My Sweet, Mortal Thoughts, Deep Cover, Reservoir Dogs, Romeo is Bleeding, Pulp Fiction,* and *The Usual Suspects* have revived the narrative devices (voice-overs and/or flashbacks) and complex structures that characterized many of the early films noirs such as *Double Indemnity, The Killers* (Robert Siodmak, 1946), and *Sorry, Wrong Number* (Anatole Litvak, 1948), co-opting them as further generic markers of "noirishness."

Indeed, comparison between texts such as the nineties neo-noir *The Two Jakes* and its seventies "prequel," *Chinatown,* are illustrative of the genre's recent evolution. *Chinatown,* produced during a period of thematic rather than stylistic or structural revival, eschewed the more obvious stylistic, iconographic, and narrative markers of classic film noir. *The Two Jakes,* a big-budget, "glossy" studio production, self-consciously evokes such markers, frequently ironizing the generic tradition to which it aspires, as witness the parody of the hard-boiled voice-over. The discrepancy between the time of the narration—the present—and the time of the events narrated—the past—classically lent films noirs a sense of inevitability, fate, and completion, as the doomed protagonist recounted events that had culminated in his present misfortune. In *The Two Jakes,* however, the often comic tone of Gittes's voice-overs ("Frankly, if I waited for an honest client, I'd be sitting around until Rocky Graziano played Rachmaninov at the Hollywood Bowl"), while suggesting the hard-boiled wit of the forties gumshoes (Marlowe in *Murder, My Sweet,* for example), and indeed the wisecracking star persona of Jack Nicholson himself, ultimately distances the film from the doom-laden voice-over narrations of classic noir texts such as *Double Indemnity, Detour, The Postman Always Rings Twice,* and *Out of the Past.* As in the original eighties studio release of *Blade Runner,* the voice-overs here in *The Two Jakes* become a device to self-consciously associate the film with and comment on the noir tradition, as well as to guide the viewer through its complex narrative ("You know, you can follow the action, which gets you good pictures, you can follow your instincts, which will probably get you in trouble, or you can follow the money, which nine times out of ten will get you closer to the truth").

Like the Hollywood renaissance filmmakers of the late sixties and seventies, and the *nouvelle vague* directors before them, the contemporary filmmakers exploit the cine-literacy of the filmgoing public and play on their awareness of the film noir genre in both its classic and contemporary incarnations. Indeed, as the film theorist Jim Collins observes:

> If the genre texts of the 1960s are distinguished by their increasing self-reflexivity about their antecedents in the Golden Age of Hollywood, the genre texts of the late 1980s–early 1990s demonstrate an even more sophisticated hyperconsciousness concerning not just narrative formulae,

but the conditions of their own circulation and reception in the present, which has a massive impact on the nature of popular entertainment.[1]

A contemporary nineties neo-noir like *The Two Jakes* demands the complicity of the viewer, playing not only on his or her familiarity with the generic tradition of the hard-boiled noir detective film but also prior knowledge of the revisionist neo-noir *Chinatown*. *The Two Jakes*, in effect, sets up an intertextual frame of reference—flashbacks to scenes in *Chinatown*, as in Gittes's encounter with the fruit farmers in the San Fernando Valley or the death of Evelyn Mulwray in Chinatown, verbal and visual allusions to the former film as in Evelyn's voice-over narration or the sign Gittes finds from the fruit farm, the reappearance of actors/characters who appeared in the original as in Kahn (James Hong) and the notary public (Allan Warnick)—that renders major plot strands in its narrative all but incomprehensible to the uninitiated.

The Two Jakes is an extreme example, but, as Collins rightly notes, in contemporary American cinema the

> foregrounded, hyperconscious intertextuality reflects changes in terms of audience competence and narrative technique, as well as a fundamental shift in what constitutes both entertainment and cultural literacy in the "Information Age" . . . The foregrounding of disparate intertexts and the all-pervasive hyperconsciousness concerning the history of both "high art" and popular representation has become one of the most significant features of contemporary storytelling. Narrative action now operates at two levels simultaneously—in reference to character adventure and in reference to a text's adventures in the array of contemporary cultural production.[2]

A film like Quentin Tarantino's *Reservoir Dogs* functions both as a contemporary counterpart to the classic film noir heist film, as in *The Asphalt Jungle* and *The Killing* (Stanley Kubrick, 1956), and as a text that self-consciously acknowledges and investigates the history and the evolution of the noir form, alluding to the *nouvelle vague*–influenced neo-noir films of the seventies and, of course, the classic noirs of "psychotic action and suicidal impulse" of the fifties. What is more, *Reservoir Dogs* alludes to the manifestation of noir in other film cultures, including references to the *nouvelle vague* films themselves and in particular to the sixties films of Jean-Luc Godard (the jewelry wholesalers where the robbery takes place is named after Anna Karina, Godard's wife and the female lead in several of his early sixties films), to the French *policiers* of the fifties and sixties such as *Du rififi chez les hommes* (Jules Dassin,

1954) and *Le Doulos* (Jean-Pierre Melville, 1962), and to the Hong Kong crime cinema of the eighties and nineties, such as *A Better Tomorrow* (John Woo, 1986) and *City On Fire* (Ringo Lan, 1989). The film thus becomes doubly ironic, referring to texts that already ironize a generic tradition, playfully catering to a knowing video-age generation of *ciné-philes* while simultaneously confounding their generic expectations in a manner that once again recalls the work of the French *nouvelle vague* and the Hollywood renaissance filmmakers.

Like the Coen Brothers' *Blood Simple,* moreover, *Reservoir Dogs* constitutes the successful fusion of independent filmmaking and mainstream American genre cinema. Like the earlier film, this is a postmodern artifact. Stylistically and thematically distinct from big-budget studio productions, especially noir pastiches like *Deceived* and *Basic Instinct,* it is connected to a number of early nineties films in the independent sector, such as *Miller's Crossing, The Grifters, After Dark, My Sweet,* and *Red Rock West* (John Dahl, 1992), that have attempted to fuse American mainstream and American art cinema filmmaking techniques in a manner intended to revive the revisionist tradition of the Hollywood renaissance filmmakers Scorsese, Penn, Altman, and Coppola. Noir, as was the case with both the *nouvelle vague*'s formal and generic reinvention of Western cinema and the Hollywood renaissance commodification of their innovation and experimentation, has become integral to this process.

In the Channel 4 documentary on contemporary film noir, *Dark and Deadly,*[3] neo-noir director James Foley has explained his intentions in *After Dark, My Sweet* in relation to this process. For Foley, a seminal period in the recent history of American cinema was the late seventies which saw the release of Steven Spielberg's *Jaws* and George Lucas's *Star Wars.* These two films effectively signaled the divorce of a stylistically and visually slick mainstream cinema, in which plot and psychological character motivation were secondary, from an art cinema in which plot, character, and an uncompromising exploration of the darker side of human existence were primary (as witness Scorsese's *Taxi Driver, New York, New York,* and *Raging Bull*). In this sense, a film like *After Dark, My Sweet* is, in Foley's words, intended to get the mainstream "back on track," combining high production values, compelling drama, and a degree of sociopolitical critique in a relatively low-budget production. Foley's conception of his neo-noir film is fascinating not only because he highlights a tendency that applies in equal measure to such independent filmmakers as John Dahl, Tamra Davis, Maggie Greenwald, Carl Franklin, and Bryan Singer, but also because he foregrounds a division between two camps of filmmakers that has been in place since the late seventies. It also echoes, to a degree, the division in classical Hollywood cinema between the A- and B-feature filmmakers.

Rendered simplistically, the division is between the mainstream Spielberg/Lucas camp and the art-house Scorsese camp. The former, in the shape of, say, Spielberg himself, Robert Zemeckis, Joe Dante, Ridley Scott, Adrian Lyne, Tony Scott, James Cameron, John McTiernan, Wolfgang Petersen, Robert Longo, and Paul Verhoeven, has dominated throughout the eighties and much of the nineties, producing generically formulaic, ideologically conservative fare characterized by cartoonlike universes in which everything is black and white, governed by clear moral boundaries that separate good from evil. The style of such films, as one critic recently observed, "favors texture, surface, layering, and insubstantiality to space, depth, dimensionality, and solidity."[4] The early nineties, however, has seen in the work of such filmmakers as Rudolph, Foley, Dahl, the Coen Brothers, Tarantino, Franklin, Mike Figgis, Bill Duke, and Spike Lee, a gradual revival of a more intellectually stimulating, less mass consumption–oriented form of filmmaking. In these films there is a greater degree of formal experimentation, and a valuation of psychological motivation, plot, and dialogue above the "image." As in Scorsese's seventies neo-noirs, expressionism is fused with realism, thematically the division between right and wrong becomes blurred, informed as in real life by ambiguities and contradictions, the darker side of the collective American psyche is explored, and, despite the postmodern artifice of the films, their inherent self-referentiality, there is in even the most self-reflexive of texts a degree of sociopolitical critique, an intersection with and reflection of prevalent cultural anxieties.

These films, produced both in the independent sector, as in Foley's *After Dark, My Sweet*, Tamra Davis's *Guncrazy*, and Bill Duke's *Deep Cover*, and by filmmakers on the periphery of the nineties mainstream, as in the Coen Brothers' *Millers Crossing*, Dennis Hopper's *The Hot Spot*, and Alan Rudolph's *Mortal Thoughts*, are intensely personal, intellectually challenging, and deeply disturbing. Like the *nouvelle vague* films of the sixties and the Hollywood renaissance films of the seventies, they delight in their self-conscious and essentially postmodern artifice, while emulating the content rather than the style of classic film noir.[5] These are films dedicated to the exploration of man's darker nature rather than an examination of the stylistic possibilities offered by "noirish" mise-en-scène and lighting. They explore the enduring sociopolitical legacy of the Reagan-Bush administrations on American society, and they are informed (an echo here of the films produced in the immediate aftermath of the Second World War) by the ideological instability that has gripped the United States since the end of the cold war.[6] They reflect deeply entrenched racial and sexual tensions in contemporary American society, rejecting the idea of political correctness, rebelling against the notion of the "caring nineties," and thematizing issues related to the corruption of corporate and governmental America, the ever-widening gap between the rich and the poor, the problems related to inner-city malaise, drug-trafficking, gang warfare, and unemployment.

Above all else, these are violent films that comment on the postmodern experience in contemporary American society. They are pulp-culture testaments to the violent fragmentation of the social fabric of the United States today. These are the cinematic counterparts to the febrile, paranoid, violent, and perversely comic fiction of contemporary pulp writers like Elmore Leonard, James Ellroy, and Carl Hiaasen. Like the early films of the *nouvelle vague* or American filmmakers like Martin Scorsese and Paul Schrader, these are films that revive the fifties noir mood of "psychotic action and suicidal impulse," similarly combining pulp-fiction narratives with B-film esthetics, and playfully reclassifying the crime movie as art film.[7]

Tarantino's *Pulp Fiction* has become emblematic of this recent noir revival in Western culture. The public's appetite for "pulp" is suggested by the popularity of recent crime writers like Ellroy, Leonard, Hiaasen, Walter Mosley, James Lee Burke, and Sara Paretsky; the sustained fascination with the twenties, thirties, and forties fiction of Dashiell Hammett, Raymond Chandler, and James M. Cain; and the "rediscovery" both in literary and cinematic circles of the low-life, paranoid fiction of fifties and sixties writers like Jim Thompson, David Goodis, Charles Williams, Chester Himes, and Charles Willeford. Aptly titled, Tarantino's film stands as a testament to the evolution both of the hard-boiled movement and film noir. Like *Reservoir Dogs* before it, *Pulp Fiction* nods, at various stages throughout its complex narrative, which interconnects three short jazzlike variations on archetypal pulp-culture narratives, to the diverse literary and cinematic manifestations of noir (from Ernest Hemingway's short story "The Killers" to the "blaxploitation" films of the seventies, from Robert Wise's late forties film noir *The Set-Up* to the literary fusion of noir fiction and black comedy in the novels of Hiaasen and Leonard)[8] that have occurred in American popular culture since the first hard-boiled short stories were published in the pulp magazine *Black Mask* in the twenties.

It is, however, the revival of interest in the violent, paranoid writings of Jim Thompson, not only as manifested in films like *The Kill-Off, The Grifters, After Dark, My Sweet,* and *The Getaway* (Roger Donaldson, 1994), which have been adapted from his work,[9] but also in such contemporary films as *Guncrazy, Reservoir Dogs,* and *One False Move,* which seems particularly appropriate in the cultural and sociopolitical context of the early-to-mid nineties. Like Thompson's novels, many recent films noirs are inward looking, characterized by an "existential vision of mistrust and refusal to acknowledge any moral centre to American life."[10] Such films share Thompson's representation of "a world where sanity and insanity, right and wrong, good and evil, are indistinguishable; where external manifestations are used to explain the horrors of life ordinarily thought to be internal to those manifestations."[11]

In the alternative, independent conception of nineties film noir, then, the noir universe is not a dark, mythical underworld domain into which the protagonist must descend, but rather it is the world we live in, a daylight world of vice, criminality, explosive violence, universal corruption, paranoia, and psychosis, a world from which the protagonists are trying to escape, as witness Collie (Jason Patric) in *After Dark, My Sweet* and Strike (Mekhi Phifer) in *Clockers.* It constitutes the externalization of the darkest recesses of the collective American psyche, presenting a world of patriarchal corruption, racial and sexual bigotry, and irrational masculine violence, a world populated by corporate gangsters, triumphantly ruthless femmes fatales, psychotic drug dealers and small-time grifters, a fractured world of uncertain relationships and unstable affiliations founded on fear and mutual distrust.

In *The Usual Suspects,* for example, a group of criminals are brought together when they are arrested on the pretext that they stand in a police line-up. Determined to avenge such effrontery, they devise a plan to heist a criminal "taxi service" operated by corrupt NYPD officers. When one of their number, Michael McManus (Stephen Baldwin), suggests laundering their haul through a contact he has in Los Angeles, the inherent distrust and suspicion that the five men hold for one another begins to surface. In California, McManus's connection offers the group another job robbing a Texan jeweler. When their mission erupts in violence and their target is killed, they discover that he was in fact a drug trafficker whose death was desired by the mysterious Keyzer Soze, a criminal mastermind of near mythical status whose own anonymity is fiercely defended and whose capacity for violent retribution is legendary in the criminal community. Keyzer Soze's contact with the group, the lawyer Kobayashi (Pete Postlethwaite), explains that in the past each of them has unwittingly infringed on Soze's criminal activities. Now they have been brought together by Soze, who engineered the police line-up, in order to make amends for their past misdemeanors by raiding a drug trafficking outfit operated by Soze's Argentinian rivals (they do not actually have drugs in their possession, but rather a man who can identify Soze). Skeptical, one of the group, Fenster (Benicio Del Toro), abandons his colleagues. When he turns up dead and Dean Keaton (Gabriel Byrne) discovers that his girlfriend, the attorney Edie Finneran (Suzy Amis), is in Kobayashi's power, the group decides to go ahead with the mission. In the ensuing battle the Argentinians' cargo ship is exploded, and twenty-seven men die. There are only two survivors, "Verbal" Klint (Kevin Spacey), one of the original group of five who is arrested and interviewed by customs official Dave Kujan (Chazz Palminteri), and the Hungarian Arkosh Kavash (Morgan Hunter) who, interviewed in his hospital bed by federal agent Jack Baer (Giancarlo Esposito), swears that he has seen Keyzer Soze at the scene of the crime.

The intricacies of the plot in *The Usual Suspects* are further compounded by the film's flashback structure. All events not pertaining to the respective interviews of Klint and Kavash are filtered through the subjective mindscreen of Klint. In this sense, therefore, given the fact that the film's ending indicates that Klint may indeed be Keyzer Soze, there is a possibility that the story Klint narrates to Kujan, in effect the plot outlined above, may be pure fabrication, lying flashbacks in the tradition of Hitchcock's *Stage Fright* (1950) and Rudolph's *Mortal Thoughts,* prompted by visual and textual stimuli in the room in which he has been interviewed. By self-consciously foregrounding the narrative process, *The Usual Suspects* illustrates the difficulties of apprehending reality, of separating fact from fiction, in postmodern culture. In Kujan's and by extension our own consumption of Klint's narrative, there is a demonstration of how postmodern esthetic constructs promote epistemological failure, constantly fragmenting the boundaries between past and present, fantasy and reality, fiction and history, illustrating the difficulties of relating to the "real" world through the medium of language (verbal, written, or cinematic), itself constructed from signs that have no direct connection with external reality. This distancing of the subject from reality, the thematization of the ineffectiveness of communication systems (verbal storytelling, literature, cinema, cybernetics, telecommunications, and so forth), instills a sense of paranoia. Indeed, in *The Usual Suspects* "Keyzer Soze" may be nothing more than an empty signifier, a linguistic construct with no correlative in diegetic reality, that Klint invokes to exploit the inherent paranoia of his fellow criminals and the investigative agents Kujan and Baer.

This motif of paranoia as it relates to the *referential,* as opposed to *truthful,* nature of contemporary man's apprehension of reality, to the gradual technological dehumanization of human interaction (radio, television, cellular phones, computers, virtual reality), and to the attendant uncertainty and dubiety that surrounds man's relationship with his environment, is self-consciously explored in Kathryn Bigelow's futuristic neo-noir *Strange Days.* In this film, set during the final days of 1999, the protagonist Lenny Nero (Ralph Fiennes), a former LAPD officer, is a black marketeer who specializes in hustling software for SQUID (or Superconducting Quantum Interference Device), a new audio-visual technology initially developed for the police state, which serves as a virtual reality link to the human brain, allowing users to experience the sights, sounds, and emotions of the original "filmmaker" whose eyes have quite literally served as a camera. Abuse of SQUID, as witness Nero's own entropic trajectory toward mental and physical dissolution, or the psychic confusion that fosters a paranoid desire for control in the corrupt music mogul played by Michael Wincott, leads us to a state "when surveillance and entertainment become indistinguishable, when escapism can be a death trip, when micro-chip assisted empathy is more likely to appeal to the worst in us than enhance our sense of humanity."[12]

Beyond its examination of mankind's increasing fetishization of spectatorship, a motif connected in classic film noir to the activities of the private investigator and the voyeuristic fantasies embodied by the figure of the sexualized femme fatale, *Strange Days* also thematizes the tenuous nature of human interaction, as witness the misunderstandings that arise between Lenny and Mace (Angela Bassett) or Lenny and Faith (Juliette Lewis), and of course the revelation that Lenny's long-standing friendship with Max (Tom Sizemore) has been a sham, the former police colleague and private detective revealed as Lenny's dark double, the psychopathic murderer of the prostitute Iris (Brigitte Bako). It points, moreover, to deeply entrenched racial tensions in American society, alluding to the recent Rodney King controversy and the subsequent Los Angeles riots. It restates the noir motif of white patriarchal America's corruption and its propensity for violence, as witness the actions of the two police officers who execute the African-American rap star Jeriko I (Glenn Plummer). What is more, the fragmentation of the narrative, as with *The Usual Suspects,* self-reflexively draws attention to the narrative processes of the film's own construction. The whole text operates within the parameters of a generic noir structure that it self-consciously acknowledges by replicating stylistic, iconographic, and narrative markers from the genre's past.

These are all motifs that, to varying degrees of importance, inform our understanding of the work, as both screenwriter (*True Romance* and *Natural Born Killers*) and director (*Reservoir Dogs* and *Pulp Fiction*), of Quentin Tarantino. As a figure who has been at the forefront of noir revisionism in recent years, he brings to American genre cinema a degree of iconoclasm that recalls the work of the Spanish filmmaker Pedro Almodóvar. Like Almodóvar, Tarantino offers "a cinema of saturation, in which vivid colour and costume compete for attention with outrageous narratives and dialogue," and his films similarly suggest a "critique of representation (of the relationship between film as presence and film as language) which is also manifest in a love of the reflexive ironies reminiscent of Sirk . . . [and] Godard."[13]

RESERVOIR DOGS

Plot Summary

Los Angeles. Mob boss Joe Cabot (Lawrence Tierney) and his son Nice Guy Eddie (Christopher Penn) are putting together a team of six criminals to rob a diamond wholesaler. Each man is known by a color-coded pseudonym: Mr. White (Harvey Keitel), Mr. Orange (Tim Roth), Mr. Pink (Steve Buscemi), Mr. Blonde (Michael Madsen), Mr. Blue (Eddie Bunker), and Mr. Brown (Quentin Tarantino). Although Mr. Pink succeeds in getting the diamonds, the robbery is botched and the men are forced to shoot their way out before reassembling at the warehouse rendezvous. Mr. Blue and Mr. Brown are killed, and Mr. Orange is badly wounded, shot in the stomach by a woman whose car he and Mr. White attempt to hijack. He is helped by Mr. White and they return to the warehouse. Mr. Pink arrives and suggests that they were set up. Mr. Blonde, in reality the ex-con Toothpick Vic Vega, a long-term employee of Cabot, returns. He has taken police officer Marvin Nash (Kirk Baltz) hostage, and they proceed to beat him up in an attempt to find out who their informant is. Nice Guy Eddie shows up. He wants Mr. Pink to retrieve the diamonds he has stashed and Mr. White to help him move the cars. In their absence Mr. Blonde proceeds to torture the cop, prompting

Mr. Orange, himself an undercover police officer, Freddy Newendyke, to kill him. When Cabot and the others return, their allegiances are divided. Cabot accuses Mr. Orange, who is defended by Mr. White, of being the informant. In a Mexican standoff all except Mr. Pink are either killed or fatally wounded. Mr. Orange/Freddy confesses his true identity to Mr. White/Larry before they both die, the former at the latter's hands. Distant gunshots suggest Mr. Pink also may have been killed.

Analysis

In his ironic revisionism of genre, his allusive intersection with American pulp/popular culture, and his sustained exploration of masculinity in crisis, Quentin Tarantino is considered by many film commentators the postmodern counterpart to Martin Scorsese, his *Reservoir Dogs* defined as a nineties correlative to Scorsese's *Mean Streets*.[14] Indeed, like *Mean Streets*, Tarantino's *Reservoir Dogs* is one of the seminal texts of the neo-noir era, itself now perceived—fairly or unfairly given the latter film's status as a screenplay going the rounds of the major studios some time before the release of *Reservoir Dogs*—as a point of reference for such films as *The Usual Suspects* and *Things To Do In Denver When You're Dead*. This is a text as much about the art of storytelling as it is a self-conscious revisionism of the film noir heist film. Above all else, in fact, Tarantino's *Reservoir Dogs* and his subsequent film *Pulp Fiction* revive that aspect of the genre that suggests "its singular concern with or awareness of the nature of narration."[15] In both films, moreover, as was the case in the Coens' *Blood Simple*, Tarantino introduces into each of his films a multiplicity of points of view that both reflects the fragmentation and schizophrenia of postmodern culture and highlights his personal predilection for the pages of crime fiction.

In fact, to a certain degree, *Reservoir Dogs* is as much an addition to the generic tradition of the literary hard-boiled caper narrative as in Lionel White's *Clean Break*, Elmore Leonard's *Swag*, and Edward Bunker's *No Beast So Fierce* (which similarly details the violent failure of the daylight robbery of a Los Angeles jewelry firm),[16] as it is to that of the heist film (noir and otherwise), as in *Armored Car Robbery* (Richard Fleischer, 1950), *The Asphalt Jungle, The Killing, Oceans 11* (Lewis Milestone, 1960), *Le Doulos, The Taking of Pelham 1-2-3* (Joseph Sargent, 1974), *Thunderbolt and Lightfoot* (Michael Cimino, 1974), and *City On Fire*. The film's principal narrative, of the assembly of the remaining criminals at the warehouse rendezvous after the jewelry robbery has been botched, comprises the bulk of the narrative and takes place in "real" time: the hour it takes for Joe Cabot to arrive on the scene is the hour the viewer spends with these men before they die. Like a novel, however, this linear space-time continuum is fragmented, interrupted by separate "chapters" from the past in which the viewer is presented with, say, Mr. Pink's escape from the police, Cabot's hiring of Mr. White, or Mr. Blonde's reunion with Cabot and his son Nice Guy Eddie after a spell in prison.

Unlike the multiple narrator classic film noir *The Killers,* however, which employed a similarly complex flashback structure, none of these insert "chapters" is cued as the mindscreen of the protagonists. As in Kubrick's *The Killing* (which does, nevertheless, employ an omniscient documentary-like voice-over narration eschewed in *Reservoir Dogs*), the "chapters" are presented objectively. The exception is the flashback within a flashback that is at the center of Mr. Orange's "chapter." Introducing yet another level to the diegesis and ultimately serving to blur the division between diegetic reality and fiction, this section of the film in a sense marks Mr. Orange as the protagonist of *Reservoir Dogs*. As his rehearsal of the "commode story" overlaps with his actual "performance" of the story and is then displaced by a visualization of its narrative, the film for the first time allows the viewer access to the psyche of one of the characters, prompting a reassessment of all that has gone before in the film's narrative.[17]

As with most films noirs, at the center of *Reservoir Dogs* is the motif of the crisis of masculine identity. Like Russell Stevens/John Hull (Larry Fishburne) in *Deep Cover,* Freddy Newendyke/Mr. Orange infiltrates the criminal underworld, fragmenting his own identity through his masquerade as a former drug dealer as well as through the weight of divided allegiances, paranoid fear of discovery, and guilt regarding the violence of his actions in his criminal guise (having been shot in the stomach by the woman whose car he and Mr. White were attempting to hijack, his reflex response was to shoot and kill her). The fragmented structure of the film's narrative can be read as a metaphor for the fragmentation of Mr. Orange's sense of identity. By the same token, the characters with whom Mr. Orange interacts in the warehouse in this sense become extensions of his own psyche, external projections of different aspects of his fragmented personality. They give expression to his inner turmoil and his own schizophrenic tendencies as he is split between the need, on the one hand, to conform to his ideologically ordained position as a law enforcer and a representative of the established patriarchal order and, on the other hand, to transgress, to explore his darker nature, and to release the irrational violence he carries within him.

As in *Point Blank* and the final sequences of *Taxi Driver*, much of *Reservoir Dogs* may be perceived as the mindscreen of a dying man, a psychic death trip in which, rather than assimilating the diverse aspects of his personality in a process of integration and rebirth, his whole sense of identity unravels, culminating in his death. In effect Mr. Orange, like Charlie in *Mean Streets*, rejects the patriarchal, authoritarian aspect of his personality as symbolized by captive police officer Marvin Nash who is beaten, tortured, and ultimately killed by the other criminals. Like Frank Keller in *Sea of Love*, he rejects the shadowy, darker side of his personality as symbolized by the psychotic Mr. Blonde, whom he kills. He dies, moreover, at the hands of Mr. White, the apparently loving figure to whom he relates most closely (and possibly the figure, to extend our analogy, that symbolizes both his own ego and his conscience), in the knowledge that he is being punished for his lack of integrity, his disloyalty, and his betrayal of an unspoken masculine code of honor. This betrayal, it could be argued, is the crux of the film's narrative. Like Charlie in *Mean Streets* or Jake La Motta in *Raging Bull*, Mr. Orange may be perceived as a masculine figure marked by guilt and a masochistic desire to make amends, hence his confession to Mr. White in the film's final sequence and the revelation of his true, now discarded, identity.[18]

In a sense, the character of Mr. Orange, at least in relation to his interaction with Mr. White, whose own loyal protection of him culminates in the Mexican standoff and slaughter with which the film concludes, evokes the mythical figure of the duplicitous shapeshifter and functions in the same way as the figure of the classic film noir femme fatale.[19] As with Klint in *The Usual Suspects*, it could be argued that Mr. Orange signifies the epistemological failure that is a characteristic feature of postmodern culture. Mr. Orange, in terms of narrative structure (the flashback within a flashback, the subjective mindscreen) and the diegesis itself (his duplicitous role as an undercover police officer, the paranoia and distrust his actions have fostered among the other criminals, his own comic-strip fueled conception of his macho persona), serves as a locus for the blurring of boundaries between reality and fiction and, by extension, the distortion of the perceptive faculties (ironically suggested by the severing of Marvin's ear). Throughout *Reservoir Dogs* this motif of man's increasing distance from reality—his difficulty in relating to the external world in postmodern culture—is conveyed by means of dialogue.

The dialogue in *Reservoir Dogs* is so dense in references to popular culture (Madonna; seventies chart hits such as "Heartbeat: It's a Lovebeat" and "The Night the Lights Went Out in Georgia"; actors like Charles Bronson, Lee Marvin, and Pam Grier; the cult film *The Lost Boys* [Joel Schumacher, 1987]; porn star John Holmes; television shows "Get Christie Love" and "Baretta"; Marvel comics; and the fast-food chain McDonalds) that it becomes a means of mediating the characters' interaction with diegetic reality. They become, then, doubly distanced from the "real" world, articulating their relationship to it not only through the referential system of the spoken word but also through their evocation of popular cultural icons to describe their own situations, as witness Mr. Blonde's evocation of the actor Lee Marvin after narrowly avoiding a fight with Mr. White, or Nice Guy Eddie's allusion to the television character Christie Love as a means of describing the beauty of one of his father's former employees. The language of these characters also becomes a marker of their masculinity in this hermetic universe, the profanity, racism, homophobia, misogyny, and machismo ("You shoot me in a dream, you'd better wake up and apologize") that characterizes their language signaling their status as lower-class or lower-middle-class white American males.[20]

Like Jake La Motta in Scorsese's *Raging Bulls* or the neighborhood characters that populate his *Mean Streets,* these are men whose sense of identity is dependent on their masculine posturings, their bravura, and their implicit capacity for violence. Even as they enjoy the homophilic fellowship of the male community suggested by the verbal banter in the diner in the pre-credits sequence or later in Nice Guy Eddie's car, however, their every action carries with it the threat of impending violence (as witness Mr. Blonde's suggestion that he shoot Mr. White when the latter confiscates Cabot's address book during the diner sequence). As in the films of Martin Scorsese and Michael Cimino that feature similar masculine communities, the narrative of *Reservoir Dogs* leads inexorably toward the eruption of this violence and the death of the protagonists (ironically foreshadowed in the mise-en-scène of the warehouse in which a hearse and coffins can be seen). In effect, *Reservoir Dogs* exploits the enduring film noir motif of the corruption of patriarchy, highlighting through the dialogue and actions of its protagonists the unstable and volatile nature of masculinity.

The film's depiction of the slow and agonizing death of Mr. Orange, Mr. Blonde's sadistic disfigurement of police officer Marvin Nash, and the absurd Mexican standoff that is a prelude to the remaining protagonists' deaths further illustrates this and epitomizes the hyperbolic, cartoonlike violence that proliferates in today's films about "men behaving badly" (*El Mariachi, Pulp Fiction, Casino, Fargo*). The films directed by Tarantino bear testament to this prevalence of *masculine* violence in American society (and indeed in pulp/popular culture from the sadism of Mickey Spillane's Mike Hammer to the excesses of Stallone and Schwarzenegger). In director Peter Medak and screenwriter Hilary Henkin's *Romeo is Bleeding,* this violence is incarnated in the *feminine* figure of Mona Demarkov (Lena Olin). Indeed, together with Catherine Tramell of *Basic Instinct* and Bridget Gregory of *The Last Seduction,* Mona constitutes the hyperbolic return to nineties film noir of the independent, sexual woman whose capacity for violence knows no bounds. In *Romeo is Bleeding,* however, the exploitation of prevalent masculine anxieties (this is, after all, the era of Lorena Bobbit's emasculation of her husband, John Wayne Bobbit) suggested by the characterization of Mona is couched in a serio-comic narrative of excess (Mona's attempt to strangle Jack as he drives, for example), the archetypal figure of the femme fatale ironized and pushed to a comic extreme.

ROMEO IS BLEEDING

Plot Summary

New York. Jack Grimaldi (Gary Oldman) is a corrupt police officer secretly accumulating wealth by selling information to mob boss Don Falcone (Roy Scheider). Having relayed the whereabouts of federal witness Nick Gazzara (Dennis Farina) to Falcone, Jack's latest mob assignment is to locate Mona Demarkov (Lena Olin), Gazzara's assassin and another potential federal witness. Mona escapes and Jack is ordered by Falcone to assassinate her or be killed himself. Mona buys him off financially and sexually, and he agrees to lie to Falcone and establish her with a new identity. At Gazzara's funeral Falcone has his men amputate one of Jack's toes as a warning. Frightened, Jack reveals his secret hoard to his wife Natalie (Annabella Sciorra) and sends her to Arizona with the money, arranging a rendezvous at the Holiday Diner outside Phoenix. When he meets Mona to collect his money, she double-crosses him, and in the ensuing struggle he shoots her in the arm. Once again she escapes. Mistaking Sheri (Juliette Lewis), his own mistress, for Mona, Jack kills her. By setting fire to the building and leaving her own amputated arm as incriminating evidence, Mona exploits the situation to make it appear that it is she who is dead. Mona has Jack captured, she makes love to him, and then forces him to bury Falcone alive before turning him over to federal agents. In custody, Jack meets Mona again. Provoked, he disarms a former colleague and kills her, but then fails in a suicide attempt. Established under a new identity (Jim Dougherty) at the Holiday Diner, Jack has now waited five years for Natalie to show up. His only keepsake is her photographic record of their marriage and his own infidelities.

Analysis

Written in 1987 but not filmed until the mid-nineties,[21] *Romeo is Bleeding* constitutes one of the most ironic of contemporary film noir palimpsests. It is a pulp-culture artifact that

- Blends noir pessimism with black comedy
- Simultaneously pays homage to, critiques, and repackages the generic traditions of the noir genre
- Deploys many of the stylistic elements (expressionist visual flourishes, chiaroscuro lighting effects, even a nostalgic jazz soundtrack by Mark Isham), the iconography (rain-slicked streets, mirrors, cigarettes, handguns, the femme fatale's long hair), the mise-en-scène (run-down hotels, an abandoned warehouse, the diners, a fairground, a gangster's mansion, a waterfront jetty), and narrative markers (voice-over narration, flashback structure, subjective fantasy sequences) traditionally associated with the classical film noir
- Represents a traditional film noir narrative of deception and entrapment enacted by archetypal noir characters (the corrupt police officer, the femme fatale, the suffering wife, the corporate gangster)
- Evokes the conventions of a number of distinct classic film noir and neo-noir subgenres (the police procedural noir, the gangster noir, the femme fatale film, the yuppie nightmare film)
- Is thematically concerned with the notion of masculinity in crisis and the broader social implications of patriarchal corruption

Like Scorsese's films, among which *Raging Bull, After Hours,* and *GoodFellas* (1990) are all points of reference in the film's intertextual allusionism, *Romeo is Bleeding* is a psychological study of character that plumbs the darker side of human nature. It is also a modern-day fable that supplies a damning critique of post-Reaganite capitalism, foregrounding the violence, greed, and individualism prevalent in contemporary American society.

Romeo is Bleeding is structured in such a way that the viewer is intended to serve as Jim Dougherty/Jack Grimaldi's interlocutor as he relates the events that have culminated in his relocation to the Holiday Diner under the federal witness program.[22] As with *Reservoir Dogs* or *The Usual Suspects,* the film is intended to self-reflexively promote an awareness of narrative construction and storytelling. Indeed, more so than the other two texts, *Romeo is Bleeding* emphasizes the referential, frequently *untruthful* nature of language. Much of what the viewer sees on screen and hears described by the protagonist is signaled as belonging to Jim/Jack's mindscreen. As the narrator becomes increasingly embroiled in the story he is telling, there is a breakdown in the cause-and-effect chain of events usually associated with a linear narrative.

Temporally and spatially distanced from the events he narrates, and emotionally troubled by them, Jack anticipates sequences that occur subsequently in the narrative, both literally (Mona's attempt to strangle Jack with her legs, for example, is visually anticipated and then quickly dismissed by the voice-over narrator early in the film: "Pretend you didn't see that") and by allusion (in reconstructing his story, Jack attributes actions such as pointing a handgun at him and then winking to Natalie, only for these actions to be reenacted by Mona later in the film). In Jack's retelling of the story, there is a subjective fusion of fantasy and reality. Dreams, such as that of his capture by Mona in the fairground, later become fulfilled, characters become blurred into one, as in the gun/wink motif that associates Natalie with Mona, or the sequence in which Sheri is mistaken for Mona and shot. There is a gradual erosion of temporal and spatial markers, as witness the appearance of first Mona and then Natalie at the Holiday Diner in Arizona. Like the narrator-protagonists of eighteenth-century picaresque novels, Jack is not to be trusted, his narrative in effect representing a disturbing/disturbed fusion of reality and fiction, as witness the narrative tensions prompted by Natalie's characterization as both a feminine ideal associated with a nostalgic past and as a manifestation of transgressive femininity.

In a sense, like Scorsese's eighties neo-noir *After Hours, Romeo is Bleeding* is best understood as a dream narrative. Indeed, there is in the text a certain degree of associational logic that tells us much about the protagonist. Like Paul Hackett in the former film, Jack seems to associate finance with potency. He even begins to mimic the rich gangster he and his colleagues monitor in his interaction with Sheri, and his narrative recalls the conflation of sex and finance suggested by Mona during their first encounter. Like Paul, he associates femininity with death. Of the two sexual women in his narrative, Mona is an assassin and Sheri suffers a violent death at Jack's hands. Love/sexual activity, as in Scorsese's film and elsewhere in the film noir canon, is related to obsession and perversion. The world Jack traverses, as was the case with Paul, proliferates with images of castration/impotence (as in Jack's inability at one stage to get an erection in Sheri's presence, the amputation of Jack's toe by Don Falcone's henchmen, the amputation of Mona's injured arm,[23] and her chainsaw severing of Sheri's arm) and symbols of phallic femininity (handguns, cigarettes, business suits, Mona's prosthetic arm), suggesting Jack's sexual anxiety and paranoia, his crisis of masculine identity.

Jack is a figure in thrall to the death instinct. This is suggested not only by his nearly obsessive involvement with the mob assassin Mona ("Can I tell you what makes love so frightening? It's that you don't own it. It owns you"), which like that of Frank Keller with Helen Cruger in *Sea of Love* is founded on masculine distrust and fear, but also by his status, as he himself suggests in his voice-over narration, as a "guy who fell in love with a hole in the ground." This is an image laden not only with sexual innuendo (once again, the conflation of sexual potency and finance) but also with ambiguity. Not only does Jack lovingly "feed the hole" in the back of his garden where he keeps the money paid to him by the mob, but he digs the grave in which Don Falcone is buried alive. Already complicit in Mona's illicit activities after providing a false identity for her and murdering Sheri, Jack, when he buries Don Falcone at gunpoint, effectively buries himself. Indeed, as Mona says to him shortly before he kills her, he *is* already a dead man. The traditional noir male protagonist, Jack is marked both by impotence (the amputated toe, the empty gun in his suicide attempt, and, as in *Blood Simple,* the burial of the corrupt/impotent patriarch), and death (the burial of the don, the shootings of Sheri and Mona).

Like Jake La Motta in *Raging Bull,* Jack is himself a corrupt patriarchal figure with whom the viewer is forced to identify, becoming in a sense implicated in the protagonist's selfish activities and paranoia.[24] Jack shares with Jake and the other masculine characters in the Scorsesean neo-noir oeuvre their duality and schizophrenia: "A man don't always do what's best for him," he observes in his voice-over commentary, "Sometimes he does the worst—he listens to a voice in his head. But what do you know, too late he finds out it's the wrong voice." Jack is a figure who repeatedly transgresses his ideologically ordained position as an upholder of the established patriarchal order, underpinned as it is by the maintenance of the law and the sanctity of the nuclear family. Despite his position as a police officer, he is intimately involved in the machinations of the criminal underworld, he is wholly immoral ("You know right from wrong," Don Falcone observes at one stage, "you just don't care"), an inveterate womanizer, and a murderer not only responsible for the deaths of both Sheri and Mona but also an accessory to the murders of the federal officers protecting Nick Gazzara, of Gazzara himself, and of Don Falcone. As with Lieutenant Colonel Oliver North, however, whose own illegal activities dominated the media at the time of Henkin's original conception of *Romeo is Bleeding,* Jack is ultimately lionized by the very establishment whose laws he transgresses, commended for his bravery in the murder of an "unarmed" woman.

In fact, as this perverse celebration of masculine activity would suggest, *Romeo is Bleeding* gives expression to the inherent misogyny of the film's protagonist Jack Grimaldi, of the masculine communities (his police colleagues, the mob figures) with which he interacts, and indeed, in general terms, of the male-dominated culture responsible for the film's production. Like *One False Move,* which plays on the assumed racism of the filmgoing public,[25] *Romeo is Bleeding* intersects with prevalent masculine anxieties, and the film can be read as a critique of the femme fatale figure, offering a narrative in which "the conventional, overdetermined fear of women is the point and not the price of the story."[26] As with *Sea of Love, Romeo is Bleeding* exploits the generic tradition of the femme fatale, in this case overinvesting the tradition, taking it to a seriocomic extreme, rather than confounding it as in the former film, as a means of foregrounding the way in which patriarchal culture endeavors to deflect the crisis in masculinity onto women. Indeed, *Romeo is Bleeding*'s self-conscious insertion in a lengthy tradition of femme fatale narratives that surreptitiously comment on and reflect patriarchal corruption is ironized within the film's diegesis itself when Jack listens to an audio police profile of Mona Demarkov, which effectively reveals that Jack follows in the footsteps of an FBI agent formerly in thrall to Mona who eventually committed suicide. History repeats itself, both generically and diegetically, the film exploiting an extradiegetic nineties context of female autonomy that parallels that of the early forties when the classic film noir

> transformed the new role of women into a negative image. Passed through the *noir* filter, the "new woman," forced by social circumstance and economic necessity to assert herself in ways that her culture had not previously encouraged, emerged on screen as a wicked, scheming creature,

sexually potent and deadly to the male. The dark thrillers record an abiding fear of strong women, women who steer men off their course, beckoning them to a life of crime, or else so disrupting their emotional poise that they are unable to function.[27]

For all Jack's attempts, in his role as the film's narrator, to denigrate (as illustrated by Sheri's nearly redundant role in his narrative) and/or demonize femininity (the life-threatening dangers posed by Mona, or more complexly, given his nostalgia and love for her, Natalie's transgression of his patriarchal authority), there is in *Romeo is Bleeding* a degree of textual tension that connects the film with other contemporary nineties femme fatale narratives. Indeed, as in *Basic Instinct,* the attempts to fetishize the female form (Mona's constant state of undress, her hair, her placement by mirrors and by windows) fail to disguise the femme fatale's dual status as both *castrator* (she is a professional assassin; at one stage in the film she wields a garrotte and later a chain saw) and *castrated* (her amputated arm). Like the ice-pick-wielding Catherine Tramell, therefore, she is both a phallic woman, at one stage threatening Jack's colleague Martie Cuchinski (Will Patton) with his own gun (the event is never seen on screen, but is related by Martie to Jack) and an erotic male fantasy figure, a fusion of both love and death (in their second meeting, for example, Jack and Mona barter over the provision of a false death certificate and then make love), a black widow figure who will kill in the wake of sexual pleasure, as witness Mona's murder of her former lover Don Falcone and her attempt to garrotte Jack.

While Mona, in keeping with the classic film noir tradition, is punished/killed by the patriarchal order whose conventions she has transgressed by usurping phallic power, accumulating financial potency, and flaunting her sexual difference, the text nevertheless closes ambiguously, suggesting a deep fissure in the masculine sense of order. If Natalie still lives (and there is a degree of uncertainty about this, given Mona's parting words to Jack), then she continues the tradition of feminine transgression. Associated with Mona by means of the aforementioned gun/wink motif, their involvement with Jack, her possession of Jack's dirty money, and their respective "appearances" at the Holiday Diner, Natalie is, nevertheless, not characterized as a femme fatale figure. Rather, like Helen Cruger in *Sea of Love,* she is presented as a woman who wishes to live outside and in spite of the corrupt male "culture of distrust." Ultimately, as Jack peruses the photographic evidence of his wife's amateur detective work cataloging his betrayal of their marriage vows, the film celebrates her independence and abandonment of him, suggesting a representation of femininity that transcends those archetypal images of the femme fatale (Mona), suffering girlfriend (Sheri), and faithful wife (Natalie) set up in Jack's narrative. This notion of a cinematic manifestation of femininity that defies neatly compartmentalized masculine preconceptions resurfaces in *One False Move,* a film that similarly thematizes the deeply entrenched racial prejudices that permeate American culture.

Unlike *Reservoir Dogs* and *Romeo is Bleeding,* both of which exemplify the prevalence of cinematic irony in the neo-noir of the nineties, *One False Move* belongs to an alternative, marginal cycle of neo-noir produced almost exclusively by African-American filmmakers. In effect, such films disrupt the postmodern chain of self-referentiality, their narratives firmly grounded in the external realities of life in American society today. Such films as *One False Move, Boyz N the Hood, Straight Out of Brooklyn* (Matty Rich, 1991), *Juice, Menace II Society,* and *Clockers* suggest a further fragmentation of the noir genre between mainstream formula and independent revisionism, and between postmodern artifice and social-realism. A film such as *One False Move* shares with *Reservoir Dogs* and *Romeo is Bleeding* their pulp-culture roots, their thematization of corruption, prejudice, and social fragmentation. But in tone it is altogether less comic, less parodic, and less self-consciously allusive. Such films are intended to serve both as examples of generic revisionism, co-opting the noir genre for a culturally specific African-American agenda, and as testaments to contemporary social malaise. They are nineties counterparts to the neo-noir texts of the seventies Anglo and Italian-American neo-modernists, further illustrative of the cyclical nature of generic evolution.

ONE FALSE MOVE

Plot Summary

Southcentral Los Angeles. Fantasia (Cynda Williams) pays a surprise visit to a friend's birthday celebrations. She lets in her white boyfriend, Ray (Billy Bob Thornton), and his partner, Pluto (Michael Beach). They proceed to beat up the guests in order to find out the whereabouts of a local drug dealer. Fantasia and Ray go to the dealer's house, where they find a drug stash and money. Ray kills all the witnesses except a young boy whom, unbeknown to him, Fantasia has spared. Meanwhile, Pluto murders the inhabitants of the original house. The trio heads for Houston, Texas, where they hope to sell the drugs to one of Pluto's connections. Detectives Cole (Jim Metzler) and McFeely (Earl Billings) are assigned the case. From a video recording that registers Fantasia's entrance into the victims' house they surmise that the gang is possibly headed for Star City, Arkansas. They fly south where they liaise with local police chief Dale "Hurricane" Dixon (Bill Paxton), a naïve family man who can barely contain his excitement at being involved in a major murder investigation. The journey of the three fugitives is plagued by disaster. When they are stopped by a suspicious patrol officer who has followed them from a convenience store, Fantasia is forced to kill him. In Houston Fantasia insists on traveling ahead to Star City to see her young son. The drug deal culminates in another slaughter. When the two men discover that Fantasia has taken all the money with her, they too head for Arkansas. From a security camera image of Fantasia, Dixon is able to identify her as local girl Lila Walker. He follows Fantasia/Lila's brother and her son to a secret rendezvous with Lila. After they depart he confronts her. They are in fact former lovers (she was a minor at the time), and she reveals that Dixon is the father of the little boy. She agrees to help Dixon capture Ray and Pluto, but when they arrive, the scene erupts in violence. The three fugitives are all killed and Dixon is seriously injured. Cole and McFeely arrive too late, having been misdirected by Fantasia's boy. The film ends with Dixon talking to his son for the first time.

Analysis

Originally entitled *Hurricane* after the male sheriff at the center of the film's narrative,[28] *One False Move* constitutes, on the one hand, a study of patriarchal corruption (male violence, the sexual abuse of minors, unfulfilled social responsibilities) and the instability of masculine identity. On the other hand, however, the film also foregrounds the issue of racial bigotry, exploring the uneasy social and physical/sexual interaction between white and black America suggested by the numerous cross-racial pairings in the film—Lila and Dale, Fantasia and Ray, Ray and Pluto, Cole and McFeely, and, ultimately, Dale and his son. To a degree, in fact, the film draws from the same sociopolitical terrain as the pulp-culture writings of Jim Thompson, William McGivern, Charles Williams, and Charles Willeford, many of whose novels similarly explore questions related to class, gender, and/or race in American society, as witness, for example, the narratives of Thompson's *Pop. 1280,* McGivern's *Odds Against Tomorrow,*

Williams's *Hell Hath No Fury,* and Willeford's *Pick-Up* (indeed, in the latter text, the author similarly plays on the reader's assumed racism, revealing only in the penultimate sentence that the protagonist with which he or she has identified is an African-American man). The film deploys, moreover, a generic noir structure (a hybrid of noir detective picture and noir road movie) which it subtly subverts as the various characters converge on Star City. Indeed, as B. Ruby Rich has remarked, the film appears "to offer itself up as one thing (urban ultraviolence) only to throw its audience a loop with bold evolutions into more complex terrain (race crossing, urban/rural dynamics, mother-love, tragedy)."[29]

Like the neo-noirs of Martin Scorsese, an acknowledged influence on the director Carl Franklin, *One False Move* is informed by a religious conception of guilt, retribution, and atonement that shapes our understanding of the actions of both Dale/Hurricane and Lila/Fantasia. Both characters are ultimately forced to make moral choices in the film's narrative, Lila's founded on a need for self-esteem after the violence of her association with Ray and Pluto, and Dale's prompted by his decision to fly in the face of white America's social construction.[30] Previously conditioned by the fear and the distrust that stems from racial bigotry (he uses the term *nigger,* for example, and constantly fails to address the African-American detective McFeely by his proper name), Dale's interaction with the L.A. detectives, his own violent encounter with Ray and Pluto, and above all, his reconciliation with Lila who serves as "the film's quiet agent of change and discovery,"[31] lead him to a position from which he can finally assume his social responsibilities and (presumably) acknowledge his fatherhood of the illegitimate Byron (Robert Anthony Bell).

In spite of its apparently upbeat ending, however, *One False Move* hardly offers a solution to the racial tensions in American society to which its narrative alludes. Filmed in 1990 but not released until 1992, *One False Move* pre-dates the Rodney King controversy, the Los Angeles race riots, the O. J. Simpson affair, and Nation of Islam demonstrations, which have all provided further evidence of an ever-widening ethnic divide in contemporary American society. What the film does do, however, a phenomenon still rare even by 1990 in the noir genre (an imbalance currently being redressed in the films of Carl Franklin, Spike Lee, Bill Duke, John Singleton, Ernest Dickerson, Mario Van Peebles, Mattie Rich, and the Hughes Brothers, among several others in the new wave of African-American filmmakers), is give a voice to African-American characters. In the past they either were absent (as in the majority of classic films noirs), were manifestations of "otherness" in threatening urban landscapes (as in Chandler's novel *Farewell, My Lovely*, which features an early sequence of violence in an African-American bar),[32] were relegated to marginal supporting roles (as in the maid in *Out of the Past*, the musicians in *D.O.A.*, and the ex-serviceman car park attendant in *The Killing*), or were present only by suggestion in the jazz scores of a number of classic films noirs (as in Alexander Mackendrick's 1957 *Sweet Smell of Success* and Orson Welles's 1958 *Touch of Evil*).[33]

The traditional noir critique of patriarchal white America is, therefore, imbued in this and other contemporary neo-noirs produced by African-American filmmakers with the added dimension of ethnic difference and a history of racial discrimination and black suffering. "Looking guilty is *being* guilty. You know that," Lila/Fantasia observes at one stage to her brother Ronnie (Kevin Hunter), reflecting her own social conditioning in a rural society dominated by a minority Anglo-American ruling class. Later, during her reunion with Dale, she points to a continuing history of white America's betrayal of black America. She reveals that she, her brother, and her son are all the progeny of miscegenation, the white father an absent and unknown quantity for each of them. Franklin has returned to this motif of miscegenation in his adaptation of Walter Mosley's period noir novel *Devil in a Blue Dress*, the activities of the novel/film's femme fatale given psychological motivation as she strives to protect her false ethnic identity, "passing" as a white person in a racist society.

Like the philosophical neo-noir thriller *Suture* (Scott McGehee and David Siegel, 1993), which refuses to acknowledge any class or ethnic differences between the half-brothers Clay Arlington (played by the African-American actor Dennis Hayshert) and Vincent Towers (played by the Anglo-American actor Michael Harris), *One False Move* offers a critique of the prejudiced social conditioning in American society and Western culture in general. Indeed, the opening sequence of *One False Move*, set in southcentral Los Angeles, an urban ghetto already associated in the world external to the diegesis with racial tension, inner-city poverty, drug wars, and violent crime,[34] plays upon the inherent racism of the filmgoing public (the expected violence of the psychotic African-American male character Pluto, the embodiment of "black rage"),[35] and also exploits class preconceptions (the primeval brutality and inarticulateness of the "white trash" male Ray) and gender prejudices (the duplicity of Fantasia) latent in American film culture. While the violence and greed of Ray and Pluto is irredeemable, however, with the gradual revelation of new plot points, the film begins to confound audience expectations regarding the role of Fantasia.

From the moment Lila is identified by Dale Dixon, in fact, she begins to take on a personality and identity that transcends the cinematic archetype of the femme fatale, a role that she has appeared to perform up to that point in the text. Unlike the majority of noir femmes fatales, Lila has a family and she is a mother. Her anti-social behavior is represented as psychologically motivated, rooted in a past of economic deprivation, sexual abuse, and failed dreams (she left Star City to try her luck as an actress in Hollywood, Dale tells Cole and McFeely). Not only is she an African-American "trapped in the darkness of white captivity,"[36] she is also a woman constrained and belittled by the gender prejudices of the dominant patriarchal order. As in *Sea of Love,* which also features a single mother figure, in *One False Move* we return to the familiar terrain of masculine distrust, and the concomitant fear and exclusion of femininity. In the sequences in which Lila and Dale are together, the distorted masculine perception of femininity prevails, the viewer effectively complicit with Dale's prejudiced point of view. Initially unable to accept the notion that he fathered Byron, comfortable in his status as the patriarch of the ideologically approved white nuclear family, Dale in effect accuses Lila of being a whore for having had a son out of wedlock. For Dale, Lila represents a past transgression he is unable to forget (early in the film Dale has ignored an interlocutor as he stares, preoccupied, at Ronnie and Byron). She constitutes a threat to the sanctity of his marriage (a woman with whom he once had an illicit sexual relationship), to his patriarchal authority (she attempts to grab his penis), and ultimately to his life (when she asks for the cigarettes in her handbag, Dale discovers the handgun she has been carrying—two iconographic markers of the classic femme fatale).

When Lila/Fantasia is not in the presence of either Dale or Ray, however, the viewer is presented with a figure concerned only for the well-being of her son. She is a mother figure who will do anything in her power to protect her offspring, so explaining her obsession (reminiscent of Paul Hackett in *After Hours* or Dorothy in *The Wizard of Oz*) to return home and offering motivation for her actions in killing the Texas Highway Patrol officer, stealing the money from Ray and Pluto, and attempting to sexually entice Dale when he shirks his responsibilities as a father and seems ready to call in the LA detectives. Indeed, this motif of mother love is foreshadowed in her sparing of the young boy in the Los Angeles-based drug dealer's house and is further emphasized in the shock cut that takes us from Los Angeles to Star City, where Dale and his wife, Cheryl Ann (Natalie Canerday), comfort their daughter after she has a nightmare. Lila/Fantasia's narrative, then, after her duplicity in the Los Angeles sequences and her violence in Texas, is ultimately one of self-sacrifice and redemption, her death effectively uniting father and son.

Although the film problematically concludes with an apparent dissolution of racial divisions in the union of Dale and Byron, one paralleled by the aforementioned pairings of Cole and McFeely or even Ray and Pluto, it fails to resolve the other social tensions and anxieties foregrounded in its text: gender prejudices (transgressive femininity is punished, while the once corrupt patriarch, presumably, survives); class distinctions governed by finance (the apparent poverty of the community in which Lila's family lives), education ("He watches TV. I read nonfiction," Cheryl Ann says of her frequently childlike husband), and regionalism (the contrast between the "sophisticated" cities of Los Angeles and Houston and the "backward" Arkansas community of Star City); urban ghettoization; the accessibility of drugs in the American inner-city; and, of course, the increasing manifestation of violent crime in American society. Like *Clockers* or the futuristic *Strange Days, One False Move* speaks of deeply-entrenched divisions in contemporary American society, reflecting the abuse of patriarchal authority, racial tensions, sexual inequality, an expanding class divide, and widespread economic deprivation, its narrative a lurid tale of greed, manipulation, power, and prejudice that has as much foundation in the generic tradition of film noir as in the history of the United States itself.

Martin Scorsese has recently commented in his documentary survey of American film history that "over the years many films address themselves to the spiritual side of man's nature. . . . It is as if movies answer an ancient quest for the common unconscious. They fulfill a spiritual need that people have—to share a common memory."[37] However, films like *One False Move, Romeo is Bleeding, Strange Days, Clockers, Sea of Love, Blood Simple, House of Games, Blue Velvet, Taxi Driver, Night Moves, The Conversation, Point Blank, Touch of Evil, Pickup on South Street, Gun Crazy,* and *Detour,* all of them examples of American film noir, address the darker side of that collective unconscious; they reflect all that is immoral and perverse in American society, cataloging a history of injustice, criminality, violence, and corruption. For all their stylistic innovation, visual flourishes, and hyperbolic narratives, such films, combining the tenets of Hollywood entertainment with sociopolitical critique, introduce a degree of realism into the American culture industry's dream-making factory. They suggest the outright failure of the American Dream and, in their thematization of social inequality, patriarchal corruption, urban malaise, and economic deprivation, they point to the violent fragmentation of American society (as witness the apocalyptic scenes in Bigelow's *Strange Days*). This is why noir has prevailed for so long, tapping into the uncertain cultural climate that is such a distinctive feature of the United States today. As with the films of the forties and fifties, the neo-noirs of the seventies, eighties, and nineties speak of a fragmented society in search of a common identity, a society fractured by ethnic, gender, and class tensions, tainted by violent crime and marked by ideological instability. The neo-noirs of recent years, like their literary and cinematic pulp-culture antecedents, offer no solutions to America's malaise. They merely give expression to a society's pain.

Notes

INTRODUCTION

1. Bill Pronzini and Jack Adrian (Eds.), *Hard-Boiled: An Anthology of American Crime Stories* (Oxford and New York: Oxford University Press, 1995): 3, 17–18.
2. Nino Frank, "Un nouveau genre 'policier': l'aventure criminelle," *L'Ecran Français* 61 (1946): 8–9, 14; Raymond Borde and Étienne Chaumeton, *Panorama du film noir américain (1941–1953)* (Paris: Éditions de Minuit, 1955).
3. Frank, "Un nouveau genre 'policier': l'aventure criminelle": 14. The term also features in an antagonistic review of *Double Indemnity, Murder, My Sweet,* and *The Lost Weekend* (Billy Wilder, 1945), published later in 1946: Jean-Pierre Chartier, "Les Américains aussi font des films 'noirs'," *Revue du Cinéma* 2 (1946): 67–70.
4. Raymond Durgnat, "Paint it Black: The Family Tree of Film Noir," *Cinema* (UK) 6/7 (1970): 49–56; Paul Schrader, "Notes on *Film Noir,*" in Kevin Jackson (Ed.), *Schrader on Schrader* (London and Boston: Faber and Faber, 1990): 80–94. First published in the Los Angeles Film Festival pamphlet for 1971 and subsequently in *Film Comment* 8, no. 1 (1972); J. A. Place and L. S. Petersen, "Some Visual Motifs of Film Noir," in B. Nichols (Ed.), *Movies and Methods,* Volume I (Berkeley, Los Angeles, and London: University of California Press, 1976): 325–38. First published in *Film Comment* 10, no. 1 (1974); Robert G. Porfirio, "No Way Out: Existential Motifs in Film Noir," *Sight and Sound* 45, no. 4 (1976): 212–17; and Alain Silver and Elizabeth Ward (Eds.), *Film Noir: An Encyclopedic Reference to the American Style* (Woodstock, N.Y.: Overlook Press, 1992, 3rd ed.). First edition published in 1979.
5. Paul Kerr, "Out of What Past?: Notes on the B Film Noir," *Screen Education* 32/33 (1979/80): 45.
6. Significantly, taking maximum advantage of the current widespread popular interest in film noir, Thomson's *Suspects,* first published in 1985, was reissued by Minerva in 1995.

7. *The Film Noir Story* was broadcast by BBC2 on 4 August 1995; the *Cinefile* documentary *Dark and Deadly* was broadcast by Channel 4 on 19 October 1995.

8. Robert C. Allen and Douglas Gomery, *Film History: Theory and Practice* (New York: McGraw-Hill, 1985): 83.

9. Raymond Chandler, "The Simple Art of Murder," in Raymond Chandler, *Pearls Are a Nuisance* (Harmondsworth: Penguin, 1964): 198.

10. Schrader, "Notes on *Film Noir*": 87.

11. On 30 March 1981, just two months after his inauguration, Ronald Reagan was shot by John Hinckley in an unsuccessful assassination attempt. Hinckley, it was revealed in his trial, had been prompted to take this action by his obsession with the character played by child actress Jodie Foster in *Taxi Driver,* Martin Scorsese's neo-noir film about an urban psychopath who at one stage is foiled in a similar attempt to murder a presidential candidate.

CHAPTER 1: INDUSTRIAL EVOLUTION

1. R. Barton Palmer, *Hollywood's Dark Cinema: The American Film Noir* (New York: Twayne, 1994): 1.

2. John Izod, *Hollywood and the Box Office, 1895–1986* (Basingstoke, England: Macmillan, 1988): 120–21.

3. Kerr, "Out of What Past?": 51.

4. Janet Staiger, "The Hollywood Mode of Production, 1930–60," in David Bordwell, Janet Staiger, and Kristin Thompson, *The Classical Hollywood Cinema: Film Style and Mode of Production to 1960* (London: Routledge, 1985): 330–32.

5. I use the term *film noir style* with certain reservations. Although classic film noir did produce some of the most visually impressive films of the forties and fifties, when the classic noir oeuvre is considered as a whole it seems that, to a certain degree, James Damico is justified in asserting that there is "no conclusive evidence that anything as cohesive and determined as a visual style exists in FN": James Damico, "Film Noir: A Modest Proposal," *Film Reader* 3 (1978): 57, n. 17. What is more, claustrophobic framing devices, tilted camera angles, mirror shots, chiaroscuro lighting, and imbalanced frame compositions are hardly unique to film noir. Nevertheless, it is taken for granted by those who consider classic film noir simply in terms of its relationship to German Expressionism and the influx of German and Hungarian filmmakers into Hollywood of the thirties and the forties, that these are the defining characteristics of the genre. It is unsurprising, therefore, that many contemporary mainstream noirs offer little more than a pastiche of these visual qualities.

6. See the television documentary *The Film Noir Story* broadcast by BBC2 on 4 August 1995.

7. In a three-part documentary, *Century of Cinema: A Personal Journey with Martin Scorsese through American Movies,* broadcast by Channel 4 between 21 May and 4 June 1995, filmmaker Martin Scorsese distinguishes between four categories of auteur: (1) the director as storyteller, (2) the director as illusionist, (3) the director as smuggler, and (4) the director as iconoclast.

8. On the early examples of television noir, see James Ursini, "Angst at Sixty Fields per Second," in Alain Silver and James Ursini (Eds.), *Film Noir Reader* (New York: Limelight Editions, 1996): 275–87. See also Palmer, *Hollywood's Dark Cinema:* 168; and John G. Cawelti, *Adventure, Mystery and Romance: Formula Stories As Art and Popular Culture* (Chicago: University of Chicago Press, 1976): 139.

9. Jim Hillier, *The New Hollywood* (London: Studio Vista, 1992): 7–9.

10. Thomas Schatz, "The New Hollywood," in Jim Collins, Hilary Radner, and Ava Preacher Collins (Eds.), *Film Theory Goes to the Movies* (New York: Routledge, 1993): 12.

11. Izod, *Hollywood and the Box Office:* 138.

12. Ibid: 141.

13. It should be noted that prior to the revival of American film noir in the late sixties there previously had been color noir productions such as *Leave Her to Heaven* (John M. Stahl, 1945), *Niagara* (Henry Hathaway, 1953), *Slightly Scarlet* (Allan Dwan, 1956), and, some would argue, *Vertigo* (Alfred Hitchcock, 1958). In the early sixties, Samuel Fuller experimented with a widescreen aspect ratio in such (predominantly) black and white films noirs as *Shock Corridor* (1963) and *The Naked Kiss* (1964).

14. Before the majors agreed to sell their films to television, many of the films broadcast on the networks were European, often from Italy and Britain.

15. Schatz, "The New Hollywood": 14.

16. Robert Phillip Kolker, *A Cinema of Loneliness: Penn, Kubrick, Scorsese, Spielberg, Altman* (New York and Oxford: Oxford University Press, 1988, 2nd ed.): 4.

17. Joseph R. Dominick, "Film Economics and Film Content: 1964–1983," in Bruce A. Austin (Ed.), *Current Research in Film: Audiences, Economics, and Law,* Volume 3 (Norwood, N.J.: Ablex, 1987): 145.

18. John Orr, *Cinema and Modernity* (Cambridge: Polity Press, 1993): 2.

19. Kolker, *Cinema of Loneliness:* 9.

20. Palmer, *Hollywood's Dark Cinema:* 172. Film noir, however, was hardly a new phenomenon in French cinema, as witness Poetic Realism and the *policier* tradition.

21. American hard-boiled fiction was an enduring attraction for the *nouvelle vague* filmmakers: Truffaut, for example, adapted *Tirez sur le pianiste* from David Goodis's novel *Down There; La Mariée était en noir* (1968) from Cornell Woolrich's *The Bride Wore Black; La Sirène du Mississippi* (1969) from Woolrich's *Waltz into Darkness;* and his last film *Vivement Dimanche!* (1983) from Charles Williams's *The Long Saturday Night.*

22. Damico, "Film Noir": 55.
23. A number of early anglophone articles about the film noir phenomenon actually analyze the neo-noirs of the late sixties and early seventies rather than the classic noir texts of the forties and fifties. See Richard T. Jameson, "Son of Noir," *Film Comment* 10, no. 6 (1974): 30–33; Charles Gregory, "Living Life Sideways," *Journal of Popular Film* 5, nos. 3/4 (1976): 289–311; and Larry Gross, "Film Après Noir," *Film Comment* 12, no. 4 (1976): 44–49. Although the term *film noir* was never employed, serious anglophone critical writings on the genre date at least from 1950 with the publication of Martha Wolfenstein and Nathan Leites's *Movies: A Psychological Study* (New York: Free Press, 1950). See especially their chapter "Killers and Victims": 175–242.
24. Schrader, "Notes on *Film Noir*": 80.
25. Peter C. Knowles, "Genre and Authorship: Two Films of Arthur Penn," *CineAction!* 21/22 (1990): 83.
26. Leighton Grist, "Moving Targets and Black Widows: Film Noir in Modern Hollywood," in Ian Cameron (Ed.), *The Movie Book of Film Noir* (London: Studio Vista, 1992): 267.
27. John Orr argues that the fifties noirs with their shift of focus from the noir love triangle to political corruption and masculine violence helped "pave the way for the noir films of the 1970s": Orr, *Cinema and Modernity:* 171. European neo-noirs of the seventies and eighties — *The American Friend* (Wim Wenders, 1977), *Coup de Torchon* (Bertrand Tavernier, 1982), and *Fanny Pelopaja* (Vicente Aranda, 1984), for example — have similarly been shaped by these cinematic and literary traditions.
28. There, are of course, exceptions to this general rule. The critically acclaimed neo-noir *The Last Seduction* (John Dahl, 1994), for example, was originally produced for cable television and only subsequently received a worldwide theatrical release. On the other hand, in addition to continuing the revisionist noir tradition of the *nouvelle vague* and Hollywood renaissance filmmakers, the independent sector of the nineties has also served up such formulaic neo-noirs as *Love Crimes* (Lizzie Borden, 1992) and *Femme Fatale* (André Guttfreund, 1991). For a more extended consideration of the very low-budget and made-for-television neo-noir, see Alain Silver, "Son of Noir: Neo-*Film Noir* and the Neo-B Picture," in Silver and Ursini, *Film Noir Reader:* 331–38.
29. Although a product of the "blockbuster mentality," *Batman* is of interest here for two reasons. First, stylistically the film suggests the influence of a gothic/expressionist/film noir artistic sensibility. Second, the film belongs to a cycle of comic strip/animated noir pastiches that includes *Who Framed Roger Rabbit?* (Robert Zemeckis, 1988), *Dick Tracy* (Warren Beatty, 1990), *Cool World* (Ralph Bakshi, 1992), and the two *Batman* sequels, *Batman Returns* (Tim Burton, 1992) and *Batman Forever* (Joel Schumacher, 1995).
30. See Susan Doll and Greg Faller, "*Blade Runner* and Genre: Film Noir and Science Fiction," *Literature/Film Quarterly* 14, no. 2 (1986): 91–92.

31. Jeremy Butler, "*Miami Vice:* The Legacy of *Film Noir*," *Journal of Popular Film and Television* 13, no. 3 (1985): 127–38. The Florida setting in the television series *Miami Vice,* with its real-life connotations of crime and corruption, is a recurrent location in contemporary noir culture. See, for example, the literature of John D. MacDonald, Elmore Leonard, Charles Willeford, Carl Hiaasen, and more recently James Ellroy (*American Tabloid*), and the neo-noir feature films *Night Moves, Body Heat, A Flash of Green* (Victor Nuñez, 1984), *Cat Chaser* (Abel Ferrara, 1989), and *Miami Blues* (George Armitage, 1990).

32. Attempts to commodify the lighting techniques of the classic black and white films noirs have been abetted by the advance in the quality of color film stock. For a more extended consideration of this issue see Todd Erickson, "Kill Me Again: Movement becomes Genre," in Silver and Ursini, *Film Noir Reader*: 314–16.

33. The distinction between seeker- and victim-heroes is borrowed from Michael Walker, "Film Noir: Introduction," in Cameron, *Movie Book of Film Noir:* 10 and 12. Walker invokes the theories of Vladimir Propp in his analysis of film noir.

34. Damico, "Film Noir": 54.

35. Shirley Smallman, Kirk Smallman, and George F. Bohrer, Jr., "*Films Noir and Their Remade Versions: Shifts in sources of evil, women's roles, and the power of fate,*" *Echoes and Mirrors* 1, no. 1 (1994): 57.

36. See Erickson, "Kill Me Again": 324.

37. Often texts like *Hammett* and *Mortal Thoughts* are the products of a brief flirtation with studio-oriented filmmaking by maverick auteurs like Rudolph and Wenders.

38. Grist, "Moving Targets and Black Widows": 281.

39. See Robert Altman's comments in the *Cinefile* documentary *Made in the USA* broadcast by Channel 4 on 25 September 1993. Altman sees today's generation of independent filmmakers as researchers and pioneers who invent new products for the Hollywood majors to clone.

40. See Ira Deutchman's comments in *Made in the USA*. Deutchman argues that there have been three "waves" of American independent filmmaking since the late fifties: the first led by John Cassavetes in the sixties and seventies, the second by John Sayles in the early eighties, the third initiated by *Sex, Lies and Videotape*.

41. William Marling, "On the Relation Between American *Roman Noir* and *Film Noir*," *Literature/Film Quarterly* 21, no. 3 (1993): 184.

42. Edward Hopper's influence is evident in the mise-en-scène of such neo-noirs as *Trouble in Mind* (Alan Rudolph, 1985), *Blue Velvet* (David Lynch, 1986), *House of Games, Kill Me Again, After Dark, My Sweet* (James Foley, 1990), and *The Last Seduction*. For a discussion of Hopper's influence on the cinema, see Erika L. Doss, "Edward Hopper, *Nighthawks* and *Film Noir*," *Post Script* 2, no. 2 (1983): 14–36; Slavoj Žižek, "At the Origins of

Noir: The Humiliated Father," in Slavoj Žižek, *Enjoy Your Symptom!: Jacques Lacan in Hollywood and out* (New York and London: Routledge, 1992): 152–54; and the *Moving Pictures* report broadcast by BBC2 on 12 February 1995. A separate *Moving Pictures* report broadcast on 30 January 1993 explores the influence of photographer Weegee on the visual style of film noir. This is evident in classic films noirs like *The Naked City* (Jules Dassin, 1948), named for one of Weegee's books, and *The Set-Up* (Robert Wise, 1949), in which he has a cameo, and the neo-noirs *Raging Bull* (Martin Scorsese, 1980) and *The Public Eye.*

43. Hal Hinson, "Joel Coen, Ethan Coen and Barry Sonnenfeld interview," *Film Comment* 21, no. 2 (1985): 18. Italics added.

CHAPTER 2: AMERICA NOIR

1. J. P. Telotte, *Voices in the Dark: The Narrative Patterns of Film Noir* (Urbana and Chicago: University of Illinois Press, 1989): 2. Italics in original.

2. The notion of time past and its relevance to the present and future is a recurrent motif in film noir and often shapes narrative structure (flashbacks, voice-overs) and plot (the races against time, for example, in *D.O.A.* and *The Big Clock*). It might be said, furthermore, that as with the lasting influence of the Depression and Second World War through the forties and fifties, the events of the sixties and early seventies (political assassinations, Vietnam, Watergate) still continue to shape the thematic content of many neo-noirs in the eighties and nineties. For a consideration of time as a motif in classic film noir, see J. P. Telotte, "The Big Clock of *Film Noir,*" *Film Criticism* 14, no. 2 (1989/90): 1–11.

3. Mike Davis, *City of Quartz: Excavating the Future of Los Angeles* (London: Vintage, 1992). See, particularly, chapter 1, "Sunshine or *Noir*?": 15–97.

4. Sylvia Harvey, "Woman's place: the absent family of film noir," in E. Ann Kaplan (Ed.), *Women in Film Noir* (London: British Film Institute, 1980, rev. ed.): 25.

5. William Luhr, *Raymond Chandler and Film* (Tallahassee: Florida State University Press, 1991, 2nd ed.): 127.

6. Davis, *City of Quartz:* 92, n. 45, also points to the personification of the city in the films of this era, a concept illustrated by the inclusion of Los Angeles in the cast credits of *Once a Thief* (W. Lee Wilder, 1950) and the numerous films that include the word *city* in their title.

7. *Night* is another word that regularly appears in the titles of films noirs. Others include *big, blue, dark, dead, kill, kiss,* and variations thereof.

8. Schrader, "Notes on *Film Noir*": 82.

9. Richard Maltby, "The Politics of the Maladjusted Text," in Cameron, *Movie Book of Film Noir:* 46.

10. On nuclear anxiety as a motif of classic film noir, see Mark Osteen, "The

Big Secret: *Film Noir* and Nuclear Fear," *Journal of Popular Film and Television* 22, no. 2 (1994): 79–90.

11. Schrader, "Notes on *Film Noir*": 87.

12. Ian Derbyshire, *Politics in the United States: From Carter to Bush* (Edinburgh: Chambers, 1990, 2nd ed.): 18.

13. Michael Ryan and Douglas Kellner, *Camera Politica: The Politics and Ideology of Contemporary Hollywood Film* (Bloomington: Indiana University Press, 1988): 17.

14. Feminist cinema, given the male dominance of the American film industry, was largely confined to experimental avant garde filmmaking throughout the seventies.

15. Ryan and Kellner, *Camera Politica:* 18.

16. For comprehensive coverage of the Watergate scandal and its aftermath, see the five-part BBC2 documentary series *Watergate,* broadcast between 8 May 1994 and 5 June 1994.

17. Grist, "Moving Targets and Black Widows": 271.

18. Robert Garson and Christopher J. Bailey, *The Uncertain Power: A Political History of the United States since 1929* (Manchester: Manchester University Press, 1990): 131.

19. Smallman, Smallman, and Bohrer, "*Films Noir* and Their Remade Versions": 68.

20. Ryan and Kellner, *Camera Politica:* 84.

21. Edward Dimendberg has recently written in "The Will to Motorization: Cinema, Highways, and Modernity," *October* 73 (1995): 131: "Lacking many of the key signifiers of the earlier urban space of film noir (an illuminated nocturnal cityscape and the detective whose mastery of it oscillates between sites of safety and danger), certain later films noir, particularly many produced after 1949, seem best described as films of centrifugal space. New territories (the interstate highway system, suburban residential districts), new expanded communication networks (the coordination of radio and television), and the fantasy escape to more "natural" and increasingly elusive settings define such films, which do not relinquish the city as much as they incorporate it into larger spatial units."

22. In an era that has also been witness to mass media hype regarding, say, Lorena Bobbit's emasculation of her husband John Wayne Bobbit, or the violent feuding of ice-skaters Tonya Harding and Nancy Kerrigan, the return of the femme fatale might also be seen as a means of adding a dimension of physicality (and therefore potential violence) to the female protagonist that is more in keeping with the modern world. Frequently the object of masculine violence, as witness two other recent media "events," namely, the trials of Mike Tyson for rape and O. J. Simpson for murder, *woman* nevertheless is now perceived, in the fantasy figure of the femme fatale at least, as being able to take care of herself by means both fair and foul. On the figure of the violent woman of contemporary (nineties) American cinema, see, for

example, Chris Holmlund, "Cruisin' for a Bruisin'": Hollywood's Deadly (Lesbian) Dolls," *Cinema Journal* 34, no. 1 (1994): 31–51.

23. The hommes fatals of *Jagged Edge, House of Games, Internal Affairs,* and *Bad Influence* are closer in spirit to the classic femme fatale than her contemporary counterpart. Like the femmes fatales of old, these men are calculating and intelligent, but they *are* ultimately outwitted and killed (this is, however, ambiguous in the case of *House of Games*). On the contemporary figure of the homme fatal, see Margaret Cohen, "The *Homme Fatal,* the Phallic Father, and the New Man," *Cultural Critique* 23 (1992/93): 111–36.

24. On the figure of the female investigator in contemporary American cinema, see Linda Mizejewski, "Picturing the Female Dick: *The Silence of the Lambs* and *Blue Steel,*" *Journal of Film and Video* 45, nos. 2/3 (1993): 6–23.

25. Marina Heung, "Black Widow," *Film Quarterly* 41, no. 1 (1987): 55.

26. Ibid: 56.

27. See Manthia Diawara, "*Noir* by *Noirs:* Toward a New Realism in Black Cinema," in Joan Copjec (Ed.), *Shades of Noir: A Reader* (London and New York: Verso, 1993): 261–78.

CHAPTER 3: SEVENTIES REVISIONISM

1. Telotte, *Voices in the Dark*: 3. Italics in original.

2. Stephen Cooper, "Sex/Knowledge/Power in the Detective Genre," *Film Quarterly* 42, no. 3 (1989): 23–31.

3. Orr, *Cinema and Modernity:* 159.

4. Christine Gledhill, "*Klute* 2: feminism and *Klute,*" in Kaplan, *Women in Film Noir:* 116.

5. B. Ruby Rich, "Dumb Lugs and Femmes Fatales," *Sight and Sound* 5, no. 11 (1995): 8.

6. Pam Cook, "Masculinity in Crisis?: Tragedy and Identification in *Raging Bull,*" *Screen* 23, nos. 3/4 (1982): 40.

7. The casting of an actor (or in Huston's case director-actor) associated with classic film noir is a common way of paying homage to America's cinematic past in the neo-noir. Lauren Bacall, for example, features in *Harper;* Lee Marvin stars in *Point Blank;* Sterling Hayden has a major role in *The Long Goodbye* (and also features in Coppola's *The Godfather,* as does Richard Conte); Robert Mitchum stars in *Farewell, My Lovely* and *The Big Sleep,* and has a minor role in the remake of *Cape Fear* (which also includes a cameo performance by Gregory Peck); Burt Lancaster stars in *Atlantic City;* Jane Greer and Richard Widmark have minor roles in *Against All Odds;* and Dorothy Malone has a minor role in *Basic Instinct.*

8. Chandler, "The Simple Art of Murder": 197.

9. Palmer, *Hollywood's Dark Cinema:* 73.

10. John G. Cawelti, "*Chinatown* and Generic Transformation in Recent Amer-

ican Films," in Gerald Mast and Marshall Cohen (Eds.), *Film Theory and Criticism: Introductory Readings* (New York: Oxford University Press, 1985, 3rd ed.): 507.

11. Cawelti, *Adventure, Mystery and Romance:* 142.

12. Cawelti, "*Chinatown* and Generic Transformation": 510. The failure of the hero adventure is a recurrent motif in seventies American cinema, particularly in the films of the political left (*Easy Rider,* in a sense, is the definitive text in this respect). Nevertheless, in right-wing cinema, especially the marginally noir vigilante films like *Dirty Harry* and *Death Wish,* and indeed militant "blaxploitation" films like *Shaft* (Gordon Parks, 1971), the hero adventure is invariably a success. In the eighties cinema of "Reaganite Entertainment," in which generic traditions are reaffirmed, the hero adventure would become the dominant narrative paradigm (*Star Wars, Rambo*).

13. Ironically the historical acts on which the water and power plot are based did serve to unify and regenerate Los Angeles while permanently damaging the Owens Valley region from which the city's water was drawn. The city, however, was owned and run by small number of wealthy men (Otis, Chandler, Hellman, Huntington). It was soon divided by class, landowners on one side and tenants on another. On the power base in Los Angeles, see Davis, *City of Quartz,* chapter 2, "Power Lines": 99–149.

14. On *Chinatown* and the Oedipus myth, see Deborah Linderman, "Oedipus in Chinatown," *Enclitic,* Special Issue (1982): 190–203. The Oedipal motif is revived in the mid-eighties noir-horror film hybrid *Angel Heart* (Alan Parker, 1987).

15. Interestingly, both films, *Once Upon a Time in the West* and *Chinatown,* infused with the European sensibilities of their respective directors Sergio Leone and Roman Polanski, offer an outsider's perspective on the United States and its history.

16. On "the rape of Owens Valley" and its relation to *Chinatown,* see Mark Cousins, "Robert Towne: On Writing," in John Boorman and Walter Donohue (Eds.), *Projections 6: Film-makers on Film-making* (London and Boston: Faber and Faber, 1996): 110–11. See also Syd Field, *Screenplay: The Foundations of Screenwriting* (New York: Dell, 1982, exp. ed.): 86–88.

17. Cawelti, "*Chinatown* and Generic Transformation": 515.

18. Michael Walker, "Night Moves," *Movie* 22 (1976): 37.

19. Tom Luddy and David Thomson, "Penn on Penn," in John Boorman, Tom Luddy, David Thomson, and Walter Donohue (Eds.), *Projections 4: Film-makers on Film-making* (London and Boston: Faber and Faber, 1995): 146.

20. Kolker, *Cinema of Loneliness:* 69.

21. Michael Walker notes that Bogart is persistently and ironically invoked in *Night Moves.* He lists the structural similarities with *The Big Sleep,* the Florida Keys setting shared with *Key Largo* (John Huston, 1948), Marty's allusion to the Sam Spade of *The Maltese Falcon,* and Paula's reference to a past boyfriend Billy Dannreuther, also the name of a Bogart character in

Beat the Devil (John Huston, 1954): Walker, "Night Moves": 38. Equally allusive is the role of Arlene Iverson (a has-been actress languishing in her personal palace and called a "black widow" by Moseby), which resembles that of Norma Desmond (Gloria Swanson) in *Sunset Boulevard* (Billy Wilder, 1950).

22. Eileen McGarry, "Night Moves," in Silver and Ward, *Film Noir:* 206.
23. The idea of counterculture is also undermined in *Taxi Driver* in the characterization of Iris (Jodie Foster).
24. Michael Powell, *Million-Dollar Movie* (London: Heinemann, 1992): 423. This book, incidentally, is dedicated to Scorsese, who befriended Powell in his later years.
25. *The Film Noir Story* was broadcast by BBC2 on 4 August 1995.
26. *Century of Cinema: A Personal Journey with Martin Scorsese through American Movies* is a three-part documentary and was broadcast by Channel 4 between 21 May and 4 June 1995.
27. Schrader, "Notes on *Film Noir*": 83.
28. Scorsese discusses the combination of styles in his audio commentary on the MGM/UA Home Video (ML104589) special edition laser disc of *New York, New York,* side 2, chap. 10.
29. Again, the pervasive influence of T. S. Eliot's narrative poem *The Waste Land* on twentieth-century Western culture manifests itself in *Taxi Driver.* The film even shares with the poem the images of fire (Travis holds his hand over the flame of a gas oven, he burns Betsy's flowers) and water (the literal, rain-washed streets, Travis's expressed desire for some kind of apocalyptic rainfall) as both destructive and purifying/regenerative.
30. Gross, "Film Après Noir": 45.
31. Bella Taylor, "Martin Scorsese," in John Tuska (Ed.), *Close-up: The Contemporary Director* (Metuchen, N.J., and London: Scarecrow, 1981): 301.
32. Julian C. Rice, "Transcendental Pornography and *Taxi Driver,*" *Journal of Popular Film* 5, no. 2 (1976): 113.
33. Marsha Kinder, *Blood Cinema: The Reconstruction of National Identity in Spain* (Berkeley: University of California Press, 1993): 141.
34. Ibid: 146.
35. Taylor, "Martin Scorsese": 342.
36. This role is played by Scorsese and is his second appearance in the film. He appears earlier outside the Palantine offices when Travis first sees Betsy. For me, these two cameos are crucial: like the young girl who takes Jesus down from the cross in *The Last Temptation of Christ* (1988), in *Taxi Driver* the Scorsese figure becomes the devil incarnate guiding Travis's reactions to his environment. It is he whose eyes follow Betsy when she first appears on screen; it is he who implants the idea of physical violence in Travis's mind. Scorsese's appearances, then, are more than simple directorial self-inscription or auteurist signature.
37. On the motif of men and their relationships with underage girls in Scorsese's

films, see Carol J. Adams, "Raging Batterer," in Steven G. Kellman (Ed.), *Perspectives on Raging Bull* (New York: G. K. Hall, 1994): 117.

38. Cook, "Masculinity in Crisis?": 39.

39. Lorraine Mortimer, "Blood Brothers: Purity, Masculinity and the Flight from the Feminine in Scorsese and Schrader," *Cinema Papers* 75 (1989): 30.

40. Pam Cook, "Scorsese's Masquerade," *Sight and Sound* 1, no. 12 (1992): 15.

41. On the religious dimension of the duality of Betsy, Iris, and Travis's characters, see Michael Bliss, *Martin Scorsese and Michael Cimino* (Metuchen, N.J.: Scarecrow, 1985): 101–2.

42. Scorsese discusses Travis's masochism in relation to the Catholic concept of sin in his audio commentary for the Voyager Company Criterion Collection *Taxi Driver* laser disc (CC1218L) on side 2, chap. 16.

43. *Taxi Driver* is the first installment in a trilogy of neo-noir films featuring the existential hero. The trilogy is completed by *American Gigolo* (1980) and *Light Sleeper* (1991), both of them written and directed by Schrader.

44. Even *Cape Fear,* the most commercial, hence least personal, of Scorsese's neo-noirs to date, is partly a psychological character study: the negative footage of Danielle Bowden's (Juliette Lewis) eyes in the opening and closing sequences demarcates the films as hers, possibly even a figment of her imagination. Moreover, the stylized mise-en-scène, lighting, sound effects, and Freddie Francis's model photography of the film's hyperbolic river sequence give the impression not of a literal voyage on the Cape Fear river but of a psychic voyage of self-discovery in which each member of the Bowden family does battle with personal demons.

45. Münch's expressionist image was first co-opted by film noir in *Among the Living* (Stuart Heisler, 1941), an early gothic exploration of duality and psychosis.

46. See Mary Scott Albert, *Towards a Theory of Slow Motion* (Master's dissertation, British Film Institute and Birkbeck College, University of London, 1993): 45. See also David Friedkin, "Blind Rage and 'Brotherly Love': The Male Psyche at War with Itself in *Raging Bull,*" in Kellman, *Perspectives on Raging Bull:* 122.

47. Scorsese briefly discusses the framing in this scene in his audio commentary on the *Taxi Driver* laser disc, side 1, chap. 11. Scorsese also describes the process by which color was manipulated in the shoot-out sequence on side 4, chap. 52 of the laser disc.

48. Bryan Bruce, "Martin Scorsese: Five Films," *Movie* 31/32 (1986): 92.

CHAPTER 4: EIGHTIES PASTICHE

1. See, for example, Steven Schiff, "Body Heat," in Richard T. Jameson (Ed.), *They Went Thataway: Redefining Film Genres—A National Society of Film*

Critics Video Guide (San Francisco: Mercury House, 1994): 31–35. First published as "Voluptuous Nightmares" in *The Boston Phoenix* (Tuesday, 22 September 1981).

2. Grist, "Moving Targets and Black Widows": 273.

3. The term *Cain-text* is borrowed from Frank Krutnik, "Desire, Transgression and James M. Cain," *Screen* 23, no. 1 (1982): 31–44.

4. Grist, "Moving Targets and Black Widows": 274.

5. Leighton Grist, "Out of the Past a.k.a. Build My Gallows High," in Cameron, *Movie Book of Film Noir:* 203.

6. Mary Ann Doane, *Femmes Fatales: Feminism, Film Theory, Psychoanalysis* (London: Routledge, 1991): 2.

7. Deborah Thomas, "How Hollywood Deals with the Deviant Male," in Cameron, *Movie Book of Film Noir:* 64. Italics in original.

8. Barbara Creed, *The Monstrous-Feminine: Film, Feminism, Psychoanalysis* (London: Routledge, 1993): 157.

9. Thomas, "How Hollywood Deals with the Deviant Male": 67.

10. Deborah Thomas, "Psychoanalysis and Film Noir," in Cameron, *Movie Book of Film Noir:* 79.

11. Carol Siri Johnson, "Constructing Machismo in *Mean Streets* and *Raging Bull,*" in Kellman, *Perspectives on Raging Bull:* 104.

12. Woody Haut, *Pulp Culture: Hardboiled Fiction and the Cold War* (London: Serpent's Tail, 1995): 17.

13. Stephen Frosh, *Identity Crisis: Modernity, Psychoanalysis and the Self* (Basingstoke and London: Macmillan, 1991): 146.

14. Grist, "Moving Targets and Black Widows": 277.

15. Bryan Bruce, "Scorsese: After Hours," *CineAction!* 6 (1986): 27.

16. Kolker, *Cinema of Loneliness:* 234.

17. For an extended consideration of the parallels with the Hades of classical mythology, see Bill Van Daalen, "After Hours," *Film Quarterly* 41, no. 3 (1988): 32.

18. Ibid: 33.

19. Bruce, "Scorsese: After Hours": 31.

20. Stephen Mamber, "Parody, Intertextuality, Signature: Kubrick, DePalma, and Scorsese," *Quarterly Review of Film and Video* 12, nos. 1/2 (1990): 32.

21. Donald Lyons, *Independent Visions: A Critical Introduction to Recent American Independent Film* (New York: Ballantine Books, 1994): 123 and 126.

22. Krutnik, "Desire, Transgression and James M. Cain": 33.

23. Frank Krutnik, *In a Lonely Street: Film noir, genre, masculinity* (London: Routledge, 1991): 163.

24. Jonathan Harkness, "The Sphinx without a Riddle," *Sight and Sound* 4, no. 8 (1994): 7. This combination of style, humor, and homage to the noir tradition has clearly inspired a number of subsequent filmmakers, most notably Andy and Larry Wachowski in their 1996 thriller *Bound.*

25. *Miller's Crossing* constitutes a remake of *The Glass Key*—Hammett's novel *and* Heisler's film—as hybridized with *The Red Harvest*—Hammett's novel and the films it inspired: *Yojimbo* (Akıra Kurosawa, 1961) and *A Fistful of Dollars* (Sergio Leone, 1964). Compare, for example, the machine-gun slaughter of soldiers in the latter film with the shoot-out at the Sons of Erin Social Club in *Miller's Crossing*. Interestingly, Bernardo Bertolucci, whose *Il Conformista* is a strong visual influence on both the Coens' *Blood Simple* and their *Miller's Crossing*, planned an adaptation of *The Red Harvest* in the early eighties that never came to fruition. See Bernardo Bertolucci and Marilyn Goldin, *Red Harvest;* photocopy of unpublished screenplay (first draft, June 1982) supplied by Hollywood Scripts, Enterprise House, Cathles Road, London SW12 9LD. The recent neo-noir *Last Man Standing,* like *Miller's Crossing,* is indebted to Hammett's *The Red Harvest* and the films it inspired.

26. Geoff Andrew, *The Film Handbook* (Harlow, England: Longman, 1989): 58.

27. Telotte, *Voices in the Dark:* 30.

28. J. G. Frazer, *The Golden Bough: A Study in Magic and Religion* (London: Papermac, 1987, abr. ed.): 362–68.

29. Ibid: 390.

30. The fishing motif also features prominently in the classic film noir *Out of the Past:* protagonist Jeff Bailey (Robert Mitchum) and his girlfriend Ann Miller (Virginia Huston) are fishing in the first scene in which they appear; Jeff and the femme fatale Kathie Moffat (Jane Greer) have a love scene set against fishing nets on an Acapulco beach; gangster Joe Stefanos (Paul Valentine) is killed with a fishing rod and line; two minor characters are named Fisher (Steve Brodie) and Eels (Ken Niles).

31. These are all motifs that resurface in the Coens' 1996 neo-noir *Fargo*. Here, as in Scorsese's *After Hours* and Medak's *Romeo is Bleeding,* male potency is conflated with financial acquisition. The motif of dismemberment is taken to a darkly comic extreme in the penultimate sequence in which Gaear Grimsrud (Peter Stormare) murders his criminal partner Carl Showalter (Steve Buscemi) with an axe and disposes of his body in a woodchipper.

32. As with sexual deviancy, obesity has been a signifier of corruption since the earliest films noirs. See, for example, the figures of Kasper Gutman (Sydney Greenstreet) in *The Maltese Falcon* and Phil Nosseross (Francis L. Sullivan) in *Night and the City*. Greenstreet's character in *The Maltese Falcon* is coded as corrupt on three counts: he is foreign, homosexual, and obese (note the name: gut-man).

33. Orr, *Cinema and Modernity:* 177.

34. See Neal Gabler, "A Special Angle of Vision: An Interview with Richard Price," in Richard Price, *Three Screenplays: The Color of Money, Sea of Love, and Night and the City* (London: Studio Vista, 1994), xvi-xvii.

35. Silver and Ward, *Film Noir:* 403.

36. My analysis of *Sea of Love* is based on the television version of the film which, in addition to being edited for language, includes supplementary

footage excluded in the theatrical release. The meeting of Frank and Denise (who never appears in the theatrical version of the film) is one such scene.

37. Nickolas Pappas, "*A Sea of Love* Among Men," *Film Criticism* 14, no. 3 (1990): 18.

38. Christopher Vogler, *The Writer's Journey: Mythic Structure for Storytellers and Screenwriters* (Los Angeles: Michael Wiese, 1992): 24–25.

39. Pacino's interpretation of Vincent Hanna in Michael Mann's 1995 *Heat* in many respects can be seen as a reprise of the *Sea of Love* role. Vincent, like Frank, is a dysfunctional character incapable of commitment to anything but his job. This *is* Frank further down the line, another crumbling marriage on from the prospective one to Helen.

40. Orr, *Cinema and Modernity:* 175.

CHAPTER 5: NINETIES IRONY

1. Jim Collins, "Genericity in the Nineties: Eclectic Irony and the New Sincerity," in Collins, Radner, and Preacher Collins, *Film Theory Goes to the Movies:* 247–48.

2. Ibid: 250 and 254.

3. The *Cinefile* documentary *Dark and Deadly* was broadcast by Channel 4 on 19 October 1995.

4. John P. Garry III, "A Reservoir of Allusions: *Reservoir Dogs* as a Really Postmodern Movie." Article downloaded from the World Wide Web internet site "Church of Tarantino," posted 6 March 1995.

5. This is an observation made by John Dahl in *Dark and Deadly*.

6. See B. Ruby Rich's comments in *Dark and Deadly*. See also, Rich, "Dumb Lugs and Femmes Fatales": 8.

7. See Gavin Smith, "Quentin Tarantino interview," *Film Comment* 30, no. 4 (1994): 33.

8. Since the commercial success of *Pulp Fiction,* Tarantino has persuaded Miramax to option four Leonard novels, *Rum Punch, Killshot, Bandits,* and *Freaky Deaky* (he began shooting *Jackie Brown,* his adaptation of *Rum Punch,* mid-1997). Leonard's fusion of black comedy and crime fiction was successfully adapted in *Get Shorty* (Barry Sonnenfeld, 1995), another commercially successful comic neo-noir featuring John Travolta. *Striptease* (Andrew Bergman, 1996), a Demi Moore star vehicle based on Carl Hiaasen's novel of the same title, is a less successful example of Hollywood's recent attempts to translate the popular comic noir writings of Leonard, Hiaasen, et al., to the big screen. Of course, as Jim Kitses has argued, film noir has often relied on comedy, the screwball comedy being as much a source of influence on the genre as the gangster picture or the western. See Jim Kitses, *Gun Crazy* (London: British Film Institute, 1996): 42–43.

9. Before the nineties cinematic revival a small number of Thompson's novels

had already been filmed: *The Getaway* was originally filmed by Sam Peck-inpah in 1972, *The Killer Inside Me* by Burt Kennedy in 1976, *A Hell of a Woman* (as *Série Noire*) by Alain Corneau in 1979, and *Pop. 1280* (as *Coup de Torchon*) by Bertrand Tavernier in 1982.

10. Orr, *Cinema and Modernity:* 176.

11. Haut, *Pulp Culture:* 47.

12. Gavin Smith, "Momentum and Design: Kathryn Bigelow interview," *Film Comment* 31, no. 5 (1995): 46.

13. Paul Julian Smith, *Desire Unlimited: The Cinema of Pedro Almodóvar* (London: Verso, 1994): 3.

14. See, for example, J. Hoberman, "Back on the Wild Side," *Premiere* (U.S.) 5, no. 12 (1992): 31–32.

15. Telotte, *Voices in the Dark:* 12.

16. An ex-con himself, Edward Bunker has a cameo in *Reservoir Dogs* as Mr. Blue. His 1973 novel *No Beast So Fierce,* written while he was in prison, was filmed in 1978 as *Straight Time* by Ulu Grosbard and starred Dustin Hoffman. The influence of Bunker's novel is acknowledged by both Quentin Tarantino and James Ellroy, two of the leading figures in the respective cinematic and literary noir revivals, on the covers of the No Exit Press edition of the book published in 1993.

17. The structure of *Reservoir Dogs* is as follows:

    A   Pre-credits sequence, followed by the credits.

    B   Mr. Orange and Mr. White on the road; aftermath of Orange's injury.

    C1   The warehouse; arrival of Mr. Orange and Mr. White, followed by the arrival of Mr. Pink.

    D   *FLASHBACK:* Mr. Pink's escape from the police.

    C2   The warehouse.

    E   Title card: "Mr. White." *FLASHBACK:* Mr. White hired by Joe Cabot.

    C3   The warehouse; Mr. White and Mr. Pink fight, followed by the arrival of Mr. Blonde.

    F   Title card: "Mr. Blonde." *FLASHBACK:* Mr. Blonde visits Cabot and Nice Guy Eddie; hired for the jewelry job.

    C4   Nice Guy Eddie on the road. The warehouse; Marvin Nash is beaten up. Eddie arrives. Eddie, Mr. White, and Mr. Pink depart. Mr. Blonde tortures Marvin. Mr. Orange kills Mr. Blonde.

    G1   Title card: "Mr. Orange." *FLASHBACK:* Freddy Newendyke/Mr. Orange undercover.

    H   *FLASHBACK WITHIN A FLASHBACK:* The commode story rehearsed with Holdaway (Randy Brooks), performed for the benefit of Cabot, Nice Guy Eddie, and Mr. White and fantasized (i.e., temporary shift from the space-time continuum of the rest of the narrative).

G2 *FLASHBACK:* Mr. Orange undercover. Mr. Orange, Mr. White, Mr. Pink, and Nice Guy Eddie drive to the briefing with Cabot. Pseudonyms are allocated. Mr. Orange and Mr. White rehearse the robbery. (N.B. Early in this sequence the POV shifts briefly to the police officers tailing Mr. Orange.)

G3 *FLASHBACK:* The aftermath of the robbery. Death of Mr. Brown. Escape of Mr. Orange and Mr. White. Mr. Orange is shot.

C5 The warehouse; the others return and are followed by Cabot. All the criminals die, in addition to Marvin and Mr. Orange. Followed by end credits.

The temporal order of *Reservoir Dogs*'s narrative is therefore as follows: E, F, [H], G1, G2, A, D, G3, B, C1–5.

18. There is a degree of irony in Mr. Orange's betrayal of Mr. White, in that it was Harvey Keitel who played Charlie in *Mean Streets* and was betrayed by De Niro's Johnny Boy. This is one of many examples of the simultaneous movie referentiality and ironization of past films that characterizes *Reservoir Dogs*.

19. Vogler, *Writer's Journey:* 78.

20. The prioritization of the spoken word in the films of twenty- and thirty-something directors like Tarantino, Hal Hartley, Richard Linklater, John Singleton, Kevin Smith, and Edward Burns is one of the most significant developments in contemporary American cinema. It is further illustrative of the independent sector's self-conscious attempt to distance itself from the high-tech gloss and verbal inanities which characterize much of the Hollywood mainstream.

21. See Hilary Henkin, *Romeo is Bleeding;* photocopy of unpublished screenplay (revised first draft, 8 November 1987) supplied by Hollywood Scripts, Enterprise House, Cathles Road, London SW12 9LD.

22. As originally conceived by Henkin, Grimaldi's interlocutor would have been seen and heard on screen. See Henkin, *Romeo is Bleeding:* 3, and 134–35.

23. In the original screenplay, Mona's left hand was also missing two middle fingers: Henkin, *Romeo is Bleeding:* 9. There is a degree of uncertainty as to whether this image is carried into the film. The arm and hand Mona places next to Sheri's body appears to be missing these fingers, but elsewhere in the film none of her fingers are missing.

24. In fact, in the slow motion sequence in which Jack attempts to commit suicide—perhaps seeking, like Jake in his final bout with "Sugar" Ray Robinson, retribution for his sins—the sound track is dominated by the animalistic noises that accompany La Motta's fights in Scorsese's film.

25. See B. Ruby Rich's comments on *One False Move* in the *Cinefile* documentary *Dark and Deadly* which was broadcast by Channel 4 on 19 October 1995.

26. Manohla Dargis, "Pulp Instinct," *Sight and Sound* 4, no. 5 (1994): 8.

27. Foster Hirsch, *The Dark Side of the Screen: Film Noir* (New York: Da Capo, 1981): 20.

28. Lyons, *Independent Visions:* 123.

29. Rich, "Dumb Lugs and Femmes Fatales": 10.

30. The concepts of moral choice, self-esteem and social construction are discussed by Carl Franklin in the *Cinefile* documentary *Dark and Deadly* which was broadcast by Channel 4 on 19 October 1995.

31. Nick James, "One False Move," *Sight and Sound* 3, no. 4 (1993): 53.

32. Significantly in the forties film version, *Murder, My Sweet,* this is a white bar.

33. I do not mean to suggest necessarily that these scores were actually performed by African-American musicians, but rather that African-American culture is present in these films through the medium of jazz or blues music. See also, for example, the jazz improvization sequence in *Phantom Lady* or even Dennis Hopper's recent neo-noir *The Hot Spot,* the sound track of which consists almost entirely of classic blues tracks.

34. See, for example, Davis, *City of Quartz:* 267–322.

35. On "black rage," see Diawara, *"Noir* by *Noirs"*: 266.

36. Ibid: 263.

37. These are Scorsese's closing remarks in *Century of Cinema: A Personal Journey with Martin Scorsese through American Movies,* a three-part documentary broadcast by Channel 4 between 21 May and 4 June 1995.

Select Filmography of American Film Noir

FORTIES AND FIFTIES

Abandoned (Joseph M. Newman, 1949)

Accused, The (William Dieterle, 1949)

Ace in the Hole/Big Carnival, The (Billy Wilder, 1951)

Act of Violence (Fred Zinnemann, 1949)

All the King's Men (Robert Rossen, 1949)

Among the Living (Stuart Heisler, 1941)

Angel Face (Otto Preminger, 1953)

Another Man's Poison (Irving Rapper, 1952)

Appointment with Danger (Lewis Allen, 1951)

Armored Car Robbery (Richard Fleischer, 1950)

Asphalt Jungle, The (John Huston, 1950)

Behind Locked Doors (Budd Boetticher, 1948)

Berlin Express (Jacques Tourneur, 1948)

Between Midnight and Dawn (Gordon Douglas, 1950)

Beware, My Lovely (Harry Horner, 1952)

Beyond a Reasonable Doubt (Fritz Lang, 1956)

Big Clock, The (John Farrow, 1948)

Big Combo, The (Joseph H. Lewis, 1955)

Big Heat, The (Fritz Lang, 1953)

Big Knife, The (Robert Aldrich, 1955)

Big Sleep, The (Howard Hawks, 1946)

Black Angel (Roy William Neill, 1946)

Black Tuesday (Hugo Fregonese, 1954)

Blackout (Terence Fisher, 1954)

Blue Dahlia, The (George Marshall, 1946)

Blue Gardenia, The (Fritz Lang, 1953)

Blues in the Night (Anatole Litvak, 1941)

Body and Soul (Robert Rossen, 1947)

Boomerang (Elia Kazan, 1947)

Border Incident (Anthony Mann, 1949)

Born to Be Bad (Nicholas Ray, 1950)

Born to Kill/Lady of Deceit (Robert Wise, 1947)

Brasher Doubloon, The (John Brahm, 1947)

Bribe, The (Robert Z. Leonard, 1949)

Brothers Rico, The (Phil Karlson, 1957)

Brute Force (Jules Dassin, 1947)

Burglar, The (Paul Wendkos, 1957)

Bury Me Dead (Bernard Vorhaus, 1947)

Caged (John Cromwell, 1950)

Call Northside 777 (Henry Hathaway, 1948)

Captive City, The (Robert Wise, 1952)

Capture, The (John Sturges, 1950)

Caught (Max Ophüls, 1949)

Champion (Mark Robson, 1949)

Chase, The (Arthur Ripley, 1946)

Chicago Deadline (Lewis Allen, 1949)

Christmas Holiday (Robert Siodmak, 1944)

City Across the River (Maxwell Shane, 1949)

City of Fear (Irving Lerner, 1959)

City That Never Sleeps (John H. Auer, 1953)

Clash by Night (Fritz Lang, 1952)

Conflict (Curtis Bernhardt, 1945)

Convicted (Henry Levin, 1950)

Cornered (Edward Dmytryk, 1945)

Crack-Up (Irving Reis, 1946)

Crime of Passion (Gerd Oswald, 1957)

Crime Wave (André de Toth, 1954)

Crimson Kimono, The (Samuel Fuller, 1959)

Criss Cross (Robert Siodmak, 1949)

Crooked Way, The (Robert Florey, 1949)

Crossfire (Edward Dmytryk, 1947)

Cry Danger (Robert Parrish, 1951)

Cry in the Night, A (Frank Tuttle, 1956)

Cry of the City (Robert Siodmak, 1948)

D.O.A. (Rudolph Maté, 1950)

Dark City (William Dieterle, 1950)

Dark Corner, The (Henry Hathaway, 1946)

Dark Mirror, The (Robert Siodmak, 1946)

Dark Passage (Delmer Daves, 1947)

Dark Past, The (Rudolph Maté, 1948)

Dark Waters (André de Toth, 1944)

Dead Reckoning (John Cromwell, 1947)

Deadline at Dawn (Harold Clurman, 1946)

Decoy (Jack Bernhard, 1946)

Destiny (Reginald LeBorg and Julien Duvivier, 1944)

Detective Story (William Wyler, 1951)

Detour (Edgar G. Ulmer, 1945)

Devil Thumbs a Ride, The (Felix Feist, 1947)

Don't Bother to Knock (Roy Baker, 1952)

Double Indemnity (Billy Wilder, 1944)

Double Life, A (George Cukor, 1948)

Edge of Doom (Mark Robson, 1950)

Enforcer, The (Bretaigne Windust and Raoul Walsh, 1951)

Fall Guy (Reginald Le Borg, 1947)

Fallen Angel (Otto Preminger, 1946)

Fallen Sparrow, The (Richard Wallace, 1943)

Fear in the Night (Maxwell Shane, 1947)

File on Thelma Jordan, The (Robert Siodmak, 1949)

Flame, The (John H. Auer, 1947)

Follow Me Quietly (Richard Fleischer, 1949)

Force of Evil (Abraham Polonsky, 1948)

Framed (Richard Wallace, 1947)

Gangster, The (Gordon Wiles, 1947)

Gilda (Charles Vidor, 1946)

Glass Key, The (Stuart Heisler, 1942)

Glass Web, The (Jack Arnold, 1953)

Gun Crazy/Deadly is the Female (Joseph H. Lewis, 1950)

Harder They Fall, The (Mark Robson, 1956)

He Ran All the Way (John Berry, 1951)

He Walked by Night (Alfred Werker and Anthony Mann, 1949)

High Sierra (Raoul Walsh, 1940)

High Wall, The (Curtis Bernhardt, 1947)

Hitch-Hiker, The (Ida Lupino, 1953)

House of Bamboo (Samuel Fuller, 1955)

House of Strangers (Joseph L. Mankiewicz, 1949)

House on 92nd Street, The (Henry Hathaway, 1945)

House on Telegraph Hill (Robert Wise, 1951)

Human Desire (Fritz Lang, 1954)

I Died a Thousand Times (Stuart Heisler, 1955)

I, the Jury (Harry Essex, 1953)

I Walk Alone (Byron Haskin, 1948)

I Was a Communist for the F.B.I. (Gordon Douglas, 1951)

In a Lonely Place (Nicholas Ray, 1950)

Johnny O'Clock (Robert Rossen, 1947)

Johnny Stool Pigeon (William Castle, 1949)

Killer's Kiss (Stanley Kubrick, 1955)

Killers, The (Robert Siodmak, 1946)

Killing, The (Stanley Kubrick, 1956)

Kiss Before Dying, A (Gerd Oswald, 1956)

Kiss Me Deadly (Robert Aldrich, 1955)

Kiss of Death (Henry Hathaway, 1947)

Kiss the Blood Off My Hands (Norman Foster, 1948)

Kiss Tomorrow Goodbye (Gordon Douglas, 1950)

Lady from Shanghai, The (Orson Welles, 1948)

Lady in the Lake (Robert Montgomery, 1947)

Laura (Otto Preminger, 1944)

Leave Her to Heaven (John M. Stahl, 1945)

Lineup, The (Don Siegel, 1958)

Locket, The (John Brahm, 1947)

M (Joseph Losey, 1951)

Maltese Falcon, The (John Huston, 1941)

Man I Love, The (Raoul Walsh, 1946)

Man in the Attic (Hugo Fregonese, 1953)

Mask of Dimitrios, The (Jean Negulesco, 1944)

Mildred Pierce (Michael Curtiz, 1945)

Mob, The (Robert Parrish, 1951)

Murder By Contract (Irving Lerner, 1958)

Murder, My Sweet/Farewell, My Lovely (Edward Dmytryk, 1944)

My Name is Julia Ross (Joseph H. Lewis, 1945)

Naked City, The (Jules Dassin, 1948)

Narrow Margin, The (Richard Fleischer, 1952)

Niagara (Henry Hathaway, 1953)

New York Confidential (Russell Rouse, 1955)

Night and the City (Jules Dassin, 1950)

Night Has a Thousand Eyes, The (John Farrow, 1948)

Night of the Hunter, The (Charles Laughton, 1955)

Nightfall (Jacques Tourneur, 1957)

Nightmare (Maxwell Shane, 1956)

Nightmare Alley (Edmund Goulding, 1947)

No Man of Her Own (Mitchell Leisen, 1950)

No Way Out (Joseph L. Mankiewicz, 1950)

Nobody Lives Forever (Jean Negulesco, 1946)

Nora Prentiss (Vincent Sherman, 1947)

Odds Against Tomorrow (Robert Wise, 1960)

On Dangerous Ground (Nicholas Ray, 1952)

Once a Thief (W. Lee Wilder, 1950)

One Way Street (Hugo Fregonese, 1950)

Out of the Past/Build My Gallows High (Jacques Tourneur, 1947)

Panic in the Streets (Elia Kazan, 1950)

Party Girl (Nicholas Ray, 1958)

Phantom Lady (Robert Siodmak, 1944)

Phenix City Story, The (Phil Karlson, 1955)

Pickup on South Street (Samuel Fuller, 1953)

Pitfall, The (André de Toth, 1948)

Place in the Sun, A (George Stevens, 1951)

Possessed (Curtis Bernhardt, 1947)

Postman Always Rings Twice, The (Tay Garnett, 1946)

Prowler, The (Joseph Losey, 1951)

Pursued (Raoul Walsh, 1947)

Pushover (Richard Quine, 1954)

Racket, The (John Cromwell, 1951)

Railroaded (Anthony Mann, 1947)

Ramrod (André de Toth, 1947)

Rancho Notorious (Fritz Lang, 1952)

Raw Deal (Anthony Mann, 1948)

Reckless Moment, The (Max Ophüls, 1949)

Red House, The (Delmer Daves, 1947)

Ride the Pink Horse (Robert Montgomery, 1947)

Road House (Jean Negulesco, 1948)

Rogue Cop (Roy Rowland, 1954)

Ruthless (Edgar G. Ulmer, 1948)

Scarlet Street (Fritz Lang, 1945)

Scene of the Crime (Roy Rowland, 1949)

Secret Beyond the Door (Fritz Lang, 1948)

Set-Up, The (Robert Wise, 1949)

711 Ocean Drive (Joseph M. Newman, 1950)

Seventh Victim, The (Mark Robson, 1943)

Shadow of a Doubt (Alfred Hitchcock, 1943)

Shanghai Gesture, The (Josef von Sternberg, 1941)

Shock (Alfred Werker, 1946)

Sleep, My Love (Douglas Sirk, 1948)

Sleeping City, The (George Sherman, 1950)

Slightly Scarlet (Allan Dwan, 1956)

So Dark the Night (Joseph H. Lewis, 1946)

Sorry, Wrong Number (Anatole Litvak, 1948)

Sniper, The (Edward Dmytryk, 1952)

Station West (Sidney Lanfield, 1948)

Strange Affair of Uncle Harry, The (Robert Siodmak, 1945)

Strange Love of Martha Ivers, The (Lewis Milestone, 1946)

Stranger, The (Orson Welles, 1946)

Stranger on the Third Floor (Boris Ingster, 1940)

Strangers on a Train (Alfred Hitchcock, 1951)

Street with No Name, The (William Keighley, 1948)

Sudden Fear (David Miller, 1952)

Suddenly (Lewis Allen, 1954)

Sunset Boulevard (Billy Wilder, 1950)

Suspense (Frank Tuttle, 1946)

Sweet Smell of Success (Alexander Mackendrick, 1957)

T-Men (Anthony Mann, 1948)

They Live By Night (Nicholas Ray, 1948)

They Won't Believe Me (Irving Pichel, 1947)

Thieves' Highway (Jules Dassin, 1949)

This Gun for Hire (Frank Tuttle, 1942)

Touch of Evil (Orson Welles, 1958)

Undercover Man, The (Joseph H. Lewis, 1949)

Undercurrent (Vincente Minnelli, 1946)

Unfaithful, The (Vincent Sherman, 1947)

Union Station (Rudolph Maté, 1950)

Unsuspected, The (Michael Curtiz, 1947)

Vertigo (Alfred Hitchcock, 1958)

Web, The (Michael Gordon, 1947)

When Strangers Marry/Betrayed (William Castle, 1944)

Where Danger Lives (John Farrow, 1950)

Where the Sidewalk Ends (Otto Preminger, 1950)

While the City Sleeps (Fritz Lang, 1956)

Whirlpool (Otto Preminger, 1949)

White Heat (Raoul Walsh, 1949)

Window, The (Ted Tetzlaff, 1949)

Woman in the Window, The (Fritz Lang, 1944)

Woman on Pier 13, The/I Married a Communist (Robert Stevenson, 1949)

Woman on the Run (Norman Foster, 1950)

Woman's Secret, A (Nicholas Ray, 1949)

SIXTIES AND SEVENTIES

All the President's Men (Alan J. Pakula, 1976)

Badlands (Terence Malick, 1973)

Big Sleep, The (Michael Winner, 1978)

Bonnie and Clyde (Arthur Penn, 1967)

Brainstorm (William Conrad, 1965)

Cape Fear (J. Lee Thompson, 1962)

Chandler (Paul Magwood, 1972)

Chinatown (Roman Polanski, 1974)

Conversation, The (Francis Ford Coppola, 1974)

Death Wish (Michael Winner, 1974)

Detective, The (Gordon Douglas, 1968)

Dirty Harry (Don Siegel, 1971)

Dog Day Afternoon (Sidney Lumet, 1975)

Driver, The (Walter Hill, 1976)

Drowning Pool, The (Stuart Rosenberg, 1976)

Farewell, My Lovely (Dick Richards, 1975)

French Connection, The (William Friedkin, 1971)

French Connection II (John Frankenheimer, 1975)

Friends of Eddie Coyle, The (Peter Yates, 1973)

Getaway, The (Sam Peckinpah, 1972)

Goodnight, My Love (Peter Hyams, 1972)

Hardcore (Paul Schrader, 1979)

Harper (Jack Smight, 1966)

Hickey & Boggs (Robert Culp, 1972)

Honeymoon Killers, The (Leonard Kastle, 1970)

Incident, The (Larry Peerce, 1967)

In Cold Blood (Richard Brooks, 1967)

Killer Inside Me, The (Burt Kennedy, 1976)

Killing of a Chinese Bookie, The (John Cassavetes, 1976)

Klute (Alan J. Pakula, 1971)

Late Show, The (Robert Benton, 1977)

Long Goodbye, The (Robert Altman, 1973)

Man-Trap (Edmond O'Brien, 1961)

Marlowe (Paul Bogart, 1969)

Mean Streets (Martin Scorsese, 1973)

Mickey One (Arthur Penn, 1965)

Mirage (Edward Dmytryk, 1965)

Money Trap (Burt Kennedy, 1966)

Naked Kiss, The (Samuel Fuller, 1964)

New York, New York (Martin Scorsese, 1977)

Night Moves (Arthur Penn, 1975)

Outfit, The (John Flynn, 1974)

Parallax View, The (Alan J. Pakula, 1974)

Play Misty for Me (Clint Eastwood, 1971)

Point Blank (John Boorman, 1967)

Rolling Thunder (John Flynn, 1977)

Serpico (Sidney Lumet, 1973)

Shock Corridor (Samuel Fuller, 1963)

Taxi Driver (Martin Scorsese, 1976)

They Shoot Horses Don't They? (Sydney Pollack, 1969)

Thieves Like Us (Robert Altman, 1974)

Third Voice, The (Hubert Cornfield, 1960)

Three Days of the Condor (Sydney Pollack, 1975)

Underworld USA (Samuel Fuller, 1961)

Yakuza, The (Sidney Pollack, 1975)

EIGHTIES AND NINETIES

After Dark, My Sweet (James Foley, 1990)

After Hours (Martin Scorsese, 1985)

Against All Odds (Taylor Hackford, 1984)

American Gigolo (Paul Schrader, 1980)

Angel Heart (Alan Parker, 1987)

Another 48 Hours (Walter Hill, 1990)

At Close Range (James Foley, 1986)

Atlantic City (Louis Malle, 1981)

Bad Influence (Curtis Hanson, 1990)

Barton Fink (Joel and Ethan Coen, 1991)

Basic Instinct (Paul Verhoeven, 1992)

Best Seller (John Flynn, 1987)

Big Easy, The (Jim McBride, 1987)

Black Rain (Ridley Scott, 1989)

Black Widow (Bob Rafelson, 1987)

Blade Runner (Ridley Scott, 1982)

Blood Simple (Joel and Ethan Coen, 1984)

Blow Out (Brian DePalma, 1981)

Blue Steel (Kathryn Bigelow, 1990)

Body Chemistry (Kristine Peterson, 1990)

Body Heat (Lawrence Kasdan, 1981)

Bound (Andy and Larry Wachowski, 1996)

Boy Called Hate, A (Mitch Marcus, 1995)

Blue Velvet (David Lynch, 1986)

Boiling Point (James B. Harris, 1993)

Breathless (Jim McBride, 1983)

Cape Fear (Martin Scorsese, 1991)

Carlito's Way (Brian DePalma, 1993)

Casino (Martin Scorsese, 1995)

Cat Chaser (Abel Ferrara, 1989)

Clockers (Spike Lee, 1995)

Close-up (Przemyslaw Reut, 1995)

Cop (James B. Harris, 1988)

D.O.A. (Rocky Morton and Annabel Jankel, 1988)

Dark Wind, The (Errol Morris, 1992)

Dead Again (Kenneth Branagh, 1991)

Dead Presidents (Albert and Allen Hughes, 1995)

Deceived (Damian Harris, 1991)

Deep Cover (Bill Duke, 1992)

Delusion (Carl Colpaert, 1991)

Desperate Hours (Michael Cimino, 1990)

Devil in a Blue Dress (Carl Franklin, 1995)

Diary of a Hitman (Roy London, 1992)

Eight Million Ways To Die (Hal Ashby and Charles Mulvehill, 1986)

Equinox (Alan Rudolph, 1993)

Fargo (Joel and Ethan Coen, 1996)

Fatal Attraction (Adrian Lyne, 1987)

Femme Fatale (André Guttfreund, 1991)

52 Pick-up (John Frankenheimer, 1986)

Final Analysis (Phil Joanou, 1992)

Flash of Green, A (Victor Nuñez, 1984)

48 Hours (Walter Hill, 1982)

Genuine Risk (Kurt Voss, 1990)

Getaway, The (Roger Donaldson, 1994)

Grifters, The (Stephen Frears, 1990)

Guilty as Sin (Sidney Lumet, 1993)

Guncrazy (Tamra Davis, 1992)

Hammett (Wim Wenders, 1983)

Hand that Rocks the Cradle, The (Curtis Hanson, 1992)

Heat (Michael Mann, 1995)

Heaven's Prisoners (Phil Joanou, 1995)

Hit List (William Lustig, 1989)

Homicide (David Mamet, 1991)

Hot Spot, The (Dennis Hopper, 1990)

House of Games (David Mamet, 1987)

House on Carroll Street, The (Peter Yates, 1988)

Impulse (Sondra Locke, 1990)

Internal Affairs (Mike Figgis, 1990)

Jade (William Friedkin, 1995)

Jagged Edge (Richard Marquand, 1985)

Jezebel's Kiss (Harvey Keith, 1990)

Johnny Handsome (Walter Hill, 1989)

Johnny Mnemonic (Robert Longo, 1995)

Kalifornia (Dominic Senna, 1993)

Kill Me Again (John Dahl, 1989)

Killing Time, The (Rick King, 1987)

Kill-Off, The (Maggie Greenwald, 1990)

Kiss Before Dying, A (James Dearden, 1991)

Kiss of Death (Barbet Schroeder, 1995)

Last Boy Scout, The (Tony Scott, 1991)

Last Man Standing (Walter Hill, 1996)

Last Seduction, The (John Dahl, 1994)

Light Sleeper (Paul Schrader, 1992)

Long Kiss Goodnight, The (Renny Harlin, 1996)

Love Crimes (Lizzie Borden, 1992)

Manhunter (Michael Mann, 1986)

Masquerade (Bob Swaim, 1988)

Miami Blues (George Armitage, 1990)

Miller's Crossing (Joel and Ethan Coen, 1990)

Morning After, The (Sidney Lumet, 1986)

Mortal Thoughts (Alan Rudolph, 1991)

Mugshot (Matt Mahurin, 1996)

Mulholland Falls (Lee Tamahori, 1995)

Narrow Margin (Peter Hyams, 1990)

New Jack City (Mario Van Peebles, 1991)

Nick of Time (John Badham, 1995)

Night and the City (Irwin Winkler, 1992)

Night of the Hunter, The (David Greene, 1991)

Nightwatch (Ole Bornedal, 1996)

No Way Out (Roger Donaldson, 1987)

Normal Life (John McNaughton, 1996)

One False Move (Carl Franklin, 1992)

P.I. Private Investigations (Nigel Dick, 1987)

Pacific Heights (John Schlesinger, 1990)

Past Midnight (Jan Eliasberg, 1992)

Postman Always Rings Twice, The (Bob Rafelson, 1981)

Presumed Innocent (Alan J. Pakula, 1990)

Public Eye, The (Howard Franklin, 1992)

Pulp Fiction (Quentin Tarantino, 1994)

Q and A (Sidney Lumet, 1990)

Rage in Harlem, A (Bill Duke, 1991)

Raging Bull (Martin Scorsese, 1980)

Red Rock West (John Dahl, 1992)

Relentless (William Lustig, 1989)

Reservoir Dogs (Quentin Tarantino, 1992)

Romeo is Bleeding (Peter Medak, 1994)

Ruby (John Mackenzie, 1992)

Rush (Lili Fini Zanuck, 1991)

Scissors (Frank De Felitta, 1991)

Sea of Love (Harold Becker, 1989)

Seven (David Fincher, 1995)

Shattered (Wolfgang Petersen, 1991)

Silence of the Lambs, The (Jonathan Demme, 1991)

Single White Female (Barbet Schroeder, 1992)

Slamdance (Wayne Wang, 1987)

Sleeping with the Enemy (Joseph Ruben, 1991)

Someone to Watch over Me (Ridley Scott, 1987)

Something Wild (Jonathan Demme, 1986)

Strange Days (Kathryn Bigelow, 1995)

Suture (Scott McGehee and David Siegel, 1993)

Terminator (James Cameron, 1984)

Thief (Michael Mann, 1981)

Things To Do In Denver When You're Dead (Gary Fleder, 1995)

Throwing Down (Lawrence O'Neil, 1996)

Thunderheart (Michael Apted, 1992)

Tightrope (Richard Tuggle, 1984)

To Live and Die in L.A. (William Friedkin, 1985)

Trespass (Walter Hill, 1992)

Bibliography

FILM NOIR

Blaser, John. *No Place for a Woman: The Family in Film Noir* (Master's dissertation, Northwestern University, 1994). Electronic edition of the dissertation downloaded from the World Wide Web site of the same title, posted in fall 1994.

Borde, Raymond, and Étienne Chaumeton. *Panorama du film noir américain (1941–1953)* (Paris: Éditions de Minuit, 1955).

———. "Towards a Definition of *Film Noir*," translated by Alain Silver, in Alain Silver and James Ursini (Eds.), *Film Noir Reader* (New York: Limelight Editions, 1996): 17–25.

Bordwell, David. "The case of film noir," in David Bordwell, Janet Staiger, and Kristin Thompson, *The Classical Hollywood Cinema: Film Style and Mode of Production to 1960* (London: Routledge, 1985): 74–77.

Brion, Patrick. *Le Film Noir* (Paris: Éditions Fernand Nathan, 1991).

Buschbaum, Jonathan. "Tame Wolves and Phoney Claims: Paranoia and Film Noir," in Ian Cameron (Ed.), *The Movie Book of Film Noir* (London: Studio Vista, 1992): 88–97. First published in *Persistence of Vision* 3/4 (1986).

Butler, Jeremy. "*Miami Vice* and the Legacy of *Film Noir*," *Journal of Popular Film and Television* 13, no. 3 (1985): 127–38. Reprinted in Alain Silver and James Ursini (Eds.), *Film Noir Reader* (New York: Limelight Editions, 1996): 289–305.

Cameron, Ian (Ed.). *The Movie Book of Film Noir* (London: Studio Vista, 1992).

Casas, Quim. "Cine policíaco: Tiempos fructíferos para gángsters y psicópatas," *Dirigido* no. 191 (1991): 54–63.

Chartier, Jean-Pierre. "Les Américains aussi font des films 'noirs'," *Revue du Cinéma* 2 (1946): 67–70.

Cieutat, Michel. "Le film noir," *CinémAction* 68 (1993): 34–45.

———. "La rue du film noir ou le mirage américain," *CinémAction* 75 (1995): 146–52.

Coma, Javier, and José Maria Latorre. *Luces y Sombras del Cine Negro* (Barcelona: Colección «Dirigido por . . . », 1981).

Cooper, Stephen. "Sex/Knowledge/Power in the Detective Genre," *Film Quarterly* 42, no. 3 (1989): 23–31.

Copjec, Joan. "The Phenomenal Nonphenomenal: Private Space in *Film Noir*," in Joan Copjec (Ed.), *Shades of Noir: A Reader* (London and New York: Verso, 1993): 167–97.

——— (Ed.). *Shades of Noir: A Reader* (London and New York: Verso, 1993).

Cowie, Elizabeth. "*Film Noir* and Women," in Joan Copjec (Ed.), *Shades of Noir: A Reader* (London and New York: Verso, 1993): 121–65.

Cozarinsky, Edgardo. "American Film Noir," in Richard Roud (Ed.), *Cinema: A Critical Dictionary,* Volume I (London: Secker and Warburg, 1980): 57–64.

Crowther, Bruce. *Film Noir: Reflections in a Dark Mirror* (London: Virgin Books, 1990). First published by Columbus Books in 1988.

Damico, James. "Film Noir: A Modest Proposal," *Film Reader* 3 (1978): 48–57. Reprinted in Alain Silver and James Ursini (Eds.), *Film Noir Reader* (New York: Limelight Editions, 1996): 95–105.

Doss, Erika L. "Edward Hopper, *Nighthawks* and *Film Noir*," *Post Script* 2, no. 2 (1983): 14–36.

Durgnat, Raymond. "Paint it Black: The Family Tree of Film Noir," *Cinema* (UK) 6/7 (1970): 49–56. Reprinted in Alain Silver and James Ursini (Eds.), *Film Noir Reader* (New York: Limelight Editions, 1996): 37–51.

Dyer, Richard. "Homosexuality and film noir," in Richard Dyer, *The Matter of Images: Essays on Representations* (London and New York: Routledge, 1993): 52–72. First published in *Jump Cut* 16 (1977).

Erickson, Todd. "Kill Me Again: Movement Becomes Genre," in Alain Silver and James Ursini (Eds.), *Film Noir Reader* (New York: Limelight Editions, 1996): 307–29.

Ewing, Dale E. Jr., "Film Noir: Style and Content," *Journal of Popular Film and Television* 16, no. 2 (1988): 60–69.

Farber, Stephen. "Violence and the Bitch Goddess," *Film Comment* 10, no. 6 (1974): 8–11.

Frank, Nino. "Un nouveau genre 'policier': l'aventure criminelle," *L'Ecran Français* 61 (1946): 8–9 and 14.

Gallafent, Edward. "Echo Park: Film Noir in the Seventies," in Ian Cameron (Ed.), *The Movie Book of Film Noir* (London: Studio Vista, 1992): 254–66.

Gledhill, Christine. "*Klute* 1: a contemporary film noir and feminist criticism," in E. Ann Kaplan (Ed.), *Women in Film Noir* (London: British Film Institute, 1980, rev. ed.): 6–21. First published in 1978.

———. "*Klute* 2: feminism and *Klute*," in E. Ann Kaplan (Ed.), *Women in Film Noir* (London: British Film Institute, 1980, rev. ed.): 112–28.

Gregory, Charles. "Living Life Sideways," *Journal of Popular Film* 5, nos. 3/4 (1976): 289–311.

Grist, Leighton. "Moving Targets and Black Widows: Film Noir in Modern Hollywood," in Ian Cameron (Ed.), *The Movie Book of Film Noir* (London: Studio Vista, 1992): 267–85.

————. "Out of the Past a.k.a. Build My Gallows High," in Ian Cameron (Ed.), *The Movie Book of Film Noir* (London: Studio Vista, 1992): 203–12.

Gross, Larry. "Film Après Noir," *Film Comment* 12, no. 4 (1976): 44–49.

Harvey, Sylvia. "Woman's place: the absent family of film noir," in E. Ann Kaplan (Ed.), *Women in Film Noir* (London: British Film Institute, 1980, rev. ed.): 22–34. First published in 1978.

Higham, Charles, and Joel Greenberg. "Black Cinema," in Charles Higham and Joel Greenberg, *Hollywood in the Forties* (Cranbury, N.J.: A. S. Barnes, 1968): 19–36.

Hirsch, Foster. *The Dark Side of the Screen: Film Noir* (New York: Da Capo, 1981).

Hollinger, Karen. "*Film Noir,* Voice-Over, and the Femme Fatale," in Alain Silver and James Ursini (Eds.), *Film Noir Reader* (New York: Limelight Editions, 1996): 243–59.

Jameson, Fredric. "The Synoptic Chandler," in Joan Copjec (Ed.), *Shades of Noir: A Reader* (London and New York: Verso, 1993): 33–56.

Jameson, Richard T. "Son of Noir," *Film Comment* 10, no. 6 (1974): 30–33.

Kaplan, E. Ann (Ed.). *Women in Film Noir* (London: British Film Institute, 1980, rev. ed.).

Kemp, Philip. "From the Nightmare Factory: HUAC and the Politics of Noir," *Sight and Sound* 55, no. 4 (1986): 266–70.

Kerr, Paul. "Out of What Past? Notes on the B Film Noir," *Screen Education* 32/33 (1979/80): 45–65. Reprinted in Alain Silver and James Ursini (Eds.), *Film Noir Reader* (New York: Limelight Editions, 1996): 107–27.

Kitses, Jim. *Gun Crazy* (London: British Film Institute, 1996).

Krutnik, Frank. "Desire, Transgression and James M. Cain," *Screen* 23, no. 1 (1982): 31–44.

————. *In a Lonely Street: Film noir, genre, masculinity* (London and New York: Routledge, 1991).

Leibman, Nina C. "The Family Spree of Film Noir," *The Journal of Popular Film and Television* 16, no. 4 (1988): 168–84.

Luhr, William. *Raymond Chandler and Film* (Tallahassee: Florida State University Press, 1991, 2nd ed.).

Lyons, Donald. "Flaws in the Iris: The Private Eye in the Seventies," *Film Comment* 29, no. 4 (1993): 44–53.

Maltby, Richard. "The Politics of the Maladjusted Text," in Ian Cameron (Ed.), *The Movie Book of Film Noir* (London: Studio Vista, 1992): 39–48. First published in *Journal of American Studies* 18 (1984).

Marling, William. "On the Relation Between American *Roman Noir* and *Film Noir,*" *Literature/Film Quarterly* 21, no. 3 (1993): 178–93.

Maxfield, James F. (Ed.). *The Fatal Woman: Sources of Male Anxiety in American Film Noir, 1941–1991* (Madison, N.J.: Fairleigh Dickinson University Press, 1996).

McArthur, Colin. *The Big Heat* (London: British Film Institute, 1992).

———. *Underworld USA* (London: Secker and Warburg/British Film Institute, 1972).

Osteen, Mark. "The Big Secret: *Film Noir* and Nuclear Fear," *Journal of Popular Film and Television* 22, no. 2 (1994): 79–90.

Ottoson, Robert. *A Reference Guide to the American Film Noir* (Metuchen, N.J.: Scarecrow, 1981).

Palmer, R. Barton. *Hollywood's Dark Cinema: The American Film Noir* (New York: Twayne, 1994).

———. *Perspectives on Film Noir* (New York: G. K. Hall, 1996).

Place, Janey. "Women in film noir," in E. Ann Kaplan (Ed.), *Women in Film Noir* (London: British Film Institute, 1980, rev. ed.): 35–67.

Place, J. A., and L. S. Petersen. "Some Visual Motifs of Film Noir," in B. Nichols (Ed.), *Movies and Methods,* Volume I (Berkeley, Los Angeles, and London: University of California Press, 1976): 325–38. First published in *Film Comment* 10, no. 1 (1974).

Polan, Dana. "Blind Insights and Dark Passages: The Problem of Placement in Forties Film," *The Velvet Light Trap* 20 (1983): 27–33.

———. "College Course File: Film Noir," *Journal of Film and Video* 37, no. 2 (1985): 75–83.

———. *In a Lonely Place* (London: British Film Institute, 1993).

Porfirio, Robert G. "*The Killers:* Expressiveness of Sound and Image," in Alain Silver and James Ursini (Eds.), *Film Noir Reader* (New York: Limelight Editions, 1996): 177–87.

———. "No Way Out: Existential Motifs in Film Noir," *Sight and Sound* 45, no. 4 (1976): 212–17. Reprinted in Alain Silver and James Ursini (Eds.), *Film Noir Reader* (New York: Limelight Editions, 1996): 77–93.

———. "Whatever Happened to the *Film Noir?*: The Postman Always Rings Twice (1946–1981)," *Literature/Film Quarterly* 13, no. 2 (1985): 102–11.

Rainer, Peter. "On Psychonoir," in Richard T. Jameson (Ed.), *They Went Thataway: Redefining Film Genres—A National Society of Film Critics Video Guide* (San Francisco: Mercury House, 1994): 26–30. First published as "Out of the Past, Darkly" in *The Los Angeles Times* (Sunday, 8 April 1990).

Reid, David, and Jayne L. Walker. "Strange Pursuit: Cornell Woolrich and the Abandoned City of the Forties," in Joan Copjec (Ed.), *Shades of Noir: A Reader* (London and New York: Verso, 1993): 57–96.

Rich, B. Ruby. "Dumb Lugs and Femmes Fatales," *Sight and Sound* 5, no. 11 (1995): 6–10.

Richardson, Carl. *Autopsy: An Element of Realism in American Film Noir* (Metuchen, N.J.: Scarecrow, 1992).

Root, Jane. "Film Noir," in Pam Cook (Ed.), *The Cinema Book* (London: British Film Institute, 1985): 93–98.

Scher, Saul N. "*The Glass Key:* The Original and Two Copies," *Literature/Film Quarterly* 12, no. 3 (1984): 147–59.

Schickel, Richard. *Double Indemnity* (London: British Film Institute, 1992).

Schrader, Paul. "Notes on *Film Noir,*" in Kevin Jackson (Ed.), *Schrader on Schrader* (London and Boston: Faber and Faber, 1990): 80–94. First published in the Los Angeles Film Festival pamphlet for 1971 and subsequently in *Film Comment* 8, no. 1 (1972).

Selby, Spencer. *Dark City: The Film Noir* (Chicago and London: St. James Press, 1984).

Shadoian, Jack. *Dreams and Dead Ends: The American Gangster/Crime Film* (Cambridge, Mass., and London: MIT Press, 1977).

Silver, Alain. "Son of *Noir:* Neo-*Film Noir* and the Neo-B Picture," in Alain Silver and James Ursini (Eds.), *Film Noir Reader* (New York: Limelight Editions, 1996): 331–38.

———, and Linda Brookover. "What Is This Thing Called *Noir?,*" in Alain Silver and James Ursini (Eds.), *Film Noir Reader* (New York: Limelight Editions, 1996): 261–73.

———, and James Ursini (Eds.). *Film Noir Reader* (New York: Limelight Editions, 1996).

———, and Elizabeth Ward (Eds.). *Film Noir: An Encyclopedic Reference to the American Style* (Woodstock, N.Y.: Overlook Press, 1992, 3rd ed.). First published in 1979.

Smallman, Shirley, Kirk Smallman, and George F. Bohrer, Jr. "*Films Noir* and Their Remade Versions: Shifts in sources of evil, women's roles, and the power of fate," *Echoes & Mirrors* 1, no. 1 (1994): 40–71.

Stephens, Michael L. *Film Noir: A Comprehensive Illustrated Reference to Movies, Terms and Persons* (Jefferson, N.C., and London: McFarland, 1995).

Telotte, J. P."The Big Clock of *Film Noir,*" *Film Criticism* 14, no. 2 (1989/90): 1–11.

———."The Fantastic Realism of Film Noir: *Kiss Me Deadly,*" *Wide Angle* 14, no. 1 (1992): 4–18.

———. *Voices in the Dark: The Narrative Patterns of Films Noir* (Urbana and Chicago: University of Illinois Press, 1989).

Thomas, Deborah. "How Hollywood Deals with the Deviant Male," in Ian Cameron (Ed.), *The Movie Book of Films Noir* (London: Studio Vista, 1992): 59–70. First published in *CineAction!* 13/14 (1988).

———. "Psychoanalysis and Film Noir," in Ian Cameron (Ed.), *The Movie Book of Film Noir* (London: Studio Vista, 1992): 71–87.

Tuska, Jon. *Dark Cinema: American Film Noir in Cultural Perspective* (Westport, Conn.: Greenwood Press, 1984).

Ursini, James. "Angst at Sixty Fields per Second," in Alain Silver and James Ursini (Eds.), *Film Noir Reader* (New York: Limelight Editions, 1996): 275–87.

Vernet, Marc. "The Filmic Transaction: On the Openings of Film Noirs," translated by David Rodowick, *The Velvet Light Trap* 20 (1983): 2–9.

———. "*Film Noir* on the Edge of Doom," translated by J. Swenson, in Joan Copjec (Ed.), *Shades of Noir: A Reader* (London and New York: Verso, 1993): 1–31.

Vincendeau, Ginette. "France 1945–65 and Hollywood: the *policier* as international text," *Screen* 33, no. 1 (1992): 50–80.

———. "Noir is Also a French Word: The French Antecedents of Film Noir," in Ian Cameron (Ed.), *The Movie Book of Film Noir* (London: Studio Vista, 1992): 49–58.

Walker, Michael. "Film Noir: Introduction," in Ian Cameron (Ed.), *The Movie Book of Film Noir* (London: Studio Vista, 1992): 8–38.

Ward, Elizabeth. "The Post-*Noir* P.I.: *The Long Goodbye* and *Hickey and Boggs,*" in Alain Silver and James Ursini (Eds.), *Film Noir Reader* (New York: Limelight Editions, 1996): 237–43.

Weinrichter, Antonio. "América violenta 1990: Tres gangsters de autor," *Dirigido por . . .* no. 185 (1990): 50–53.

Whitney, J. S. "A Filmography of Film Noir," *Journal of Popular Film* 5, nos. 3/4 (1976): 321–71.

Williams, Tony. "*Phantom Lady,* Cornell Woolrich, and the Masochistic Aesthetic," *CineAction!* 13/14 (1988): 56–63. Reprinted in Alain Silver and James Ursini (Eds.), *Film Noir Reader* (New York: Limelight Editions, 1996): 129–43.

Williamson, Judith. "Consuming Passions," *City Limits* 16 (1982): 34–37.

Wolfenstein, Martha, and Nathan Leites. "Killers and Victims," in Martha Wolfenstein and Nathan Leites, *Movies: A Psychological Study* (New York: Free Press, 1950): 175–242.

Wood, Michael. "The Interpretation of Dreams," in *America in the Movies* (London: Secker and Warburg, 1975): 97–125.

Wood, Robin. "Creativity and Evaluation: Two Film Noirs of the Fifties," *CineAction!* 21/22 (1990): 4–20.

.——— "*Rancho Notorious:* A Noir Western in Colour," *CineAction!* 13/14 (1988): 83–93.

Younger, Richard. "Song in Contemporary Film Noir," *Films in Review* 45, nos. 7/8 (1994): 48–50.

Žižek, Slavoj. "At the Origins of *Noir:* The Humiliated Father," in Slavoj Žižek, *Enjoy your symptom!: Jacques Lacan in Hollywood and out* (New York and London: Routledge, 1992): 149–65.

GENERAL

Albert, Mary Scott. *Towards a Theory of Slow Motion* (Master's dissertation, British Film Institute and Birkbeck College, University of London, 1993).

Reprinted in Colin MacCabe and Duncan Petrie (Eds.), *New Scholarship from BFI Research* (London: British Film Institute, 1996).

Allen, Robert C., and Douglas Gomery. *Film History: Theory and Practice* (New York: McGraw-Hill, 1985).

Alton, John. *Painting with Light* (Berkeley, Los Angeles, and London: University of California Press, 1995). First published by Macmillan in 1949.

Andrew, Geoff. *The Film Handbook* (Harlow, England: Longman, 1989).

———. "Too Weird for Words," *Time Out* 1120 (5–12 February 1992): 18–21.

Atkinson, Michael. "Crossing the Frontiers," *Sight and Sound* 4, no. 1 (1994): 14–17.

Austin, Bruce A., and Thomas F. Gordon. "Movie Genres: Toward a Conceptualized Model and Standardized Definitions," in Bruce A. Austin (Ed.), *Current Research in Film: Audiences, Economics, and Law,* Volume 3 (Norwood, N.J.: Ablex, 1987): 12–33.

Babington, Bruce, and Peter William Evans. *Biblical Epics: Sacred Narrative in the Hollywood Cinema* (Manchester and New York: Manchester University Press, 1993).

Balio, Tino (Ed.). *The American Film Industry* (Madison and London: University of Wisconsin Press, 1985, 2nd ed.).

Barker, Adam. "Cries and Whispers," *Sight and Sound* 1, no. 10 (1992): 24–25.

Bernard, Jami. *Quentin Tarantino: The Man and his Movies* (London: Harper-Collins, 1995).

Berry, Betsy, "Forever in My Dreams: Generic Conventions and The Subversive Imagination in *Blue Velvet,*" *Literature/Film Quarterly* 16, no. 2 (1988): 82–90.

Bertolucci, Bernardo, and Marilyn Goldin. *Red Harvest.* Photocopy of unpublished screenplay (first draft, June 1982) supplied by Hollywood Scripts, Enterprise House, Cathles Road, London SW12 9LD.

Biskind, Peter. "An Auteur Is Born," *Premiere* (U.S.) 8, no. 3 (1994): 94–102.

Bliss, Michael. *Martin Scorsese and Michael Cimino* (Metuchen, N.J., and London: Scarecrow, 1985).

———. *The Word Made Flesh: Catholicism and Conflict in the Films of Martin Scorsese* (Lanham, Md., and London: Scarecrow, 1995).

Bordwell, David, Janet Staiger, and Kristin Thompson. *The Classical Hollywood Cinema: Film Style and Mode of Production to 1960* (London: Routledge, 1985).

Bourguignon, Thomas. "*Blood Simple:* Blood Brothers," *Positif* no. 399 (1994): 24–26.

Boyd, David. "Prisoner of the Night," *Film Heritage* 12, no. 2 (1976/77): 24–30.

Braudy, Leo. "The Sacraments of Genre: Coppola, DePalma, Scorsese," *Film Quarterly* 39, no. 3 (1986): 17–28.

Breitbart, Eric. "Joel and Ethan Coen," *American Film* 10, no. 7 (1985): 49–51.

Britton, Andrew. "Blissing Out: The Politics of Reaganite Entertainment," *Movie* 31/32 (1986): 1–42.

Bruce, Bryan. "Martin Scorsese: Five Films," *Movie* 31/32 (1986): 88–94.

——. "Scorsese: After Hours," *CineAction!* 6 (1986): 26–31.

Buck-Morss, Susan. "The City as Dreamworld and Catastrophe," *October* 73 (1995): 3–26.

Campbell, Joseph. *The Hero with a Thousand Faces* (London: Paladin, 1988). First published by Princeton University Press in 1949.

Cawelti, John G. *Adventure, Mystery and Romance: Formula Stories as Art and Popular Culture* (Chicago: University of Chicago Press, 1976).

——. "*Chinatown* and Generic Transformation in Recent American Films," in G. Mast and M. Cohen (Eds.), *Film Theory and Criticism: Introductory Readings* (New York and Oxford: Oxford University Press, 1985, 3rd ed.): 503–20.

Chandler, Raymond. "The Simple Art of Murder," in Raymond Chandler, *Pearls are a Nuisance* (Harmondsworth: Penguin, 1964). First published in *Atlantic Monthly* in 1944.

Christie, Ian. *Arrows of Desire: The Films of Michael Powell and Emeric Pressburger* (London and Boston: Faber and Faber, 1994, rev. ed.). First published by Waterstone in 1985.

——. "Martin Scorsese's Testament," *Sight and Sound* 6, no. 1 (1996): 7–11.

——. "The Scorsese Interview," *Sight and Sound* 4, no. 2 (1994): 10–15.

Chute, David. "Tropic of Kasdan," *Film Comment* 17, no. 5 (1981): 49–52.

Ciment, Michel, and Hubert Niogret. "A chacun sa couleur," translated into French by Michel Ciment, *Positif* no. 379 (1992): 28–35.

——. "Entretien avec Quentin Tarantino," translated into French by Michel Ciment, *Positif* no. 405 (1994): 10–15.

Coates, Paul. *The Gorgon's Gaze: German Cinema, Expressionism and the Image of Horror* (Cambridge: Cambridge University Press, 1991).

Cocks, Jay, and Martin Scorsese. "Joseph H. Lewis: High Style on a Low Budget," *The New York Times* (Sunday, 12 May 1991), Section 2: 17 and 20.

Coen, Joel, and Ethan Coen. *Barton Fink and Miller's Crossing* (London and Boston: Faber and Faber, 1991).

——. *Blood Simple* (New York: St. Martin's Press, 1988).

——. *Fargo* (London and Boston: Faber and Faber, 1996).

Cohen, Margaret. "The *Homme Fatal,* the Phallic Father, and the New Man," *Cultural Critique* 23 (1992/93): 111–36.

Collins, Jim. "Genericity in the Nineties: Eclectic Irony and the New Sincerity," in Jim Collins, Hilary Radner, and Ava Preacher Collins (Eds.), *Film Theory Goes to the Movies* (New York and London: Routledge, 1993): 242–63.

——, Hilary Radner, and Ava Preacher Collins (Eds.). *Film Theory Goes to the Movies* (New York and London: Routledge, 1993).

Conant, Michael. *Antitrust in the Motion Picture Industry* (Berkeley: University of California Press, 1960).

Cook, David A. *A History of Narrative Film* (New York and London: W. W. Norton, 1990, 2nd ed.).

Cook, Pam. "Masculinity in Crisis?: Tragedy and Identification in *Raging Bull*," *Screen* 23, nos. 3/4 (1982): 39–46.

———. "Scorsese's Masquerade," *Sight and Sound* 1, no. 12 (1992): 14–15.

Corliss, Richard. "Our Town," *Film Comment* 22, no. 6 (1986): 9–17.

Corrigan, Timothy. *A Cinema Without Walls: Movies and Culture After Vietnam* (London: Routledge, 1991).

Cousins, Mark. "Robert Towne: On Writing," in John Boorman and Walter Donohue (Eds.), *Projections 6: Film-makers on Film-making* (London and Boston: Faber and Faber, 1996): 109–22.

Creed, Barbara. "From Here to Modernity: Feminism and Postmodernism," *Screen* 28, no. 2 (1987): 47–67.

———. *The Monstrous-Feminine: Film, Feminism, Psychoanalysis* (London and New York: Routledge, 1993).

Cross, Robin. *B Movies* (New York: St. Martin's Press, 1981).

Dargis, Manohla. "Dark Side of the Dream," *Sight and Sound* 6, no. 8 (1996): 16–18.

———. "Pulp Instinct," *Sight and Sound* 4, no. 5 (1994): 6–9.

———. "Roads to Freedom," *Sight and Sound* 1, no. 3 (1991): 14–18.

Darke, Chris. "Inside the Light," *Sight and Sound* 6, no. 4 (1996): 18–20.

Davis, Mike. *City of Quartz: Excavating the Future in Los Angeles* (London: Vintage, 1992). First published by Verso in 1990.

Dawson, Jeff. *Tarantino: Inside Story* (London: Cassell, 1995).

Deleyto, Celestino. "Postmodernism and Parody in Pedro Almodóvar's *Mujeres al borde de un ataque de nervios* (1988)," *Forum for Modern Language Studies* 31, no. 1 (1995): 49–63.

Derbyshire, Ian. *Politics in the United States: From Carter to Bush* (Edinburgh: Chambers, 1990, 2nd ed.).

Desser, David. "*Blade Runner:* Science Fiction and Transcendence," *Literature/Film Quarterly* 13, no. 3 (1985): 172–79.

Dimendberg, Edward. "The Will to Motorization: Cinema, Highways, and Modernity," *October* 73 (1995): 91–137.

Dixon, Wheeler W. *The "B" Directors: A Biographical Directory* (Metuchen, N.J.: Scarecrow, 1985).

Doane, Mary Ann. *Femmes Fatales: Feminism, Film Theory, Psychoanalysis* (London and New York: Routledge, 1991).

Doll, Susan, and Greg Faller. "*Blade Runner* and Genre: Film Noir and Science Fiction," *Literature/Film Quarterly* 14, no. 2 (1986): 89–100.

Dominick, Joseph R. "Film Economics and Film Content: 1964–1983," in Bruce A. Austin (Ed.), *Current Research in Film: Audiences, Economics, and Law*, Volume 3 (Norwood, N.J.: Ablex, 1987): 136–53.

Ehrenstein, David. *The Scorsese Picture: The Art and Life of Martin Scorsese* (New York: Birch Lane Press, 1992).

Elley, Derek. "Quentin Tarantino," in Peter Cowie (Ed.), *Variety International Film Guide 1995* (London: Hamlyn, 1994): 39–44.

Evans, Peter William. *The Films of Luis Buñuel: Subjectivity and Desire* (Oxford: Clarendon Press, 1995).

Farber, Stephen. "Five Horsemen After the Apocalypse," *Film Comment* 21, no. 4 (1985): 32–35.

Field, Syd. *Screenplay: The Foundations of Screenwriting* (New York: Dell, 1982, exp. ed.).

Fox, Terry Curtis, et al. "Hardboiled Hollywood," *Film Comment* 20, no. 5 (1984): 29–49.

Francke, Lizzie. "Screen Dreams of Beautiful Women," *The Observer* (Sunday, 16 January 1994), *Review* Section: 14–15.

———. "Virtual Fears," *Sight and Sound* 5, no. 12 (1995): 6–9.

Frazer, J. G. *The Golden Bough: A Study in Magic and Religion* (London: Papermac, 1987, abr. ed.). First published by Macmillan in 1922.

Frosh, Stephen. *Identity Crisis: Modernity, Psychoanalysis and the Self* (Basingstoke and London: Macmillan, 1991).

Fuller, Graham. "Answers first, questions later," in John Boorman and Walter Donohue (Eds.), *Projections 3: Film-makers on Film-making* (London and Boston: Faber and Faber, 1994): 174–95.

———. "Kasdan on Kasdan," in John Boorman and Walter Donohue (Eds.), *Projections 3: Film-makers on Film-making* (London and Boston: Faber and Faber, 1994): 111–50.

Garry, John P. III. "A Reservoir of Allusions: *Reservoir Dogs* as a Really Postmodern Movie." Internet article downloaded from the World Wide Web site "Church of Tarantino," posted 6 March 1995.

Garson, Robert, and Christopher J. Bailey. *The uncertain power: A political history of the United States since 1929* (Manchester and New York: Manchester University Press, 1990).

Gomery, Douglas. *The Hollywood Studio System* (London: British Film Institute/Macmillan, 1986).

Goulding, Daniel J. (Ed.). *Five Filmmakers: Tarkovsky, Forman, Polanski, Szabó, Makavejev* (Bloomington and Indianapolis: Indiana University Press, 1994).

Harkness, Jonathan. "The Sphinx without a Riddle," *Sight and Sound* 4, no. 8 (1994): 7–9.

Harvey, David. *The Condition of Postmodernity: An Enquiry into the Origins of Cultural Change* (Cambridge, Mass., and Oxford: Blackwells, 1990).

Haskell, Molly. *From Reverence to Rape: The Treatment of Women in the Movies* (Chicago and London: University of Chicago Press, 1987, 2nd ed.).

Haut, Woody. *Pulp Culture: Hardboiled Fiction and the Cold War* (London and New York: Serpent's Tail, 1995).

Henkin, Hilary. *Romeo is Bleeding*. Photocopy of unpublished screenplay (revised first draft, 8 November 1987) supplied by Hollywood Scripts, Enterprise House, Cathles Road, London SW12 9LD.

Heung, Marina. "Black Widow," *Film Quarterly* 41, no. 1 (1987): 54–58.

Hickenlooper, George. *Reel Conversations: Candid Interviews with Film's Foremost Directors and Critics* (New York: Citadel Press, 1991).

Hillier, Jim (Ed.). *Cahiers du Cinéma, The 1950s: Neo-Realism, Hollywood, New Wave* (London: Routledge and Kegan Paul/British Film Institute, 1985).

———— (Ed.). *Cahiers du Cinéma, The 1960s: New Wave, New Cinema, Reevaluating Hollywood* (London: Routledge and Kegan Paul/British Film Institute, 1986).

————. *The New Hollywood* (London: Studio Vista, 1993).

Hinson, Hal. "Bloodlines," *Film Comment* 21, no. 2 (1985): 14–16.

————. "Joel Coen, Ethan Coen and Barry Sonnenfeld interview," *Film Comment* 21, no. 2 (1985), 16–19.

Hoberman, J. "Back on the Wild Side," *Premiere* (U.S.) 5, no. 12 (1992): 31–32.

Holmlund, Chris. "Cruisin' for a Bruisin': Hollywood's Deadly (Lesbian) Dolls," *Cinema Journal* 34, no. 1 (1994): 31–51.

Hopper, Dennis. "Blood Lust Snicker Snicker in Wide Screen," *Grand Street* 13, no. 1 (1994): 11–22.

Horowitz, Mark. "Coen Brothers A-Z: The Big Two-Headed Picture," *Film Comment* 27, no. 5 (1991): 27–32.

————. "Fault Lines," *Film Comment* 26, no. 6 (1990): 52–58.

Izod, John. *Hollywood and the Box Office, 1895–1986* (Basingstoke and London: Macmillan, 1988).

Jackson, Kevin (Ed.). *Schrader on Schrader* (London and Boston: Faber and Faber, 1990).

Jacobs, Diane. *Hollywood Renaissance* (South Brunswick, N.J.: A. S. Barnes, 1977).

Jacobs, Lea. "The B Film and the Problem of Cultural Distinction," *Screen* 33, no. 1 (1992): 1–13.

James, Nick. "One False Move," *Sight and Sound* 3, no. 4 (1993): 52–53.

Jameson, Fredric. "Postmodernism, or The Cultural Logic of Late Capitalism," *New Left Review* 146 (1984): 53–92.

Jameson, Richard T. (Ed.). *They Went Thataway: Redefining Film Genres—A National Society of Film Critics Video Guide* (San Francisco: Mercury House, 1994).

Kaminsky, Stuart. *American Film Genres* (Dayton, Ohio: Pflaum Publishing, 1974).

Kawin, Bruce F. *Mindscreen: Bergman, Godard, and First-Person Film* (Princeton, N.J.: Princeton University Press, 1978).

Kellman, Steven G. (Ed.). *Perspectives on Raging Bull* (New York: G. K. Hall, 1994).

Kellner, Douglas. "Film, Politics and Ideology: Reflections on Hollywood Film in the Age of Reagan," *The Velvet Light Trap* 27 (1991): 9–24.

Kerr, Paul. "My Name is Joseph H. Lewis," *Screen* 24, nos. 4/5 (1983): 48–66.

Keyser, Les. *Martin Scorsese* (New York: Twayne, 1992).

————, and Barbara Keyser. *Hollywood and the Catholic Church: The Image of Roman Catholicism in American Movies* (Chicago: Loyola University Press, 1984).

Keyssar, Helene. *Robert Altman's America* (New York and Oxford: Oxford University Press, 1991).

Kindem, Gorham (Ed.). *The American Movie Industry: The Business of Motion Pictures* (Carbondale: Southern Illinois University Press, 1982).

Kinder, Marsha. "Back to the Future in the 80s with Fathers & Sons, Supermen & PeeWees, Gorillas & Toons," *Film Quarterly* 42, no. 4 (1989): 2–11.

———. *Blood Cinema: The Reconstruction of National Identity in Spain* (Berkeley, Los Angeles, and London: University of California Press, 1993).

Kirkham, Pat, and Janet Thumin (Eds.). *You Tarzan: Masculinity, Movies and Men* (London: Lawrence and Wishart, 1993).

Kline, T. Jefferson. *Screening the Text: Intertextuality in New Wave French Cinema* (Baltimore and London: Johns Hopkins University Press, 1992).

Knowles, Peter C. "Genre and Authorship: Two Films of Arthur Penn," *CineAction!* 21/22 (1990): 76–83.

Kolker, Robert Phillip. *A Cinema of Loneliness: Penn, Kubrick, Scorsese, Spielberg, Altman* (New York and Oxford: Oxford University Press, 1988, 2nd ed.).

Leff, Leonard J., and Jerold L. Simmons. *The Dame in the Kimono: Hollywood, Censorship, and the Production Code from the 1920s to the 1960s* (New York: Grove Weidenfeld, 1990).

Leitch, Thomas M. "Twice-Told Tales: The Rhetoric of the Remake," *Literature/Film Quarterly* 18, no. 3 (1990): 138–49.

Linderman, Deborah "Oedipus in Chinatown," *Enclitic,* Special Issue (1982): 190–203.

Lourdeaux, Lee. *Italian and Irish Filmmakers in America: Ford, Capra, Coppola, and Scorsese* (Philadelphia: Temple University Press, 1990).

Luddy, Tom, and David Thomson. "Penn on Penn," in John Boorman, Tom Luddy, David Thomson, and Walter Donohue (Eds.), *Projections 4: Film-makers on Film-making* (London and Boston: Faber and Faber, 1995): 113–60.

Lyons, Deborah, and Adam D. Weinberg (Eds.). *Edward Hopper and the American Imagination* (New York and London: W. W. Norton, 1995).

Lyons, Donald. *Independent Visions: A Critical Introduction to Recent Independent American Film* (New York: Ballantine Books, 1994).

Mamber, Stephen. "Parody, Intertextuality, Signature: Kubrick, DePalma, and Scorsese," *Quarterly Review of Film and Video* 12, nos. 1/2 (1990): 29–35.

Martin, Adrian. *Phantasms* (Ringwood: McPhee Gribble, 1994).

Massood, Paula J. "Mapping the Hood: The Genealogy of City Space in *Boyz N the Hood* and *Menace II Society,*" *Cinema Journal* 35, no. 2 (1996): 85–97.

McCarthy, Todd, and Charles Flynn (Eds.). *Kings of the Bs: Working Within the Hollywood Studio System* (New York: E. P. Dutton, 1975).

McGilligan, Patrick. *Jack's Life: A Biography of Jack Nicholson* (London: HarperCollins, 1995). First published by Hutchinson in 1994.

Miller, Don. *"B" Movies* (New York: Curtis Books, 1973).

Mizejewski, Linda. "Picturing the Female Dick: *The Silence of the Lambs* and *Blue Steel*," *Journal of Film and Video* 45, nos. 2/3 (1993): 6–23.

Monaco, James. *American Film Now: The People, The Power, The Money, The Movies* (New York: New York Zoetrope, 1984, 2nd ed.).

Mortimer, Lorraine. "Blood Brothers: Purity, Masculinity and the Flight from the Feminine in Scorsese and Schrader," *Cinema Papers* 75 (1989): 30–36.

Motion Picture Association of America. *Code of Self-Regulation* (1966).

———. *The Motion Picture Production Code* (1956).

Motion Picture Producers and Distributors of America, Inc. *A Code to Govern the Making of Motion and Talking Pictures: The Reasons Supporting It and the Resolution for Uniform Interpretation* (1934).

Mulvey, Laura. "The Oedipus Myth: Beyond the Riddles of the Sphinx," in *Visual and Other Pleasures* (London: Macmillan, 1989): 177–201.

Murray, Abigail. *The Films of Alan Rudolph* (Master's dissertation, British Film Institute and Birkbeck College, University of London, 1994).

Neve, Brian. *Film and Politics in America: A Social Tradition* (London and New York: Routledge, 1992).

Newman, David, and Robert Benton. *Bonnie and Clyde,* additional material compiled and edited by Sandra Wake and Nicola Hayden (London and Boston: Faber and Faber, 1995). First published by Lorrimer Publishing in 1972.

Occhiogrosso, Peter. *Once a Catholic: Prominent Catholics and Ex-Catholics Discuss the Influence of the Church on Their Lives and Work* (Boston: Houghton Mifflin, 1987).

Orr, John. *Cinema and Modernity* (Cambridge: Polity Press, 1993).

Pappas, Nickolas. "*A Sea of Love* Among Men," *Film Criticism* 14, no. 3 (1990): 14–26.

Phillips, Mike. "Chic and Beyond," *Sight and Sound* 6, no. 8 (1996): 25–27.

Pierson, John. *Spike, Mike, Slackers & Dykes: A Guided Tour Across a Decade of American Independent Cinema,* with the conversational collaboration of Kevin Smith (London: Faber and Faber, 1996). First published by Hyperion/Miramax in 1995.

Pileggi, Nicholas, and Martin Scorsese. *Casino* (London and Boston: Faber and Faber, 1996).

Pirie, David (Ed.). *Anatomy of the Movies* (London: Windward, 1981).

Polan, Dana. *Power and Paranoia: History, Narrative, and the American Cinema* (New York: Columbia University Press, 1986).

Powell, Michael. *Million-Dollar Movie* (London: Heinemann, 1992).

Price, Richard. *Three Screenplays: The Color of Money, Sea of Love, and Night and the City* (London: Studio Vista, 1994).

Pronzini, Bill, and Jack Adrian (Eds.). *Hard-Boiled: An Anthology of American Crime Stories* (Oxford and New York: Oxford University Press, 1995).

Propp, Vladimir. *Morphology of the Folktale,* translated by Lawrence Scott (Austin: University of Texas Press, 1968, 2nd ed.).

Pye, Michael, and Lynda Myles. *The Movie Brats: How the Film Generation Took Over Hollywood* (New York: Holt, Rinehart and Winston, 1979).

Rapping, Elayne. *Media-tions: Forays into the Culture and Gender Wars* (Boston: South End Press, 1994).

Rattigan, Neil, and Thomas P. McManus. "Fathers, Sons, and Brothers: Patriarchy and Guilt in 1980s American Cinema," *Journal of Popular Film and Television* 20, no. 1 (1992): 15–23.

Ray, Robert B. *A Certain Tendency of the Hollywood Cinema, 1930–1980* (Princeton, N.J.: Princeton University Press, 1985).

Rice, Julian C. "Transcendental Pornography and *Taxi Driver*," *Journal of Popular Film* 5, no. 2 (1976): 109–23.

Rich, B. Ruby. "Art House Killers," *Sight and Sound* 2, no. 8 (1992): 5–6.

Rodriguez, Robert. *Rebel Without a Crew: Or How a 23-Year-Old Filmmaker with $7,000 Became a Hollywood Player* (New York: Dutton, 1995).

Romney, Jonathan. "How Did We Get Here?," *Sight and Sound* 5, no. 2 (1995): 32–34.

———, and Adrian Wootton (Eds.). *Celluloid Jukebox: Popular Music and Movies since the 50s* (London: British Film Institute, 1995).

Ryan, Michael, and Douglas Kellner. *Camera Politica: The Politics and Ideology of Contemporary Hollywood Film* (Bloomington and Indianapolis: Indiana University Press, 1988).

Saada, Nicolas. "Série B: Contre quelques idées reçues," *Cahiers du cinéma* no. 441 (1991): 44–49.

Salt, Barry. *Film Style and Technology: History and Analysis* (London: Starword, 1992, 2nd ed.).

Schatz, Thomas. *The Genius of the System: Hollywood Filmmaking in the Studio Era* (New York: Pantheon, 1988).

———. "The New Hollywood," in Jim Collins, Hilary Radner, and Ava Preacher Collins (Eds.), *Film Theory Goes to the Movies* (New York and London: Routledge, 1993): 8–36.

Schrader, Paul. *Taxi Driver* (London and Boston: Faber and Faber, 1990).

———. *Transcendental Style in Film: Ozu, Bresson, Dreyer* (New York: Da Capo, 1988). First published by University of California Press in 1972.

Scorsese, Martin. "Martin Scorsese's Guilty Pleasures," *Film comment* 14, no. 5 (1978): 63–66.

———. "Our Generation," in John Boorman and Walter Donohue (Eds.), *Projections 7: Film-makers on Film-making—In Association with Cahiers du Cinéma* (London and Boston: Faber and Faber, 1997): 60–65. First published in French in *Cahiers du Cinéma* no. 500 (1996).

———. "Personal Best," *Premiere* (U.S.), Special Issue: New York and the Movies (1994): 109.

———. "Tapping the Intensity of the City: Creativity as a natural resource," *The New York Times Magazine* (Sunday, 9 November 1986), Part 2: 28 and 82–84.

Sharrett, Christopher (Ed.). *Crisis Cinema: The Apocalyptic Idea in Postmodern Narrative Film* (Washington, D.C.: Maisonneuve Press, 1993).

Siegel, Robert L. "Mentors and Godfathers: The Offer Directors Can't Refuse," *The Independent: Film and Video Monthly* 17, no. 6 (1994): 20–25.

Sklar, Robert. *Movie-Made America: A Cultural History of American Movies* (New York: Random House, 1975).

Smith, Gavin. "Momentum and Design: Kathryn Bigelow interview," *Film Comment* 31, no. 5 (1995): 46–50 and 55–60.

———. "Quentin Tarantino interview," *Film Comment* 30, no. 4 (1994): 32–43.

Smith, Paul Julian. *Desire Unlimited: The Cinema of Pedro Almodóvar* (London and New York: Verso, 1994).

Sonnenfeld, Barry. "Shadows and Shivers for *Blood Simple*," *American Cinematographer* 66, no. 7 (1985): 70–74.

Stern, Lesley. *The Scorsese Connection* (London, Bloomington, and Indianapolis: British Film Institute/Indiana University Press, 1995).

Tarantino, Quentin. *Pulp Fiction* (London and Boston: Faber and Faber, 1994).

———. *Reservoir Dogs* (London and Boston: Faber and Faber, 1994).

Taubin, Amy. "The Allure of Decay," *Sight and Sound* 6, no. 1 (1996): 23–24.

———. "The Men's Room," *Sight and Sound* 2, no. 8 (1992): 2–4.

Taylor, Bella. "Martin Scorsese," in John Tuska (Ed.), *Close-up: The Contemporary Director* (Metuchen, N.J., and London: Scarecrow, 1981): 292–368.

Thompson, David. "I Make Films for Adults," *Sight and Sound* 5, no. 4 (1995): 6–11.

———, and Ian Christie (Eds.). *Scorsese on Scorsese* (London and Boston: Faber and Faber, 1996, rev. ed.). First published in 1989.

Thompson, Richard. "Screen Writer: *Taxi Driver*'s Paul Schrader," *Film Comment* 12, no. 2 (1976): 6–19.

Thumin, Maureen. *Flashbacks in Film: Memory and History* (London and New York: Routledge, 1989).

Towne, Robert. *Chinatown*. Photocopies of unpublished screenplay (third draft, 9 October 1973) and treatment (no date) supplied by Hollywood Scripts, Enterprise House, Cathles Road, London SW12 9LD.

Tuska, John (Ed.). *Close-up: The Contemporary Director* (Metuchen, N.J., and London: Scarecrow, 1981).

Van Daalen, Bill. "After Hours," *Film Quarterly* 41, no. 3 (1988): 31–34.

Van Wert, William F. "Psychoanalysis and Con Games: *House of Games*," *Film Quarterly* 43, no. 4 (1990): 2–10.

Vatrican, Vincent. "*Blood Simple* de Joel et Ethan Coen," *Cahiers du Cinéma*, numéro hors-série: 100 films pour une vidéothèque (1993): 30.

Vidler, Anthony. "Bodies in Space/Subjects in the City: Psychopathologies of Modern Urbanism," *Differences* 5, no. 3 (1993): 31–51.

Vogler, Christopher. *The Writer's Journey: Mythic Structure for Storytellers and Screenwriters* (Los Angeles: Michael Wiese, 1992).

Walker, Michael. "Night Moves," *Movie* 22 (1976): 34–38.

Weaver, David. "The Narrative of Alienation: Martin Scorsese's *Taxi Driver*," *CineAction!* 6 (1986): 12–16.

Westerbeck, Colin L. Jr., "Beauties and the Beast," *Sight and Sound* 45, no. 3 (1976): 134–39.

Wilder, Billy, and Raymond Chandler. *Double Indemnity*. Photocopy of unpub-
    lished screenplay (25 September 1943) supplied by Hollywood Scripts, En-
    terprise House, Cathles Road, London SW12 9LD.
Winokur, Mark. "Eating Children Is Wrong," *Sight and Sound* 1, no. 7 (1991):
    10–13.
Wood, Robin. *Hollywood From Vietnam to Reagan* (New York: Columbia Uni-
    versity Press, 1986).
Yakir, Dan. "Lawrence Kasdan interview," *Film Comment* 17, no. 5 (1981):
    52–56.

Index

About the Author

Richard Martin was educated at the University of Newcastle upon Tyne (England) and the University of Zaragoza (Spain) and gained his Ph.D. in Film Studies in 1996. He has taught film studies courses at the Tyneside Cinema and the University of Warwick (England). Martin currently works as a freelance editor and writer, specializing in reference publishing and film books.